Barbecue

PILLSBURY'S BARBECUE COOKBOOK

Pillsbury

To the chef:

Outdoor cooking conjures up images of fresh air, hearty appetites and casual mealtimes. It is the time when culinary skills are at their best and even rain cannot dampen spirits.

Most people do much of their outdoor cooking in their own backyard, but we show it is just as easy to have a tailgate party, using one or two small grills. A patio brunch or a boating excursion or a camping trip are all good times made even better by cooking outdoors.

Pillsbury moves the good flavor of barbecuing indoors, too. Fireplaces, indoor grills, or outdoor grills placed in a well ventilated garage make barbecuing a year 'round pleasure.

We offer you menus for the American Barbecue — five terrific examples of the way outdoor cooking is not only a tradition in America but grew with America.

Come venture with us into a world of delicious food and great times. Barbecuing is all-American!

The Pillsbury Kitchens

Contents

Barbecuing Basics

HOT OFF THE GRILL: Familiar method of cooking over direct heat used for most barbecue cooking. For the beginner, the first rule to know is that a good, even bed of coals is the key to success.

- Light the charcoal about one half hour before you wish to cook food.

- To reduce heat when cooking, raise the height of the grill. To increase heat near the end of cooking time, tap the ashes off the coals because they tend to blanket the fire.

- For controlling flare-ups and smoke, trim as much fat from meat as possible before placing on grill. Have water available to extinguish any flames.

ROTISSERIE ROASTING: When using a rotisserie, coals are arranged along the back of the grill. Place a drip pan (you can make one from several thicknesses of foil) under the meat. The juices from the meat can be used as a sauce to serve along with meat or for basting. Follow use-and-care instructions for using your specific rotisserie; however, here are some extra tips:

- Center meat on rotisserie so that weight is balanced equally.

- Thread ribs on spit in accordion fashion

- When threading a cut of meat containing bone that runs the length of the meat, follow the bone, if possible.

- Meats over 12 lbs. generally do not cook well by rotisserie.

COVERED GRILL ROASTING: In covered kettle or wagon cookers, large cuts of meat can be roasted without a rotisserie. For the kettle cooker, coals are arranged around the sides of the meat and a drip pan is placed underneath. For the wagon cooker, charcoal is placed at one end, with the meat and drip pan at the other end.

FOIL COOKING: The "no clean-up" convenience of wrapping foods in foil before grilling gives barbecue cooking another dimension. One dish meals make their appearance as vegetables, fruits, rice and sauces are added to these handy packets. Other foil baking or roasting pans can be used, too. When testing recipes for this book, we used a single thickness of heavy duty foil. For steaks and chops with small bones that might tear the foil when handled, two thicknesses can be used.

Building a Fire

Your fire can be one of the most crucial factors to a successful barbecue. If the heat is too intense, the food will burn on the outside while remaining raw on the inside. And if it is too cool, your food will dry out before it is cooked. Obviously a good cut of meat can be ruined with an improper fire.

PREPARING THE GRILL BED. Some people prefer to line the inside of their grill with foil. This serves two purposes. The obvious result is easier cleanup; the other bonus is that shiny foil will reflect the heat towards the food. In addition some barbecue chefs layer the bottom of the grill with sand or gravel. This protects the metal of the grill bottom from overheating. Gravel also gives a certain amount of bottom draft. Any of these methods for preparing the grill bed are particularly good with light metal and solid-bottomed barbecue units.

THE CHARCOAL. Charcoal comes in two forms — briquets and lump. Lump charcoal is exactly that: lumps of irregularly-shaped pieces direct from the charcoal kiln. Briquets are lump charcoal which has been ground and pressed back into uniform shapes. Briquets have several advantages over lump charcoal: they are easier to arrange, burn more evenly and give off uniform heat. Charcoal varies widely in composition, which is stated on the bag. Most barbecue chefs prefer a hardwood base for its ease in lighting. Each type of charcoal burns a little differently. Therefore, we suggest that when you find a brand you like, stay with it so you won't have any unexpected surprises.

LIGHTING YOUR FIRE. Charcoal has a tendency not to want to light without a little help. Thus, there are a few products on the market to help you with this process. *Electric starters* come in many styles. They are simple to use and start fires in 20 to 25 minutes. *Inflammable liquids* are sold specifically for lighting charcoal. Arrange coals in a pile, pyramid style and douse. Wait a minute or two for the liquid to soak in, then light. *Jellied alcohol* such as canned heat is stuffed into the crevices between briquets. Arrange coals in a pyramid and stuff in 2 or 3 table-spoons, making sure it is well under the briquets; light. Both liquid and jelly take from 30 to 40 minutes to get coals to the ash stage.

ARRANGING THE COALS. Your fire is ready for cooking when the coals are ashen gray. Do not start to cook if there any coals spotted with black as they give off uneven heat and are more likely to flare up and smoke. There are two basic arrangements for coals depending on the type of food you are cooking.

The *direct grilling method* is used for quickly cooked foods such as hamburgers, steaks, hot dogs — anytime you wish to broil. To

arrange coals for this type of grilling simply spread out the pyramid so that there is a good layer of coals under all areas of the food.

A variation of this arrangement is used when grilling skewered foods. Chefs often like to arrange the coals in rows under each skewer, giving intense heat in a small area.

The *indirect method* of coal arrangement is used chiefly with thicker pieces of meat and roasts which take long, slow cooking. Arrange coals in a ring around the outside of the meat with a drip pan underneath. If your barbecue unit does not come equipped with a cover it would help to make a dome out of heavy duty aluminum foil. The cover will trap and reflect heat to help cook the top and sides.

A variation of the indirect method can be used when you have a barbecue unit equipped with a rotisserie. Place the coals evenly at the rear of the fire box and put a drip pan near the front, under the meat. (See page 156 for directions for making a drip pan.)

If you find it necessary to add more coals during cooking, place them at the edge of the fire. Allow them to turn ashen before moving them in toward the food.

DETERMINING THE TEMPERATURE. A grill thermometer is the most accurate way of determining the temperature of your fire. If your grill is not equipped with one of these, use the hand test method. Hold your hand at grill level and start counting the seconds. If you can leave your hand there for only three seconds, the temperature is around 350°-400° and is considered a hot fire which is just right for most foods cooked with the direct grilling method. If the temperature is any hotter, space out the briquets a little. If you can hold your hand over the grill about four seconds, it is a moderate fire; five or six seconds indicates a slow fire. Add more briquets if the temperature is any cooler.

One of the easiest ways to change the temperature is to raise or lower the rack on the grill. If you have a unit which does not offer different rack levels, the temperature may be changed by the addition or subtraction in the number of charcoal pieces used.

Remember: you are not cooking in an oven equipped with a thermostat to regulate your temperature. So do check your food often.

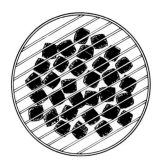

METHOD A

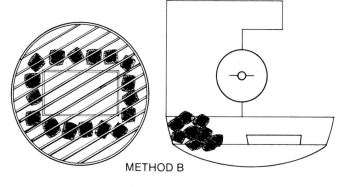

METHOD B

...when the kids do the cooking

Menu

Barbecued Hamburgers
Crisp Vegetable Relishes
*Individual Bean 'N Apple Pots, page 107
*Doughnuts S'Mores, page 113
Beverage

Barbecue cooking requires some degree of skill and patience, but by the time you're 12 and on through the teens this kind of cooking is the fun way to learn, in *any* kind of weather.

Kids can follow Dad's lead in learning to start the fire and doing the actual cooking. They can also make the meal plans, do the "before grilling" preparations and attractively serve the food with Mom's assistance. Choose simple meals at first, then as skill increases surprise your family with other foods!

MEATS: Try other hamburger ideas such as those for international hamburgers, pages 26-28. Or, if chicken sounds good to you, begin with some of the pre-cooked ones, page 68.

VEGETABLES: Beans baked in foil packets, like Individual Bean 'N Apple Pots, are fun to assemble and easy to serve. Other hot or cold barbecue favorites you like such as potato salad, baked beans or corn-on-the-cob are always good. Or, develop some salad specialties of your own.

DESSERTS: S'Mores are a favorite; these have a new twist of being made with doughnuts. Or, have an ice cream social to entertain friends. The old-fashioned kind of freezer you crank by hand can be fun. If you don't have a freezer, have a sundae extravaganza with different kinds of ice cream and toppings.

...when the tailgate's the table

Menu

Barbecued Wieners
Potato Chips
*Zippy Baked Beans, page 107
Vegetable Relishes
*Smokey Barbecue Buns, page 103
*Tato Flake Cheese Buns, page 104
Brownies
Beverage

Tailgate no longer refers only to the back entry of a station wagon. Today it's a special kind of picnic popularized by football fans — or any other sport's enthusiasts — to beat the traffic and have a party at the same time.

Seasons for these picnics extend from spring well into winter. Weather is no deterrent — umbrellas, rain coats, parkas, even camping heaters have been seen at tailgate gatherings.

Keeping foods hot — or cold — is one important consideration when planning foods for tailgating. See Tips, below.

Tailgating menus can be simple fare, or as fancy as you like! Your friends, equipment, experience and the season will be determining factors. Our menu uses fairly common equipment — a hibachi grill, insulated cooler, assorted-sized baskets and a heavy casserole. The foods, although simple, have exciting flavors that give them a new twist. That's really all it takes.

When planning the menu for a large group of tailgaters, consult the chapter on Cooking for Crowds for recipes that serve up to 25!

MEATS: Wieners and sausages fit any season's tailgating picnic. Kabobs are ideal, too. Meat cubes can be carried along in a flavorful marinade, so they're all ready for the skewer. Sauces for meats can be made at home and kept in an insulated container. Hot meat sandwiches are hearty for cold days and easy to eat.

VEGETABLES: All kinds of baked beans (ours is sparked with a carbonated beverage) are good served either hot or cool. Earthenware or pottery casseroles hold in heat. Hot potato salads — heat the canned variety — are a good change. If the weather's warmer, select vegetables in vinaigrette because these carry easily in covered plastic containers.

BREAD: Homemade rolls, one flavored with liquid smoke, the other with cayenne and cheese, make a hit without taking too much time to prepare. French bread slices filled with cheese and toasted are an easy idea from the breads section; look there for other suggestions.

DESSERT: Fingers, not forks, are the rule when choosing desserts: bars, easy-to-carry cakes, fruit turnovers, sweet rolls and coffee breads are among the possibilities.

BEVERAGES: Water and ice top this list. Be sure someone is responsible for plenty of both. Depending on the weather, icy beer or hot cider may be popular. Soups, hot or on-the-rocks, can be considered.

...dinner at the captain's table

Menu

*Steak Strips Sauterne, page 47
*Red Pickled Potato Salad, page 92
 French Bread
 Fresh Fruit
 Pound Cake
 Bordeaux, Cabernet Sauvignon or Rosé
 Wine

Boats and lakes come in many sizes . . . but one thing is sure — eating out on the open water on a sunny day or in the marina once the sun is going down will make seafarers of your most landlubberly friends.

Even if your boat's large enough to have cooking facilities, there are still many foods you'll prepare at home and bring aboard. There are barbecue grills designed especially for boats with ash catchers to prevent sparks or, a hibachi can easily fit along in with other gear.

On a very small boat, cooking will be impossible. Picnics are the best answer, unless you wait until you're back on shore to use a grill.

Larger boats that can accommodate a half dozen people or so, usually have enough room so you can drop anchor and cook dinner on board. Refrigerated storage is at a premium, so make special consideration when planning the menu. Ours requires an ice chest since only the meat and salad need chilling.

If your boat has a galley, more mealtime possibilities are available. Hot casseroles that heat in the oven or one-dish meals that cook quickly in a pressure cooker on a gas burner can be served. Because of the ups and downs of cooking on the open sea, it's best to save most cooking for dockside or a quiet portage.

Simple meals . . . however elegant . . . are the key in menu planning. Ours is easy, yet includes items even the most discerning guest would enjoy. It will be easy to include a few extras for dinner if need be. Boat-to-boat hospitality is to be expected — and welcomed.

SNACKS AND DRINKS: Plenty of cold drinks and snacks should be kept on hand. Look for spreads, cocktail appetizers, nuts and snack crackers that come in cans, so there's no chance for moisture to ruin the crunch!

MEATS: Kabobs are ideal for serving on board. They cook quickly, and can be stretched to feed a few extra people if the need arises. Other recipes you might like are Wine Marinated Beef Kabobs, page 44, or Picnic Kabobs, page 62.

SALADS: Make ahead salads like Red Pickled Potato Salad take to toting in large covered plastic containers. Since the containers are the serving dishes, they save space, too. Other salads to take are Minty Melon Bowl, page 89, or Summertime Bean Salad, page 94.

DESSERT: Fruit with pound cake completes a perfect dockside supper. For heartier appetites when meals are served on the open water, try Apricot Banana Bars, page 117, or other fruit-filled bar cookies.

...cook-out that moves indoors

Menu

*Tomato Noggins, page 111
*Cheese Fondue, page 32
 Wieners
*Grapefruit Spinach Toss, page 91
*Caesarettes, page 109
 Hot Fruit Compote

More and more homes are being built with indoor barbecue grills. However, if you don't have a built-in grill, this need not prevent you from enjoying the fun of a barbecue during the winter months.

Hibachi grills are especially suited for use indoors, as are the all-purpose grills with an adjustable pole (see photograph) that can be used outdoors or in the fireplace.

The fireplace is the best place for cooking inside because the chimney carries away any smoke; however, the range hood is a good substitute. Hibachi grills can be used almost anyplace as long as ordinary fire precautions are observed. Keep them away from curtains and always have a window in the room slightly open. Get rid of any hot coals that might be left by using tongs to drop them into a bucket of cold water. To start the fire, use an electric starter or starter fluid; avoid using newspaper since it is difficult to control the flame.

Space will probably allow that only the meat be cooked on the grill. Care in choosing lean meats, and careful trimming of excess fat to prevent flare-up are even more important considerations when cooking indoors than out. Cuts of meat that require long cooking aren't recommended either, since the amount of coals is usually small.

Cooking indoors offers many chances to entertain since the foods you could prepare range from appetizers to desserts. Our menu was planned with New Year's Day in mind. No-fuss foods that can be cooked as they're eaten make this buffet meal ideal for the hours of parades and football games. It's also easy on after-Christmas budgets!

MEATS: Quick-cooking beef and lamb which includes meat cubes for kabobs, fish, lean ground beef and wieners are good selections. If bacon is used, partially cook it to remove excess fat. The Cheese Fondue in this menu is quickly made using condensed Cheddar cheese soup.

SALAD: Combine greens with winter fruits for a tossed salad. The tangy dressing is a good contrast with Cheese Fondue. For a buffet, it's usually best to let guests add their own dressing, so the greens stay crisp.

BREADS: Snack size breads or crackers make good nibbling. Caesarettes are crunchy triangles that get their flavor from Caesar salad dressing and herb stuffing. One recipe using refrigerated Crescent rolls makes lots of good eating.

DESSERT: Fruit completes this meal best. Guests will appreciate this kind of dessert, especially if you are entertaining just after the big meals of the holidays. Serve warm, with steaming cups of coffee, then send guests homeward bound.

...cooked ahead for the fellows

Menu

*Kentucky Barbecued Ribs, page 52
*Baked Potatoes, page 106
 Coleslaw
*Cheese 'n Chili Cornbréad, page 103
 Lemon Meringue Pie
 Cold Drinks

When the men get together for their evenings of poker or bowling — or before an evening at the baseball game — a stag supper of their own cooking can be a huge success.

The homemaker can leave the scene after making a few foods ahead for the evening's feast. Men can be counted on to prepare the potatoes for roasting, toss the coleslaw together and concoct the marinade for Kentucky Barbecued Ribs.

Making meals ahead for cooking later is a big part of barbecuing. Meats that marinate for several hours before they're cooked, like the ribs in this menu; bread that can be made ahead to reheat on the grill; and desserts made early, then refrigerated or stored until ready for eating, make advance preparation a breeze.

Some tips to remember when marinating: time is fairly flexible; however the longer the time, the greater the flavor. If you perceive a long marinating time — over 12 hours — consider using less of such ingredients as vinegar and lemon juice since they tend to build up in strength.

Cover all foods before placing in refrigerator. This prevents foods from drying out and flavors from mingling.

To store breads, wrap securely in foil or place in plastic bags. Reheat breads, wrapped loosely in foil, at 375° or on the grill, 10 to 15 minutes.

...even when it rains

Menu

*Savory Smoked Steak, page 46
*Baked Stuffed Potatoes, page 106
*Creamy Burgundy Cherries, page 95
  Hot Rolls
  Beverage

Even when there's no chance to eat outside — planned or unplanned — a meal cooked on the barbecue need not be cancelled. With a little inventiveness, the day can be even more fun than the original party plan!

Room enough for everyone to eat inside may be the biggest problem to overcome. A picnic served on the floor in the basement or garage may suit children fine, but adults are more likely to prefer chairs. Perhaps, one of your guests has more space, and the whole party can change location — with you providing the food, of course. Sheltered picnic areas are another alternative. Even if eating indoors is a little crowded, your guests probably won't notice too much — and you can plan the rest of the day far away from your home.

Lots of activities are available in most communities and make excellent choices for outings on rainy days. Museums, art galleries or indoor skating can be enjoyed even when the weather is bad. Check the newspaper for ideas — maybe there's a circus or special exhibit in town. If it's a small group, brainstorm for ideas. Choose a movie or play you wouldn't normally attend; it's sure to spark some lively discussion. Or, visit some point of historical interest, out-of-the way shops, antique stores, or, get out in the country, provided the weather's not too threatening. A hike takes on

a whole new outlook in the rain and can be just as much fun if everyone's dressed in boots and slickers.

MEATS: Depending on your equipment, no change in menu needs to be made. Tips for Cooking in Cold Weather, page 19, may apply. The smokey flavored steak in this menu is sure to bring good thoughts of outdoor cooking to even the grayest day.

POTATOES: Cook these along with the meat or in the oven. All recipes in this book that can be cooked on the grill, have indoor cooking methods, too. Other baked potatoes with savory seasoned butter are on page 106.

SALAD: Fruit in a salad offers a change from traditional vegetable tossed salads. The salad in this menu is made with gelatin and cherry pie filling, sparkled with wine. Others to try are Roquefort Tossed Fruit Salad, page 91, or Cardinal Coleslaw, page 93.

...breakfast in the park

Menu

*Breakfast Bunwiches, page 56
Fresh Fruit
Cold or Hot Beverages

The sun's just coming up — and you're there
to catch the sights and sounds of those
early hours and to follow the pursuits of
summer: fishing, hiking, photography, bird
watching or, just that ''got to get up'' feeling.
When it's time to stop for some hot coffee
and something to eat, have breakfast in the
open air. It needs to be hearty . . . though
not necessary traditional.

A tiny portable grill can be carried along
for this sandwich breakfast. The Canadian
bacon slices cook quickly and when placed
inside a toasted bun with cheese and tomato
give real stick-to-the-ribs goodness.

Fresh fruit along with a hot or cold drink,
depending on the weather, is all you need
to add to the Bunwiches. Instant drink mixes,
coffee, bouillon or soups, are easy to carry;
then all you need is one container for the
water! Don't forget a pot for heating the water.

Self-lighting charcoal kits are compact and
easy to carry. Keep equipment to a minimum;
no plates are needed for this easy meal.

...a "plug-in brunch"

Menu

Blender Orange Juice
*Maple Ham Dinner, page 59
Skillet Scrambled Eggs
Streusel Cinnamon Coffee Cake
Breakfast Danish Rolls
Coffee

Weekends give the homemaker a chance to spend more time with the first meal of the day. Brunch need not be formal. Traditional breakfast foods take on new dimensions when served outdoors. Enjoy these favorites — but let appliances do the work.

Small kitchen appliances can be used for all the cooking. Just be sure your patio has adequate electrical wiring for the number of appliances you want to use. If an extension cord is necessary, be sure it's heavy duty and placed well out of the way of all possible traffic.

Popular appliances you can use in planning "plug-in meals" are given below with suggestions for foods you might like to try.

A blender whips orange juice or mixtures of juices, milk drinks, chilled soups and dips for fruits to frothy goodness. Cordless blenders are available for those who do lots of entertaining — no matter how far they happen to be from an electrical outlet.

A griddle or grill cooks ham or Canadian bacon slices along with pancakes, waffles, French toast, fruit slices or kabobs. Canadian Bacon Brunch, basted with rich cranberry glaze, page 56, is delicious prepared on a rotisserie that accompanies this electric grill.

An electric skillet offers scrambled eggs made special, if desired, by adding cheese or cream soups. Use the skillet for grilled meat or cheese sandwiches, too.

Bun warmers heat breads you make or buy from the bakery.

Use an electric ice crusher or blender to crush ice that surrounds a fresh fruit bowl or is mixed with fruit drinks or juices.

Cordless electric knives slice meats and vegetables extra thin for summer sandwiches and salads.

...picnic on the go

Menu

*Circle Burgers, page 24
*Cheese Potatoes, page 106
*Onion Corn on the Cob, page 99
Easy Salad Wedges
Instant Dessert Torte

Suddenly it's a beautiful day — when it was supposed to rain — and someone mentions a picnic. Why not? Today's food companies offer many prepared foods that make instant picnicking possible at the push of a grocery cart.

Recipes are developed as you wheel down the supermarket aisles, so what you need to remember is your equipment. Some families even keep a hibachi grill in their car trunks all the time for spur-of-the-moment picnics. A list similar to ours, tucked in the picnic hamper, can be referred to before leaving home, so nothing as essential as a can opener gets left behind.

Our menu includes doughnut-shaped burgers filled with a squeeze of cheese spread; easily cut wedges or slices of iceberg lettuce — topped with a refrigerated dressing or flavored dip; corn on the cob, roasted in onion-butter; frozen French fries, heated in foil — and an unbelievably fancy cake! We were so excited, we almost forgot to leave the shopping cart behind!

MEATS: Choose those that cook quickly, since equipment will be simple and there won't be pre-preparation time. Tender steaks, cube steaks, ground beef, brown-and-serve sausages, wieners, ham slices or the "fixings" for kabobs make good choices. Salad dressings, prepared sauces and fruit preserves make good brush-on sauces.

VEGETABLES: Use foil cooking to good advantage for frozen potato products as well as other vegetables.

SALADS: Salad mixtures can be found in cans, jars or packages in the produce section, dairy case or grocery shelf. Toss together greens or slaw mixtures with dressing or just serve canned bean salad. Fruit ambrosia can be quickly made with chilled fruit sections and a sprinkle of coconut. No need to be in the carrot and celery stick rut! Vegetables and fruit miss too many picnics without very good reasons, so give these fun salads special thought.

DESSERT: Can be the crowning touch with so many easy-to-use convenience products. Ours is a prepared cake layered with canned pudding, sliced bananas and ice cream topping. These are versatile products that need no refrigeration. Frozen desserts that need only thawing before eating can be taken, too.

PICNIC EQUIPMENT CHECKLIST

Paper tablecloth, napkins, plates
Plastic spoons, forks and sharp plastic knives
Plastic cups
Roll of heavy-duty aluminum foil
5-pound bag of charcoal briquets and lighter fluid or two self-lighting kits
Potholders
Paper towels
Long sharp knife
Paring knife
Kitchen fork
Pancake turner or tongs
Can opener and bottle opener
Bread board (or use foil to protect some other flat surface)
Pail filled with ice or ice chest
Drinking water
Large paper bags or cartons for trash

Meats

Indoors or out, any time of year, there are few limits to the kind of meat or cooking methods for the barbecue chef. Meat is the main attraction whether it be hamburgers, wieners, beef, pork, lamb, poultry or seafood.

Four methods are used when cooking over coals. Familiarity with these helps in making meat selections.

HOT OFF THE GRILL applies to the most common cooking method. Meat cooks quickly to the desired doneness on a rack supported a few inches from the coals.

ROASTING larger cuts requires a shielded, or covered, grill or a rotisserie. Temperature control is important since a slow steady fire must be maintained.

The popularity of FOIL for barbecue cooking grows with the added bonus — no grills to clean. Browning meats over hot coals for a few minutes before wrapping with foil gives a better flavor.

SMOKED FLAVOR is added by using dampened wood chips, then covering the grill while cooking. This method is often combined with roasting since the longer cooking time allows the smoke to penetrate.

Each section of this chapter gives help in choosing meats and cooking methods. Information on buying grills and accessories, as well as specific information on using charcoal for fires, is on pages 152-155.

Once this information is at hand, you can coordinate the recipe with other meal plans. Think through the preparation time you will need. Learning to arrange time for those parts of the meal that need kitchen preparation with actual cooking time on the grill, is what makes barbecuing a carefree cooking experience. The recipes and information in the pages that follow will give greater variety to your barbecue meals. As any seasoned chef will say — tender meat plus great barbecue flavor are the beginnings of cooking triumphs that will become your own specialties.

FACTORS AFFECTING COOKING TIME — cooking times have been given in recipes and on charts for meats used in this chapter. These will vary depending on several factors:

1. The meat cut, size and shape.

2. Temperature of meat when cooking begins.

3. Equipment used.

4. Heat maintained during cooking which can be affected by both wind and temperature.

5. Degree of doneness desired.

While it is possible to control these factors to some extent, it's always a good idea to leave flexibility in your meal schedule. Plan activities or snacks to busy family and guests if the cooking seems to be longer than expected; wrap meats in foil and place at the back of the grill to keep them hot until serving time if they're done before you're ready. It's that simple.

Cooking in Cold Weather — When developing recipes for this book, we had a chance to test recipes when the temperature outside was around 40 degrees. At this temperature, we found that covered grills were almost essential to keep meats hot on one side while the other side was cooking. Cooking times increased about 5 minutes on each side for hamburgers and steaks, longer for larger cuts. Be sure to allow extra time in your schedule. The eating, however, was always worth the cold fingers and red noses of our taste testers.

Serving Size — The number of servings given for a recipe is a guide to the average number of servings that recipe will make, not an indication of the number of people it will serve. In general, we have allowed larger servings for recipes in this book. Barbecue menus tend to be more simple and appetites are larger! You, however, are the best judge as to the amount your family or guests require.

A good general guide when purchasing meats to barbecue is allowing ¾ to 1 pound per serving for bone-in cuts; ⅓ to ½ pound for boneless cuts. Poultry can be purchased according to this guide or in portions. Have the butcher cut birds into half or quarter bird servings. Servings of fish may be smaller; although regional preferences must be considered.

MEAT THERMOMETERS

Meat thermometers register the internal temperature (degree of doneness) of the meat. They should be inserted into the center of the thickest portion of meat, being sure that the bulb of the thermometer doesn't rest in fat or on bone. See specific recipes for the approximate roasting times.

Seasoning sorcery

Although there is a certain aura to any food cooked over the coals, not all the good flavor can be attributed to that source. The creative cook knows that other seasonings — whether in basting sauces, marinades or herb flavored oils — are necessary to further enhance foods cooked on the grill.

Imagination, along with a few basic guidelines, will aid you in developing a wide repertoire of these specialties.

MARINADES: Accomplish both tenderizing and flavoring. Meats are marinated by letting them stand in a mixture of oil and either vinegar, wine or fruit juice along with herbs and spices.

When tenderizing is needed, longer marinating times are used. The meat may be pierced with a fork to allow the marinade to penetrate.

Marinating can be done either in the refrigerator or at room temperature just prior to cooking time. Since barbecues are in many settings, we make the following recommendations to protect against the possibility of spoilage: *any marinating over an hour's time in an outdoor situation — or two hours in the home — should be done in the refrigerator or an insulated cooler.* If you do marinate at room temperature, do not put the meat in direct sunlight or in a very warm place.

The easiest way to marinate meat is to put it in a plastic bag. Just make sure the bag is tightly closed, so the liquid doesn't leak. You may also place the contents in a glass or plastic bowl and then cover. If you use an aluminum pan, the vinegar portion of the marinade will make the pan turn dark although the food will not be harmed.

Selection of ingredients for marinades needs some consideration. The following are guidelines for using a variety of ingredients:

OILS: See HERB FLAVORED OILS, below.

VINEGARS, WINES AND FRUIT JUICES: As a general rule, make a choice that is a natural partner to the meat you're cooking. Cider, wine, garlic or other herb flavored vinegars go well with meats. These are generally better to use than distilled white vinegar used for pickling.

Alcohol evaporates during the cooking process so wine is used only for its rich flavor. A good sound rule is to cook with the wine you drink — and vice versa. Small amounts of leftover dinner wines are great to use in cooking, and every wine type can be used.

Fruit juices are more likely to flavor than tenderize meats, so are best used with tender cuts, poultry and seafood. Lemon juice is an exception. Other juices such as orange, apple, apricot and peach nectars are sometimes substitutes for wines; however, these cannot be expected to give as rich a flavor.

HERBS AND SPICES: See chart.

BASTING SAUCES: Flavor meat while it cooks. These are usually thick enough to coat the meat, but not to penetrate.

Some sauces which have a high sugar content cannot be used during the entire cooking process because they tend to burn. Adding these during the last 30 minutes will give meats a sparkling glazed appearance without overpowering the meat flavor.

HERB FLAVORED OILS: Cooking oils, whether corn, safflower, peanut or another you might choose, or even melted butter or margarine, are mixed with herbs to become flavored brush-ons for kabobs, poultry and fish. These are leaner meats which would readily dry out from the heat of the coals. The oil serves as a carrier for herbs as well, so their value can't be disputed. Cooking oil, rather than butter, should be used in marinades because it will not solidify when cool.

USE OF TENDERIZERS IN BARBECUING: To minimize food costs, these chapters contain many recipes using less tender cuts of meat. However, less tender cuts usually require long, slow cooking. Cooking times and methods can be varied by use of meat tenderizers. When using tenderizers, follow manufacturer's directions carefully for best results. Most meats which have been treated with tenderizers are cooked to medium rare because heat will stop the action of the tenderizer.

Instant meat marinades come in individual packages and contain tenderizer as well as seasoning. These need only the addition of water or wine, and marinating time is short. Use these as directed on label.

Pre-tenderized meats are now available in some supermarkets. Cooking times for roasts and larger cuts take less time when they are pre-tenderized.

Many sauce mixes, prepared sauces and marinades are available today. We've taken advantage of these in our recipes as well as giving many recipes for sauces you can make from scratch. Here are three basic ones you can use for a start. Develop your own specialties from them.

EASY BARBECUE SAUCE

1½ cups sauce

    1 cup (8-oz. can) tomato sauce
    ¼ cup prepared barbecue sauce
    1 tablespoon instant minced onion
    1 lemon, thinly sliced
    2 tablespoons brown sugar
    1 teaspoon garlic salt
    ½ teaspoon dry mustard
    ⅛ teaspoon pepper

Combine all ingredients; mix well. Let stand 15 to 20 minutes to blend flavors. Store leftover sauce, covered, in refrigerator.

HERBS AND SPICES

Basil	Beef and lamb roasts, hamburgers, lamb chops, chicken, duck, turkey, shrimp, lobster, salmon
Marjoram	Lamb, stuffings, turkey, duck, shrimp, salmon
Oregano	Hamburger, beef and lamb roasts, chicken, fish and shrimp
Rosemary	Lamb or pork roast, turkey, duck, salmon
Sage	Pork, chicken, duck, turkey, salmon
Savory	Beef and pork roasts, hamburgers, spareribs, fish
Tarragon	Chicken, duck, turkey, fish and seafood
Thyme	Roasts, hamburgers, chicken, lobster, scallops, shrimp

BEEF TERIYAKI MARINADE

1⅓ cups marinade

    1 cup soy sauce
    ¼ cup sugar
    2 tablespoons finely chopped onion or
      2 teaspoons instant minced onion
    1¼ teaspoons ground ginger
    4 bay leaves, crushed
    4 cloves garlic, crushed

Combine all ingredients; stir until blended.

QUICK AND EASY TOMATO SAUCE

1½ cups sauce

    1 cup (8-oz. can) tomato sauce
    ½ cup water
    1 teaspoon Worcestershire sauce
    ½ teaspoon salt
    Dash pepper

Combine ingredients in saucepan. Heat and serve.

SUBSTITUTIONS

1 med. Lemon — 2 to 3 tsps. grated fresh peel and 2 to 3 Tbsp. juice; or 1½ tsp. lemon flavoring; or 1 to 1½ tsp. prepared lemon peel; or 2 to 3 Tbsps. bottled lemon juice

1 med. Orange — 1 to 2 Tbsp. grated fresh peel and ¼ to ⅓ cup juice or frozen orange juice, reconstituted; or ½ to 1 Tbsp. grated prepared orange peel

1 med. clove Garlic — ⅛ tsp. instant minced garlic; or ⅛ tsp. garlic powder; or ½ tsp. garlic salt

1 Tbsp. Herbs, fresh — 1 tsp. dried herbs

Individual Seasonings — Blended, packaged seasonings for salad dressings, spaghetti sauce and other dishes

1 tsp. prepared Mustard — ½ tsp. dry mustard

1 med. Onion — ½ cup chopped or sliced; 2 Tbsp. instant chopped or minced or onion flakes; or 1½ tsps. onion powder; or 2 Tbsp. onion salt

1 cup Tomato Sauce — 8 oz. can; or 1¼ cups (10¼-oz. can) condensed tomato soup; or 1 cup catsup; or ¾ cup tomato paste plus ¼ cup water

Ground Beef

Summertime, U.S.A. — and the aroma drifting along any street about suppertime is barbecue flavored. Chances are it's sizzling hamburgers that account for most of the smells. It's said that Americans dream of charcoal broiled steaks, but hamburgers top the list for family fare.

Ground beef is available in several different types:

"Hamburger" can contain up to 30% fat. This can include the addition of beef fat above that which is attached to the meat. Because of the large amount of fat, the meat may shrink after cooking.

Ground beef, regular ground beef or chopped beef: consists of ground or chopped fresh and/or frozen beef with or without seasoning and without the addition of beef fat as such. It does not contain more than 30 percent fat. It does not contain water or any by-products. Lean ground beef, lean regular ground beef or lean chopped beef: meets the requirements of ground beef but does not contain more than 22 percent fat.

Extra lean ground beef, extra lean regular ground beef, or extra lean chopped beef: meets the requirements of ground beef but does not contain more than 15 percent fat.

Occasionally ground meat is sold in meatloaf mixtures or other such pre-combined foods. If these mixtures include ingredients other than meat, the ingredients will be listed on the label.

Generally, leaner types of ground beef have better flavor, but any will do. Dripping fat that causes flare-up and excessive smoking is another reason for choosing a leaner cut. Check the recipe before making a choice. Ingredients like bread crumbs help absorb fat, and added liquid moistens leaner types that sometimes seem dry.

Handle ground beef gently — the less it's handled during mixing and shaping the more tender the burgers will be.

Cooking hamburgers for a crowd? Make patties ahead, stacking between sheets of waxed paper; refrigerate until ready for grilling. Or, freeze days ahead by wrapping stacked patties in foil; thaw before grilling for juicier burgers.

For easy shaping, use a ½ to 1-cup measure. Meat mixture can also be shaped into a rectangle, then divided and shaped into equal portions.

Use imagination in shaping patties — rounds, squares, doughnuts, ovals, wiener shapes can all make the barbecue scene. Just remember to handle gently!

HAMBURGERS
4 servings

>1 lb. ground beef
>1 tablespoon Worcestershire sauce
>Dash Tabasco sauce
>Salt
>Pepper

BEFORE GRILLING: Combine ground beef with Worcestershire sauce and Tabasco sauce. Shape into patties.

ON THE GRILL: Place patties on grill 3 to 4 inches from hot coals. Cook on each side, until browned to desired doneness. Season with salt and pepper. If desired, serve with onion slices, mustard and catsup.

Tips: Patties can be fried in fry pan or oven broiled, as directed.

The following seasonings can be used for the Worcestershire sauce and Tabasco sauce: 2 to 4 tablespoons chopped onion, 1 tablespoon instant minced onion or 1 tablespoon onion salt. 1 tablespoon garlic salt, ⅛ teaspoon garlic powder or ⅓ teaspoon instant minced garlic. 1 tablespoon barbecue sauce. 1 teaspoon prepared mustard and/or 1 tablespoon catsup.

For Cheeseburgers, top each hamburger with 1 slice cheese during last minute of frying. Cover until cheese begins to melt.

Filled hamburgers: Form each patty into two thin patties. Place desired filling between patties; seal edges well.

Filling Suggestions:
Slices of cheese
Chopped canned mushrooms
Mustard
Catsup
Pickle relish
Chopped or sliced pickle

SALISBURY STEAK SPECIAL

4 to 5 servings

    2 lbs. ground beef
 ½ cup bread or cracker crumbs
 ¼ cup chopped onion
   1 teaspoon salt or seasoned salt
 Dash pepper
 Dash garlic salt
   3 tablespoons prepared mustard
   2 tablespoons catsup or steak sauce
   2 tablespoons Worcestershire sauce

BEFORE GRILLING: In large bowl, combine ground beef, bread crumbs, onion, salt, pepper and garlic salt; blend well. Shape into a large patty, about 1½-inches thick. Combine mustard, catsup and Worcestershire sauce for basting sauce.

ON THE GRILL: Brush with basting sauce. Place patty on grill 4 to 6 inches from hot coals. Cook 20 to 25 minutes until browned on both sides and of desired doneness, brushing several times with basting sauce.

Tip: Steak can be broiled, as directed, in oven.

Meat balls make quick hors d'oeuvres grilled on a hibachi in the fireplace anytime of year. These are also fun to fondue and serve with your favorite sauce.

SPICY APPETIZER MEAT BALLS

24 meat balls

    1 lb. ground beef
    ¼ teaspoon garlic salt
    ½ teaspoon salt or seasoned salt
    2 teaspoons prepared mustard
    2 teaspoons soy sauce
    1 teaspoon Worcestershire sauce

BEFORE GRILLING: Combine all ingredients; mix well. Form into 1-inch meat balls. Thread on skewers.

ON THE GRILL: Place skewers on grill 3 to 4 inches above hot coals. Cook for 8 to 10 minutes, turning occasionally, until meat is browned and of desired doneness. If desired, serve with cocktail or barbecue sauce.

> **Tips:** Meat balls can be broiled in oven, browned in 1 tablespoon cooking oil in fry pan or cooked in hot oil in fondue pot.
> For patties, form meat into three to four patties. Cook 10 to 15 minutes, turning once.

CIRCLE BURGERS

4 sandwiches

    1 lb. ground beef
    1 teaspoon salt
    2 English muffins
    Mustard
    1 jar (8 oz.) pasteurized process cheese
       spread

BEFORE GRILLING: Combine meat and salt; form into 4 doughnut-shaped patties. Split English muffins; have mustard and cheese ready at grill.

ON THE GRILL: Place patties on grill 3 to 4 inches from hot coals. Cook until browned on both sides and of desired doneness. Toast split side of English muffin on grill. Spread muffins with mustard; top with patties. Spoon cheese spread into center of patties. Place on grill until cheese melts.

> **Tips:** If desired, top cheese with relish or chopped onion.
> Serve on toasted buns for easy eating.
> Burgers can be broiled, as directed, in oven.

CHEESEBURGER LOAF

6 servings

    1 can (10¾ oz.) condensed Cheddar
       cheese soup
    ½ cup dry bread or cracker crumbs
    ½ cup chopped onion or 2 tablespoons
       instant minced onion
    2 tablespoons finely chopped green
       pepper
    1 tablespoon prepared mustard
    1 teaspoon salt or seasoned salt
    ¼ teaspoon pepper or seasoned pepper
    2 eggs
    2 lbs. ground beef
    2 tablespoons milk
    Green pepper rings, if desired

BEFORE GRILLING: In large mixing bowl, combine ½ can (½ cup) soup with remaining ingredients except milk and green pepper; mix well. Place in greased foil-lined 9x5-inch loaf pan or disposable foil pan. Shape into a loaf.

ON THE GRILL: Place on grill 6 to 8 inches from hot coals; cover with hood of grill or foil tent (see page 156). Cook for 1 to 1½ hours until done. Transfer meat to platter. If desired, heat remaining soup with 2 tablespoons milk. Serve over meat loaf; decorate with green pepper rings. For easier slicing, let set 10 to 15 minutes before serving.

> **Tips:** Meat loaf can be baked in oven at 350° for 40 to 50 minutes.
> Cream of mushroom and celery soups can be used for Cheddar cheese soup. Add sliced mushrooms that have been cooked in butter to sauce, if desired.

LEMONY BURGERS

4 servings

    1 lb. ground beef
    1 package Pillsbury Brown Gravy Mix
    ¼ cup chopped onion or 1 tablespoon
       instant minced onion
    2 tablespoons lemon juice
    1 tablespoon Worcestershire sauce
    ½ teaspoon pepper or 1 to
       2 teaspoons lemon pepper marinade

BEFORE GRILLING: In large bowl, combine all ingredients; blend well. Shape into 4 patties.

ON THE GRILL: Place patties on grill 3 to 4 inches from hot coals. Cook on both sides until browned or of desired doneness.

> **Tip:** Burgers can be broiled, as directed, in oven.

HAMBURGER TOPPER

½ cup

½ cup dairy or imitation sour cream
½ teaspoon prepared mustard
½ teaspoon dill weed or 1 teaspoon
  dill seed

Combine all ingredients; mix well. Store, covered, in refrigerator after use.

> **Tip:** Sour cream topper can be used as dip for beef fondue or meatballs.

Covered grills can take the place of an oven during warm summer months. Baked right in the pan, this easy dish has added smokey barbecue flavor. Add foil cooked vegetables and heat brown 'n serve rolls on the grill, too.

COOKOUT HAMBURGER PIE

4 to 6 servings

1½ lbs. lean ground beef
¼ cup dry bread or cracker crumbs
¼ cup milk
¼ cup chopped onion or 1 tablespoon
  instant minced onion
1 tablespoon parsley flakes
1 tablespoon Worcestershire sauce
1 teaspoon salt or seasoned salt
Dash pepper
1 can (15 oz.) Spanish rice
Parsley flakes, if desired

BEFORE GRILLING: In large bowl, combine all ingredients except Spanish rice and parsley flakes; mix well. Pat mixture into greased 9-inch metal or foil pie pan; gently press up sides of pan to make a crust. Spoon Spanish rice into meat crust.

ON THE GRILL: Place on grill 6 to 8 inches from hot coals; cover with hood of grill or a foil tent. (See page 156.) Cook 20 to 25 minutes until done. If desired, sprinkle with additional parsley flakes.

> **Tips:** 4 servings Pillsbury Hungry Jack Mashed Potatoes can be used for Spanish rice. After cooking, brush top of potatoes with melted butter and sprinkle on paprika or parsley flakes.
>
> Other cooked flavored rice mixes, prepared as directed, can be used for Spanish rice.
>
> For 8-inch pie pan, use 1 lb. ground beef.
>
> Hamburger Pie can be baked, as directed, in 350° oven.

A favorite main dish made on the grill! Great for getting out of the kitchen on a summer day and takes enough time to roast potatoes, too!

SMOKEY MEAT LOAF

6 servings

2 lbs. ground beef
½ cup dry bread or cracker crumbs
½ cup chopped onion or 2 tablespoons
  instant minced onion
1 tablespoon prepared mustard
1 teaspoon salt or seasoned salt
¼ teaspoon pepper or seasoned pepper
¼ teaspoon liquid smoke, if desired
2 eggs

Glaze:

¼ cup catsup or chili sauce
2 tablespoons chopped onion or
  1 teaspoon instant minced onion
1 tablespoon brown sugar
1 tablespoon cooking oil

BEFORE GRILLING: In mixing bowl, combine all ingredients for meat loaf; mix well. Shape meat mixture into a loaf. Combine Glaze ingredients; mix well.

ON THE GRILL: Place meat loaf on grill 6 to 8 inches from medium coals. Cover with hood of grill or foil tent (see page 156). Cook 50 to 60 minutes until desired doneness, turning once and brushing occasionally with Glaze.

> **Tips:** Meat loaf can be shaped on a piece of heavy duty foil. Bring sides of foil up around loaf to form a pan. Place on grill and bake as directed.
>
> Meat loaf can be baked, as directed, in 350° oven.

NORTHWOODS BURGERS
6 servings

    2 lbs. ground beef
    1 egg
    2 tablespoons Worcestershire sauce
1½ teaspoons salt
    ½ teaspoon garlic salt
    ¼ teaspoon pepper
    ⅓ cup (3 oz.) blue cheese
    2 tablespoons oil and vinegar salad
       dressing
    1 teaspoon Worcestershire sauce

BEFORE GRILLING: Combine ground beef, egg, Worcestershire sauce, salt, garlic salt and pepper; mix well. Divide into 6 portions. Flatten each portion into a 5½-inch circle. Blend blue cheese, salad dressing and 1 teaspoon Worcestershire sauce and place 1 tablespoon of the mixture on one half of each meat patty, leaving a ½-inch edge of the meat uncovered. Gently fold uncovered portion of meat over cheese, pressing edges of meat together to seal.

ON THE GRILL: Place patties on grill 3 to 4 inches from hot coals. Cook until browned on both sides and of desired doneness.

Tip: Burgers can be broiled, as directed, in oven.

CHEESEBURGER CANTONESE
6 sandwiches

    1 lb. ground beef
    1 can (1 lb.) bean sprouts, drained
    2 tablespoons soy sauce
    ½ teaspoon onion salt or ¼ teaspoon
       onion powder
    6 slices American pasteurized process
       cheese
    6 hamburger buns, split
    Salad dressing

BEFORE GRILLING: Combine beef, bean sprouts, soy sauce and onion salt; mix well. Form mixture into 6 patties.

ON THE GRILL: Place patties on grill 3 to 4 inches from hot coals. Cook until browned on both sides to desired doneness. For each sandwich, place bun tops on grill to toast. When toasted, place a piece of cheese on each patty and top with toasted bun. While cheese melts, toast bottom half of buns. If desired, spread with salad dressing before topping with patty.

Tip: Burgers can be broiled in oven or browned in fry pan.

Hamburgers in the best German tradition, filled with wieners, topped with cheese and sauerkraut! Heat the sauerkraut, if you like, in its open can or in foil right on the grill.

CHEESEBURGERS, FRANKFORT-STYLE
6 servings

1½ lbs. ground beef
4 wieners, finely chopped
⅓ cup steak sauce
3 tablespoons dry onion soup mix
1 tablespoon mustard
12 slices rye bread or 6 rye buns
4 slices crisp bacon, crumbled, if desired
1 can (1 lb.) sauerkraut, drained
6 slices Swiss cheese

BEFORE GRILLING: In large bowl, combine beef, wieners, soup mix, steak sauce and mustard; blend well. Shape into 6 patties. Have bread, bacon, sauerkraut and cheese ready to serve.

ON THE GRILL: Place patties on grill 3 to 4 inches from hot coals. Cook until browned on both sides and of desired doneness. Serve on bread with sauerkraut, bacon and cheese.

Tip: Burgers can be broiled, as directed, in oven.

Ladies especially like these fruit topped burgers. Try serving them when your group gets together for lunch on the patio.

FRUIT 'N BEEF POLYNESIAN
4 servings

1½ lbs. ground beef
1½ teaspoons salt or seasoned salt
½ teaspoon pepper or seasoned pepper
¼ cup butter or margarine, melted
½ cup prepared sweet and sour sauce
2 bananas
4 pineapple slices

BEFORE GRILLING: In large bowl, combine beef, salt and pepper; blend well. Shape into 4 oval patties. Melt butter in saucepan; stir in sauce. Have banana and pineapple slices ready at grill.

ON THE GRILL: Brush patties with sauce. Place on grill 3 to 4 inches from hot coals. Cook until browned on one side; turn. Meanwhile, cut bananas lengthwise and crosswise in quarters. Lay a pineapple slice and 2 banana quarters on each burger. Spoon on remaining sauce. Continue cooking until of desired doneness.

Tips: Burgers may be broiled, as directed, in oven.

These burgers are best served open-faced on toasted English muffins.

CHILES RELLENOS BURGERS

6 servings

>   1 lb. ground beef
>   1 can (8 oz.) tomato sauce with onions
>   ½ teaspoon pepper
>   1 cup (4 oz.) shredded Cheddar cheese
>   1 tablespoon canned diced green chiles*
>   6 hot dog buns, toasted

BEFORE GRILLING: In large bowl, combine meat, ½ cup tomato sauce (reserve remaining for sauce), salt and pepper. Form into 6 long patties, ¼-inch thick. Combine cheese with chiles. Place 1 tablespoon cheese mixture lengthwise down center of each patty; reserve remaining cheese. Fold sides together and seal securely. Refrigerate until cooking time.

ON THE GRILL: Place patties on grill 3 to 4 inches from hot coals. Cook 15 to 20 minutes until browned on both sides and of desired doneness. (Meanwhile, heat remaining tomato sauce with reserved cheese mixture.) Keep warm until serving time. Place burgers on buns and top with sauce.

> **Tips:** *If your family prefers a milder flavored filling, substitute chopped stuffed green olives for the chiles. Burgers can be broiled, as directed, in oven.

Serve this to a hungry bunch of teenagers for a hearty party, Italian-style. Add individual servings of relishes, Seasoned Chipper Snacks, page 109, and home made ice cream.

HAMBURGER PIZZA-RIFFIC

4 to 6 servings

>   1½ lbs. ground beef
>   1 can (8 oz.) tomato sauce with
>   mushrooms
>   1 clove garlic, minced or ¼ teaspoon
>   instant minced garlic
>   2 teaspoons sugar
>   ½ teaspoon Italian seasoning
>   1 unsliced loaf Italian or French bread
>   2 to 4 tablespoons butter or margarine
>   Salt or seasoned salt
>   4 slices American or Mozzarella cheese,
>   cut into triangles
>   3 tablespoons Parmesan cheese

BEFORE GRILLING: Shape beef into 8 patties.

Combine tomato sauce, garlic, sugar and seasoning in saucepan; simmer 5 minutes. Keep warm until serving time. Slice bread in halves lengthwise; spread with butter.

ON THE GRILL: Place patties on grill 3 to 4 inches from hot coals. Cook until browned on both sides and of desired doneness. Season with salt. To assemble sandwich, place bottom half of loaf on large piece of heavy duty foil. Dip patties in sauce, then overlap lengthwise down loaf. Place a cheese triangle between each patty. Pour remaining sauce over patties; sprinkle with Parmesan cheese. Shape foil around loaf, but do not cover. Heat on grill along with top half of loaf for 10 to 15 minutes until bread is hot. Top with other half of loaf; secure with toothpicks and cut into serving size pieces.

> **Tip:** Burgers can be broiled in oven or browned in fry pan. Heat sandwich in oven or under broiler. If desired, serve sandwich open-face.

MEDITERRANEAN BURGER STACK UPS

6 large servings

>   2 lbs. ground beef
>   1 teaspoon salt
>   ½ teaspoon oregano or Italian seasoning
>   1 small eggplant, cut in ½-inch slices
>   ½ cup Italian salad dressing
>   1 to 2 large tomatoes, sliced

BEFORE GRILLING: In large bowl, combine ground beef, salt and oregano; blend well. Shape into 6 large patties. Have eggplant, dressing and tomatoes ready at grill.

ON THE GRILL: Brush patties and eggplant slices with salad dressing. Place on grill 3 to 4 inches from hot coals. Cook patties until browned on both sides and of desired doneness. Brush eggplant slices occasionally with salad dressing during grilling, turning once and topping with tomato. To serve, stack tomato and eggplant on top of hamburger. Garnish with crumbled Roquefort cheese or onion.

> **Tips:** Burgers can be broiled, as directed, in oven.
> Or, cook patties and eggplant slices in small amount of oil in fry pan.

SESAME SURPRISE MEATBALLS

    1 lb. ground beef
    2 teaspoons sugar
    ¼ teaspoon garlic salt
    ¼ teaspoon pepper
    1½ teaspoons soy sauce
    16 to 24 cocktail onions
    ¼ to ½ cup sesame seeds

BEFORE GRILLING: In large bowl, combine all ingredients except onions and sesame seeds; blend well. Shape into 16 to 24 meatballs with an onion in the center of each; coat with sesame seed. Thread meatballs on small skewers.

ON THE GRILL: Place skewers on grill 3 to 4 inches from hot coals. Cook until browned and of desired doneness.

    Tip: Meatballs can be broiled in oven or browned in fry pan.

Cover an oven proof Dutch oven with foil to save clean-up time when making this hearty casserole. Corn chips take on tamale characteristics!

CHILI SUPPER DISH

6 to 8 servings

    1 package (6 oz.) corn chips, crushed
    3 cans (1 lb. 5 oz. each) chili con carne
       with beans
    1 cup (1 bunch) green onions, chopped,
       including tops
    ½ cup ripe olives, drained and sliced
    4 tomatoes, sliced
    Salt
    Pepper
    1 cup shredded Cheddar or American
       cheese

BEFORE GRILLING: Place corn chips in bottom of generously buttered 3-quart Dutch oven. Add chili con carne. Sprinkle chopped onions over chili. Arrange olives and tomatoes in alternate layers, ending with tomatoes. Sprinkle with salt and pepper. Top with shredded cheese; cover.

ON THE GRILL: Place on grill 6 to 8 inches from hot coals. Cook about 1 hour or until thoroughly heated and tomatoes are cooked.

    Tip: Casserole can be heated, in 350° oven, as directed.

Double quick hamburgers with no shaping needed. Sure to please the camping crowd because they cook in about 10 minutes. Serve with potato salad.

EASY CHEESEBURGERS

3-4 servings

    1 to 1½ lbs. ground beef
    ½ cup (1 med.) chopped onion or
       2 tablespoons instant minced onion
    Salt or seasoned salt
    Pepper or seasoned pepper
    1 jar (5 oz.) pasteurized process cheese
       spread with hickory smoke flavor

ON THE GRILL: In fry pan, 3 to 4 inches from hot coals, brown ground beef and onion; drain. Season to taste. Add cheese, stir until cheese begins to melt. Serve on buns.

    Tips: Cheeseburgers can be prepared, as directed, in fry pan.

    1½ cups (6 oz.) shredded American or Cheddar cheese can be used for cheese spread. Or, try another favorite spread.

POTATO ONION BURGER DINNER

4 to 5 servings

    1 package Pillsbury Au Gratin Potato Mix
    1½ lbs. ground beef
    1 teaspoon salt or seasoned salt
    ½ teaspoon pepper or seasoned pepper
    ¼ teaspoon sage, if desired
    ¼ teaspoon thyme, if desired
    1 small onion, sliced
    ½ cup water

BEFORE GRILLING: Boil potatoes from au gratin mix in enough water to cover for 5 minutes. (Or, rehydrate potatoes by letting stand in cold water for 1½ hours.) Drain potatoes. Combine remaining ingredients except onion; blend well. Shape into 8 to 10 patties. Insert onion slice between 2 patties; seal edges. Place patties on squares of heavy duty foil. Spoon potatoes onto each patty. Mix water with cheese sauce mix; spoon over patties. Wrap tightly in foil.

ON THE GRILL: Place packets on grill 3 to 4 inches from hot coals. Cook for 20 to 25 minutes.

    Tips: Packets may be heated, as directed, in oven.

    To make ahead, assemble packets, as directed; refrigerate until ready to cook. Cook as directed.

Wieners and Sausage

A squirt of catsup, some pickles and a roasted wiener inside a toasted bun. The all-American hot dog has won universal acceptance as a handy and flavorful sandwich. Choices of wieners and other members of the sausage family for barbecuing go all the way from midget cocktail franks to king-size loaves of bologna.

Wieners, along with their sausage and luncheon meat partners, have in common their minced or ground meat base, which is blended with spices and other seasonings and usually stuffed into a casing.

1. WIENERS: Also called frankfurters, frank and Vienna-style sausage. They are available in varying sizes from the plump dinner franks to midget cocktail franks. Wieners are cured, spiced, packed in casings, smoked and cooked. Several types of wieners are available — all beef, all meat (made with a combination of beef, pork, and/or veal), and wieners with cereal and/or nonfat dry milk added. Manufacturers are required by law to list the ingredients which are added, so the labels tell you exactly what you are buying.

2. BOLOGNA: A cooked, smoked sausage made of all beef or beef and pork with mild seasonings similar to wieners. It is available in rings to cut in chunks for kabobs or large side rolls to rotisserie.

3. KNACKWURST: A garlic flavored sausage similar to wieners. It is usually larger in size than wieners.

4. SMOKED COUNTRY-STYLE SAUSAGE OR PORK SAUSAGE: Coarsely ground pork and beef combination, or pork only, that has been mildly cured and smoked, but not cooked. These and other uncooked smoked sausages must be precooked *before* grilling to assure doneness. One easy method is to drop the sausages into boiling water; cover and simmer over low heat, to prevent the casings from breaking, until heated through, about 5 to 10 minutes. This can be done ahead of time, if desired, then the sausage can be cooked on the grill like wieners.

5. POLISH SAUSAGE OR KIELBASA: Coarsely ground lean pork with beef added. It is cured, highly seasoned with garlic and smoked, but must be cooked as directed for Country Style Sausage before grilling. It comes in links either 4 to 5-inches or 8 to 10-inches long.

6. BRATWURST: Pork or a combination of pork with beef or veal which is seasoned with salt and spices similar to wieners. It is usually parboiled though not fully cooked or smoked. Bratwurst should be heated as directed for Country-Style Sausage before grilling. Bratwurst links may be plumper than frankfurters or pork sausage links.

SEASONED HOT DOG BUNS: Toast wiener buns along with the wieners until golden brown and crispy. For some extra zip, try mixing Parmesan cheese, Italian seasoning, caraway seeds or thyme with softened butter; spread on the inside of the buns before toasting.

CHUCKWAGON BEAN BAKE
4 to 5 servings

    1 can (12 oz.) luncheon meat
    2 cans (1-lb. each) pork and beans in
      tomato sauce
    ¼ cup catsup or chili sauce
    1 tablespoon brown sugar
    1 teaspoon prepared mustard or
      ½ teaspoon dry mustard
    1 teaspoon instant minced onion,
      if desired

BEFORE GRILLING: Slice luncheon meat into 4 to 5 slices. Combine all ingredients except luncheon meat; blend well. On squares of heavy duty foil, spoon beans into 4 to 5 portions; top with meat. Seal packets securely.

ON THE GRILL: Place packets on grill 3 to 4 inches from hot coals. Cook 20 to 25 minutes until heated.

Tips: Packets can be heated, as directed, in 350° oven.

To make ahead, assemble and refrigerate. Cook as directed. If refrigerated, allow about 5 minutes extra cooking time.

Fun to cook hot dogs and buns—all in one on a stick! Try these with Pillsbury Refrigerated Buttermilk or Country Style Biscuits, too.

CAMPFIRE WIENER CRESCENTS

6 to 8 servings

> 1 can (8 oz.) Pillsbury Quick Crescent Dinner Rolls
> 12 to 16 wieners
> 12 to 16 strips Cheddar or American cheese

BEFORE GRILLING: Separate crescent dough into 4 rectangles; press perforations to seal (this prevents separation during baking). Cut each into 3 or 4 strips lengthwise. Cut a narrow slit, lengthwise, in wieners, to make a pocket. Insert strip of cheese in each. Wind a strip of crescent dough around each wiener, spiral-fashion; secure each end with a toothpick. Place wieners on skewers, long-handled fork or green stick. (Or place on greased grill.)

ON THE GRILL: Hold wieners or place on grill 2 to 3 inches from hot coals. Cook 3 to 5 minutes, until crescent is dark golden brown, turning to bake crescent on all sides.

> **Tips:** Wiener crescents can be baked on cookie sheet in 375° oven for 10 to 15 minutes.
>
> To use Pillsbury Refrigerated Buttermilk or Country Style Biscuits, roll biscuits into strips; wind around 10 wieners and cook as directed.
>
> Try spreading split wiener with mustard or barbecue sauce before inserting cheese or press crescent dough in cornmeal or crushed flavored potato chips before winding to add extra crispness to rolls.
>
> Recipe can be halved. Extra crescent triangles can be baked, as directed, on the grill.

CHEESY CONEY ISLANDS

6 to 8 servings

> 1 can (15 oz.) chili
> 1 can (10¾ oz.) condensed Cheddar cheese soup
> 1 teaspoon Worcestershire sauce
> Dash garlic powder

Combine all ingredients in saucepan. Heat until bubbly. Spoon over grilled wieners on toasted buns.

TACO INSIDE OUTS

4 to 5 servings

> 1 cup shredded Cheddar or American cheese
> ½ cup crushed corn chips
> ¼ cup taco or barbecue sauce*
> 1 lb. wieners

BEFORE GRILLING: In small bowl, combine cheese, corn chips and taco sauce. Cut a narrow slit, lengthwise in wieners, to make a pocket. Insert about 2 tablespoons cheese mixture in each wiener. Place wieners on skewers, long-handled forks or green sticks.

ON THE GRILL: Hold wieners 2 to 3 inches from hot coals. Cook for 3 to 5 minutes, until heated and cheese melts.

> **Tips:** Wieners can be broiled, as directed, in oven.
>
> *Try part taco sauce mixed with catsup or barbecue sauce. This amount taco sauce may be too highly seasoned for some families.

Perfect for a fireplace cook-out. Cook wieners on a hibachi or in the fireplace, then dip in this tasty Cheddar fondue. Recipe is pictured on page 11.

CHEESE FONDUE

2 cups

> ½ cup Sauterne or other dry white wine
> 1 medium clove garlic, minced
> 4 slices (4 oz.) Swiss cheese, torn into pieces
> 2 tablespoons flour
> 1 can (10¾ oz.) condensed Cheddar cheese soup
> 1 lb. cocktail or bite-size pieces of wieners*

In saucepan or fondue pot, simmer wine and garlic over low heat. Combine cheese and flour; gradually blend into wine. Heat until cheese melts, stirring occasionally. Blend in soup; heat, stirring until smooth. Spear wieners with fork or toothpick and dip into fondue.

> **Tips:** *Also good with bite-size pieces of French or Italian bread cubes; lobster, shrimp or artichoke hearts.
>
> 1 cup shredded Swiss cheese can be used for slices.
>
> Recipe can be doubled.

As hostess, provide these four platters, metal skewers, garlic bread, a simple dessert, beverage . . . and a bed of hot coals.

PETITE SUPPER ON A SKEWER

PLATTER NO. 1 — *Meat:* Cubes of bologna, cervelat, salami, ham and other favorite cold cuts; skinless cocktail frankfurters and pork sausage links; bacon.

PLATTER NO. 2 — *Vegetables:* Tomato wedges or tiny whole tomatoes; green pepper squares; thickly sliced canned sweet potatoes, cooked carrots or squash; onion slices or whole cooked onion; and small canned (or cooked) Irish potatoes.

PLATTER NO. 3 — *Garnishes:* Canned (or cooked) mushroom caps, stuffed green olives, pitted ripe olives, pickles.

PLATTER NO. 4 — *Fruit:* Pineapple chunks, apple wedges, apricot halves, orange sections, lime or lemon slices, maraschino cherries.

Dress up canned meats with this tart 'n tangy glaze! Choose this one for an extra special camping treat. It's delicious brushed on canned ham, too!

ZESTY GRILLED LUNCHEON SLICES

3 to 4 servings

    1 can (12 oz.) luncheon meat
    ¼ cup apple or currant jelly
    ¼ cup firmly packed brown sugar
    1 tablespoon horseradish
    6 to 8 canned pear halves, peach halves
      or pineapple slices, if desired

BEFORE GRILLING: Slice luncheon meat into 4 to 5 slices. Combine jelly, mustard, brown sugar and horseradish in saucepan; heat over low heat until jelly is melted.

ON THE GRILL: Brush glaze on meat slices and fruit. Place on grill 3 to 4 inches from hot coals. Cook 3 to 5 minutes on each side, brushing frequently with glaze.

    Tip: Meat and fruit can be broiled, as directed, in oven.

BOLOGNA CROWD PLEASER

6 to 8 servings

    2 tablespoons butter or margarine
    2 tablespoons catsup
    2 tablespoons orange marmalade
    1 teaspoon Worcestershire sauce
    4 lbs. unsliced bologna

BEFORE GRILLING: Combine all ingredients except bologna to make basting sauce. Insert spit rod through center of meat; secure with holding forks.

ON THE GRILL: Arrange coals for roasting meat; see method B, page 5. Center meat on grill 6 to 8 inches from coals; cover. Roast over slow fire until heated through (about 1½ hours) basting with sauce during last 30 minutes. If desired, serve slices on toasted hamburger buns.

    Tip: Bologna can be heated, as directed, in 325° oven about 1 hour.

A sweet-sour barbecue sauce gives a sensational flavor to these kabobs. Do them on the grill or in the broiler. They make fun picnic fare with a potato or macaroni salad and a vegetable.

SMOKIE ISLAND KABOBS

10 kabobs

    1 cup (13½-oz. can) pineapple tidbits,
      drain and reserve ⅔ cup liquid
    Reserved ⅔ cup pineapple liquid
    1 package (¾ oz.) barbecue sauce mix
    1 cup (8-oz. can) tomato sauce
    1 lb. (10) smokie links, cut into thirds*
    1 green pepper, cut into cubes
   10 sweet pickles, cut in half

Preheat broiler. In small saucepan, combine pineapple liquid, barbecue sauce mix and tomato sauce. Heat, stirring occasionally, until mixture comes to a boil. Thread wieners, pineapple, green pepper and pickle alternately on skewers. Broil or grill 2 to 3 inches from heat, brushing occasionally with sauce, for 3 to 4 minutes on each side until heated through and lightly browned.

    Tips: *Wieners can be used for the smokie links. Cook thoroughly.

    Prepared barbecue sauce can be used for the sauce mixture in recipe. Or, barbecue sauce mix can be prepared as directed on package, if desired.

    Kabobs can be broiled, as directed, in oven.

Wieners curl up as they grill from cuts made along one side. Fill the center with sauerkraut for a German-style dinner, or see Tips for other filling suggestions.

FRANKS 'N KRAUT IN THE ROUND

4 servings

    3 to 4 cups (1 lb. 12-oz. can or 1 quart)
      sauerkraut
    2 tart cooking apples, peeled and
      chopped
    8 wieners
    Prepared barbecue sauce

BEFORE GRILLING: Spoon sauerkraut on four squares of foil. Top with chopped apple. Close; seal securely. Place each seam-side down on another square of foil. Close tightly. On outside curved edge, slice wieners almost through, on diagonal at ½-inch intervals.

ON THE GRILL: Place foil packets 4 to 6 inches from hot coals. Cook, turning every 15 minutes, for 30 to 45 minutes until heated through. Cook wieners on grill during last 10 minutes, brushing with barbecue sauce and turning occasionally. To serve, arrange 2 wieners in circle at base of sauerkraut.

> **Tips:** For variety, try two 1-lb. cans pork and beans, chili or spaghetti in place of sauerkraut and apple.
> Wieners can be broiled, as directed, in oven.

FAR EASTERN FRANKS AND PEACHES

4 to 5 servings

    1 can (29 oz.) peach halves
    ¼ cup vinegar
    ¼ cup molasses
    1 teaspoon cornstarch
    ¼ teaspoon salt
    ⅛ teaspoon ginger
    ½ teaspoon soy sauce, if desired
    1 lb. wieners

BEFORE GRILLING: Drain peaches, reserving ¼ cup syrup. In saucepan, combine syrup with remaining ingredients except wieners. Heat to boiling; reduce heat and simmer 5 minutes, stirring occasionally.

ON THE GRILL: Brush wieners and peach halves with sauce. Place on grill 3 to 4 inches from hot coals. Cook about 5 to 10 minutes until heated through, brushing frequently with sauce.

> **Tip:** Wieners and peaches can be broiled as directed in oven.

Summer or winter, bratwurst's a favorite of sports fans. Our ski picnic (on the opposite page), features this zesty sausage treat.

BEER 'N BRATWURST

4 to 5 servings

    1 lb. (6 to 8) bratwurst or other smoked
      sausage
    1 can (12 oz.) beer
    1 medium onion, sliced
    1 teaspoon celery seed, if desired
    1 bay leaf, if desired
    1 tablespoon butter or margarine

BEFORE GRILLING: In saucepan, heat bratwurst, beer, onion, celery seed and bay leaf to boiling; reduce heat and simmer gently for 5 minutes. Remove from heat. If desired, leave sausage in beer until ready to grill*; or drain, reserving bratwurst and onion. Melt butter in same saucepan; cook onions in butter until tender, but not browned. Keep warm for serving with bratwurst.

ON THE GRILL: Place bratwurst on the grill 3 to 4 inches from hot coals. Cook about 5 minutes on each side until sausages are done. Serve on buns with onions.

> **Tips:** Bratwurst can be broiled, as directed for 2 to 3 minutes on each side in oven.
> Recipe can be doubled.
>
> *Bratwurst can be marinated in cooled beer mixture overnight in refrigerator.

HOT FRUIT DOGS

    Wieners
    Fresh or dried fruit*

BEFORE GRILLING: Cut a narrow slit, lengthwise, in wieners to make a pocket. Insert pieces of fruit; secure with toothpicks.

ON THE GRILL: Place wieners, fruit-side down, on grill 3 to 4 inches from hot coals. Cook for 2 to 3 minutes on each side until heated through. If desired, serve with a prepared sweet and spicy sauce.

> **Tips:** Fruit Dogs can be broiled, as directed, in oven.
>
> *For a real taste treat, try wedge-shaped pieces of fresh pineapple, banana, apple, orange, cooked dried apricots or grapefruit.

Provincial Steak with Tomatoes, page 38; Marinated Artichoke Salad, page 91.

Beef

Beef is the undisputed favorite for barbecues — whether it appears on the table as thick steak, tender roast or flavorful kabob. Since a variety of cooking methods can be used there's no need to worry any more about the strain on the budget when the request for meat at your house always ends with "steak." Most beef cuts can be cooked to melt in your mouth tenderness if they are properly grilled.

Tender cuts can be cooked to rare or well-done; less tender cuts (unless pre-tendered) can be tenderized by marinating or using a tenderizer. Recipes in the chapter have been grouped according to the tenderness of cuts used.

A guide to choosing the method of cooking needed for barbecuing various beef cuts is the same as that used for the kitchen range. The following chart serves as a guide. Names given beef cuts sometimes vary from store to store and in different parts of the country. Moreover, the same name may mean different things in different areas. In most of the recipes we have given different cuts as options so that you will be able to choose a cut that will not only work satisfactorily in the recipe, but may even be a weekend special.

- Rub fat trimmings over grill or brush grill with cooking oil before cooking to prevent meat from sticking.

- To prevent loss of meat juices use tongs to turn steaks to avoid piercing the meat surface while cooking. If a fork must be used, insert it in the fat at the edge of steak.

- To check doneness, make a small cut in the meat near the bone. Timing, once you have experience, is actually a better cooking method since there will be less loss of meat juices.

- Remove meats, especially thick steaks, from refrigerator about an hour before cooking. It's easier to achieve the doneness desired than when these cuts are cooked right from the refrigerator.

ROAST HINTS

- Less tender roasts should be treated with meat tenderizer or marinated before cooking.

- Thin roasts up to 3 inches thick can be cooked on a regular grill; larger pieces can be cooked on a covered grill or rotisserie.

- Boneless, rolled roasts are generally better choices for the barbecue than bone-in roasts, since the even shape of rolled roasts cooks to a more even doneness throughout.

- Meat thermometers are the most accurate test of doneness, since many factors such as wind or distance of food from the heat source affect the time roasts cook on the grill.

Cut	Cooking Method
Tender steaks — T-bone, Rib, Tenderloin, Sirloin, Club, Porterhouse	Grill — Cook quickly at least 3 inches from hot coals
Tender roasts — Rib, Rib Eye, Tenderloin	Rotisserie or Covered Grill Grill
Less tender steaks — Round, Chuck, Family Flank Cube	Rotisserie or Covered Grill
Less tender roasts — Rump, Sirloin Tip Blade Bone, Arm Bone	Grill — thin roasts up to 3 inches
Brisket, Short ribs	Precook simmered in liquid; Grill or Covered Grill
Beef liver	Grill

STEAK HINTS

- Select well-marbled steaks cut at least one inch thick. This will help you achieve the desired doneness more easily than with thinner steaks.

- Trim excess fat so drippings will not catch fire; slash the fat edge at 1 to 2-inch intervals, without cutting through the lean tissue, to prevent steaks from curling during cooking.

- Marinate or tenderize less tender cuts. When using prepared meat tenderizers or instant marinades follow label directions carefully.

Subtle wine-flavored tomatoes enhance tender steaks. Simple enough for the budding gourmet!

PROVINCIAL STEAK WITH TOMATOES
3 to 4 servings

> 3 to 4 tender steaks*
> 2 tablespoons butter or margarine
> 2 tablespoons chopped green onions
> 2 tablespoons chopped parsley, if desired
> 2 tablespoons dry white wine or dry vermouth
> ½ teaspoon garlic salt
> 2 tomatoes, thinly sliced
> Salt or seasoned salt
> Pepper or seasoned pepper

ON THE GRILL: Place steaks on grill 3 to 4 inches from hot coals. Cook to desired doneness. About 5 minutes before steak is done, place 8-inch fry pan over hottest coals. Melt butter; add onions, parsley, wine and garlic salt; bring to boiling. Add tomatoes. Cook just until tomatoes are heated. To serve, season steaks with salt and pepper; spoon tomatoes on or along side steaks.

> **Tips:** Steaks can be broiled, as directed, in oven; prepare tomatoes on top of stove.
>
> *Club, tenderloin, T-bone, porterhouse or two sirloin steaks can be used.

GRILLING TIME FOR TENDER STEAKS*
(approximate time in minutes)

Size	Rare	Medium	Well
1 inch	8 to 12	14 to 20	20 to 30
1½ inches	14 to 18	16 to 25	25 to 35
2 inches	16 to 20	30 to 35	40 or more

*Timetable can also be used for pre-tenderized meat cuts, or less tender cuts that have been seasoned with meat tenderizer, as directed on label.

A superbly easy steak — one of our favorites. Serve this one with buttered mushrooms.

GREAT CAESAR'S STEAK
2 to 3 servings

> 1 sirloin steak, 1½ to 2-inches thick
> ½ cup Caesar salad dressing
> 2 to 3 tablespoons Parmesan cheese
> Salt or seasoned salt
> Pepper or seasoned pepper

ON THE GRILL: Brush both sides of steak with part of salad dressing. Center steak on grill 3 to 4 inches from hot coals. Cook 25 to 30 minutes for medium rare or until of desired doneness, turning once and brushing with remaining salad dressing. Sprinkle with Parmesan cheese and seasoning when removed from grill. To serve, remove bone and cut across grain into slices. If desired, sprinkle with more cheese.

> **Tips:** Steak can be broiled, as directed, in oven.
>
> Round or family steak, treated with meat tenderizer can be used for sirloin.
>
> Creamy Onion or other creamy salad dressings can be used for Caesar salad dressing.

SIRLOIN STEAK WITH ROQUEFORT
6 to 8 servings

> ¼ cup butter or margarine
> ¼ cup (2 oz.) Roquefort or blue cheese
> Salt
> Dash pepper
> 2 lbs. sirloin steak, cut 1½-inches thick

BEFORE GRILLING: In small bowl, cream all ingredients, except steak. Trim excess fat from steak. Slash fat edge to prevent curling.

ON THE GRILL: Place steak on grill 6 inches from hot coals. Cook 10 to 15 minutes; turn. Spread with cheese mixture and cook 15 minutes longer for medium steak or until of desired doneness.

> **Tip:** Steak can be broiled, as directed, in oven.

Hawaiian Teriyaki Beef; Polynesian Fruit Punch, page 111.

HAWAIIAN TERIYAKI BEEF

4 to 6 servings

    1 cup (8 oz.) prepared teriyaki marinade
    1 tablespoon grated lemon peel
    2 lbs. sirloin steak, cut into 1-inch cubes
    1 pineapple

BEFORE GRILLING: Prepare Beef Teriyaki Marinade as directed, using lemon peel for onion. Pour marinade over steak cubes in non-metallic bowl or plastic bag. Marinate at least two hours at room temperature or overnight in refrigerator. Drain meat; save marinade for basting sauce. Peel and cut pineapple into 1-inch cubes. Thread steak and pineapple on six skewers.

ON THE GRILL: Place skewers on grill 3 to 4 inches from hot coals. Cook 15 to 20 minutes or until of desired doneness, basting with marinade, until beef is browned.

    Tips: Kabobs can be broiled, as directed, in oven.

If fresh pineapple is not available, 1 cup (13-oz. can) frozen pineapple chunks can be used.

Red wine or pineapple juice can be used for part of teriyaki marinade if milder flavor is desired.

Rib roast marinated in wine with seasonings you choose yourself. No better way to enjoy this delectable cut of meat.

CONTINENTAL RIB ROAST

8 to 12 servings

>   1 cup red wine
> ¼ cup cooking oil
>   2 tablespoons soy or Worcestershire sauce
>   1 tablespoon (3 teaspoons) ground mustard
> ½ teaspoon instant minced garlic or
>   2 cloves garlic, minced
> ½ teaspoon marjoram*
>   4 to 6 lbs. rolled rib roast, 4-inches in diameter

BEFORE GRILLING: Combine all ingredients except roast to make marinade. Pour marinade over roast in non-metallic bowl or plastic bag. Marinate 12 to 24 hours in refrigerator, turning several times to season. Remove roast; reserve marinade for basting sauce. Dry roast with paper towel. Insert meat thermometer; see directions on page 19.

ON THE GRILL: Arrange coals for roasting meat; see method B, page 5. Center meat on grill 6 to 8 inches from coals; cover. Roast over slow fire to 160° for medium rare (about 2½ hours) or until of desired doneness, basting with marinade every 30 minutes. For ease in carving, let stand 15 minutes.

> **Tips:** For rotisserie, see method B, page 5.
>
> For oven roasting, roast at 325° for 2 to 2½ hours until of desired doneness.
>
> *Thyme, basil, tarragon, ground ginger, savory, horseradish or parsley can be other optional ingredients. Vary and combine seasonings as desired, being careful to start with a small amount — adding more as desired. With occasional exceptions, no one seasoning should be obvious. A subtle blend is best.

BEER BASTED BEEF ROAST

8 to 12 servings

>   1½ cups (12-oz. can) beer
>   2 tablespoons instant minced onion or
>   ½ cup chopped onion
>   1 tablespoon lemon peel
>   1 teaspoon ground or leaf sage, if desired
>   4 lbs. rolled rump, sirloin tip or top round, 4-inches in diameter
>   1 package (4/5 oz.) instant meat marinade

BEFORE GRILLING: Combine all ingredients except roast and meat marinade to make marinade. Pour marinade over roast in large non-metallic bowl or plastic bag. Marinate at least 2 hours at room temperature or overnight in refrigerator, piercing roast generously with fork and turning several times to season. Fifteen minutes before grilling, sprinkle roast with instant meat marinade. Turn roast several times to coat and mix marinade with beer. Remove roast; save marinade for basting sauce. Insert meat thermometer; see directions on page 19.

ON THE GRILL: Arrange coals for roasting meat; see method B, page 5. Center meat on grill 6 to 8 inches from coals; cover. Roast over slow fire to 160° for medium rare (about 1¾ hours) or until of desired doneness, basting with marinade every 30 minutes. For ease in carving, let stand 15 minutes.

> **Tips:** For rotisserie; see method B, page 5.
>
> For oven roasting, roast at 325° for 2 to 2½ hours until of desired doneness.

BEEF ON A SPIT

6 to 8 servings

>   1 can (10½ oz.) condensed onion soup
>   ½ soup can water
>   1 tablespoon bleu cheese, crumbled
>   3 to 4 lbs. rolled loin roast

BEFORE GRILLING: In shallow non-metallic bowl or plastic bag, combine soup, water and cheese; add beef. Marinate at room temperature for 2 hours or in refrigerator overnight; turn once. Save marinade. Mount and balance beef on spit. Insert meat thermometer into beef.

ON THE GRILL: Place roast on spit, following directions for rotisserie roasting, page 5. Roast until meat thermometer reads 140° F. for rare (about 1½ to 2 hours). Meanwhile, in saucepan, heat marinade until cheese is melted; stirring occasionally. If desired, thicken with 1 tablespoon flour and add a little kitchen bouquet for richer color. Serve with meat.

>   **Tip:** Roast can be prepared, as directed, in 325° oven.

POT-ROAST BARBECUE

6 to 8 servings

>   1 cup prepared barbecue sauce
>   3 tablespoons flour
>   1 tablespoon brown sugar
>   4 lbs. blade-bone chuck roast, cut
>   1½-inches thick
>   1 teaspoon salt
>   Dash pepper
>   1 or 2 stalks celery, sliced on bias
>   1 or 2 medium carrots, sliced
>   1 medium onion, sliced

BEFORE GRILLING: Blend barbecue sauce, flour and sugar. Have ready at the grill.

ON THE GRILL: Center roast 6 to 8 inches from hot coals. Cook about 8 to 10 minutes on each side. (Use soaked hickory chips on briquettes, if desired.) Season with salt and pepper. Spoon half of sauce onto large sheet of double thickness heavy duty foil. Add meat, vegetables and remaining sauce. Place packet on grill. Cook about 1½ hours, until meat is tender.

>   **Tip:** Roast can be prepared in 350° oven as directed. Cook for 1½ to 2 hours. Omit browning meat before wrapping in foil, if desired.

GUIDE FOR GRILLING BEEF ROASTS

A good general rule to follow is that roasting over coals takes a *little less time than in the oven.* There is considerable variation between roasts and different types of equipment. For best results, consult the manufacturer's information booklet that came with your grill.

Use a meat thermometer as the best assurance of desired doneness. Insert as directed on page 19.

Cooking on a rotisserie generally takes longer than in covered grills.

Diameter of rolled roasts, not weight, determines roasting time. For example, a 6 lb. 4-inch diameter rolled roast cooks in the same time as a 4 lb. 4-inch diameter roast. Added pounds in length do not increase cooking time.

For a larger party, choose two smaller roasts instead of one large one. Roast one to medium, the other to rare, giving guests whichever they prefer.

HONEY 'N SPICE BRISKET

8 to 10 servings

> 3 to 4 lbs. boneless beef brisket
> 2 teaspoons leaf basil or 1 bay leaf
> 1 teaspoon coarsely ground black pepper
>   or peppercorns
> ¼ cup barbecue sauce
> ¼ cup soy sauce
> 2 tablespoons honey

BEFORE GRILLING: In large saucepan, cover brisket with water. Add basil and pepper. Cover and simmer over low heat 3 to 3½ hours until tender. Drain; dry brisket with paper towels. Combine barbecue sauce, soy sauce and honey for basting sauce.

ON THE GRILL: Center brisket on grill 6 to 8 inches from coals; cover. Cook 1 hour for medium rare or until of desired doneness, turning occasionally and basting frequently during last 30 minutes. Cut on the diagonal, across grain, into very thin slices.

> **Tips:** For oven preparation, roast at 325° for 1½ hours until tender. Brush with sauce, as directed.
>
> Brisket can be cooked ahead and refrigerated before grilling. Leave at room temperature an hour before grilling or increase cooking time ½ hour.

STEAK DINNER ITALIAN

4 to 5 servings

> 2 lbs. chuck (arm or blade) steak, cut
>   1½ to 2-inches thick
> ½ cup French dressing or sweet-and-
>   spicy French dressing
> 4 small potatoes, thinly sliced
> 4 small onions, thinly sliced
> ½ cup sliced stuffed olives
> ¼ cup water
> 1 teaspoon salt
> ½ teaspoon pepper

ON THE GRILL: Brush both sides of steak with part of salad dressing. Center steak on grill 3 to 4 inches from hot coals. Cook 8 to 10 minutes on each side. Place meat in center of large piece of heavy duty foil; add remaining ingredients and salad dressing. Bring edges of foil together and seal securely. Roast over slow fire 1½ to 2 hours, until meat is tender.

> **Tips:** For oven roasting, brown steak in ¼ cup salad dressing in skillet over high heat. Wrap in foil as directed. Roast at 350° for 1½ to 2 hours.

WINE 'N GARLIC ROLLED ROAST

8 to 12 servings

> ½ cup red wine vinegar or red wine
> ½ cup cooking oil
> 1 clove garlic, minced or ¼ teaspoon
>   instant minced garlic
> 1 teaspoon dry mustard or 1 tablespoon
>   prepared mustard
> 3 to 4 lbs. rolled rump, sirloin tip or top
>   round roast, 4-inches in diameter
> 3 to 4 tablespoons coarsely ground black
>   pepper

BEFORE GRILLING: Combine all ingredients except roast and pepper to make marinade. Pour marinade over roast in non-metallic bowl or plastic bag. Marinate 12 to 14 hours or overnight in refrigerator, turning several times to season. Remove roast; reserve marinade for basting sauce. Dry roast with paper towel; press pepper into all sides of roast. Insert meat thermometer; see directions on page 19.

ON THE GRILL: Arrange coals for roasting meat; see method B, page 5. Center meat on grill 6 to 8 inches from coals; cover. Roast over slow fire to 160° for medium rare (about 1¾ hours) or until of desired doneness, basting with marinade every 30 minutes. For ease in carving, let stand 15 minutes.

> **Tips:** For rotisserie, see method B, page 5.
>
> For oven roasting, roast at 325° for 2 to 2½ hours until of desired doneness.

Perfect for the lunch box, these hearty sandwiches have man-pleasing proportions and flavors. Wrap in foil and send along with Salad On A Stick, page 94 and Banana Apricot Bars, page 117.

BEEFEATERS' SANDWICHES

4 sandwiches

> 2 tablespoons butter or margarine
> 1 onion, thinly sliced
> 4 slices cooked roast beef
> Horseradish Cream Sauce, page 49
> 4 hot dog buns or French rolls

Melt butter in fry pan; cook onion in butter until tender; drain on paper towel. Place onion on beef slices; roll up. Prepare sauce. Spread on buns. Place a beef roll on each bun.

CHIPPER CUBE STEAKS

4 servings

  4 cube steaks or frozen beef steaks,
      thawed
  ½ cup Creamy Onion salad dressing
  ½ to 1 cup crushed potato chips
      Salt
      Pepper

ON THE GRILL: Brush steaks with salad dressing. Place on greased grill 3 to 4 inches from hot coals. Cook until browned on both sides and of desired doneness, turning once and sprinkling top with potato chips. Season with salt and pepper.

> **Tips:** Cube steaks can be broiled, as directed, in oven. Sprinkle potato chips on steaks after broiling.

ORANGE GRILLED CHUCK STEAK

4 to 5 servings

  1½ to 2 lbs. chuck steak, about 2-inches
      thick
      Meat tenderizer
  1 cup orange or pineapple juice
  ½ cup finely chopped onion or
      2 tablespoons instant minced onion
  1 teaspoon ground mustard or
      1 tablespoon prepared mustard
  ½ teaspoon leaf or ground thyme
  ½ teaspoon pepper or seasoned pepper
  ½ cup orange marmalade
  ¼ cup cooking oil

BEFORE GRILLING: Trim excess fat from meat. Sprinkle with meat tenderizer as directed on label. Combine orange juice, onion, mustard, thyme and pepper to make marinade. Pour marinade over meat in shallow non-metallic container or plastic bag. Cover; marinate at least two hours at room temperature or over-night in refrigerator. Drain marinade from steak; combine with orange marmalade and cooking oil to use for basting sauce.

ON THE GRILL: Center steak on grill 4 to 6 inches from hot coals. Cook 30 to 40 minutes for medium rare or until of desired doneness, turning once and brushing occasionally with basting sauce. To serve, remove bone and cut across grain into slices.

> **Tips:** Basting sauce can be thickened by adding 1 tablespoon cornstarch. Cook, stirring constantly, until mixture comes to a boil and thickens. Spoon over steak slices.

Meat marinade mix provides the seasoning base for a wine marinade and helps to tenderize a less tender, more economical cut of meat for these kabobs.

WINE MARINATED BEEF KABOBS

4 to 6 servings

  1½ lbs. family steak, cut into 1-inch cubes
      Meat marinade
      Red wine
  1 cup (8 oz. or 1 pt.) whole mushrooms
  2 green peppers, cut into 2-inch squares
      Salt or seasoned salt
      Pepper or seasoned pepper

BEFORE GRILLING: Prepare marinade as directed on package, adding wine for the liquid called for. Marinate meat as directed on package. Remove meat from marinade. Thread meat, green pepper and mushrooms on skewers; season with salt and pepper.

ON THE GRILL: Place skewers on grill 3 to 4 inches from hot coals. Cook 6 to 8 minutes on each side until of desired doneness, basting occasionally with marinade. Season mildly with salt and pepper before serving, if desired.

> **Tip:** Kabobs can be broiled, as directed, in oven.

LONDON BROIL WITH MUSHROOM-TOMATO SAUCE

6 servings

  1½ lbs. flank steak
  ½ cup (1 med.) sliced onion
  1 tablespoon butter or margarine
  1 can (10½ oz.) condensed golden
      mushroom soup
  ⅓ cup water or tomato liquid
  ⅓ cup chopped canned tomatoes
  2 tablespoons chopped parsley or
      1 tablespoon parsley flakes
  1 tablespoon Dijon mustard or
      ½ tablespoon prepared mustard

BEFORE GRILLING: In saucepan, cook onion in butter until tender. Add remaining ingredients. Heat, stirring occasionally. Keep warm to serve over meat slices.

ON THE GRILL: Place steak on grill 3 to 4 inches from hot coals. Cook 5 minutes on each side for medium rare. Thinly slice meat diagonally across the grain. Serve with sauce.

> **Tip:** Meat can be broiled, as directed, in oven.

GINGER STEAK BURGUNDY

½ cup cooking oil
½ cup Burgundy or red wine
2 tablespoons catsup
2 tablespoons molasses or soy sauce
2 teaspoons ground ginger or
   2 tablespoons finely chopped candied
   ginger or grated ginger root
½ teaspoon salt
½ teaspoon pepper
2 cloves garlic, minced or ¼ teaspoon
   instant minced garlic
2 lbs. family, round or chuck steak, cut
   into 1-inch cubes
2 green peppers
2 cups whole mushrooms

BEFORE GRILLING: Combine all ingredients except steak, green pepper and mushrooms to make marinade. Pour marinade over steak in non-metallic bowl or plastic bag. Marinate at least 2 hours at room temperature or overnight in refrigerator. Drain meat; reserve marinade for basting sauce. Cut green peppers in 1-inch pieces; wash mushrooms. Thread steak and vegetables on six skewers.

ON THE GRILL: Place skewers on grill 3 to 4 inches from hot coals. Cook 15 to 20 minutes or until of desired doneness, basting with marinade, until beef is browned.

   Tip: Steak can be broiled, as directed, in oven.

Dill pickle lovers will delight in these quick cube steak roll-ups. They're attractive and good with potato salad and sliced tomatoes.

DILLY MEAT ROLL-UPS

4 servings

2 tablespoons butter or margarine
¼ cup chopped onion or 1 teaspoon
   instant minced onion
2 cups soft bread cubes
2 tablespoons dill pickle liquid or water
1 teaspoon caraway seed, if desired
½ teaspoon salt or seasoned salt
Dash pepper or seasoned pepper
4 cube steaks (about 1 lb.) or frozen
   beef steaks, thawed
2 large dill pickles, cut into quarters
½ cup prepared barbecue sauce,
   or see Plantation Barbecue Sauce,
   page 49.

BEFORE GRILLING: Melt butter in fry pan; cook onion until tender. Combine onion with bread cubes, pickle liquid, caraway seed, salt and pepper; mix well. Place about ¼ cup stuffing on each cube steak. Roll 2 pickle quarters inside each; tie string around roll in two places to hold together.

ON THE GRILL: Place steak rolls on grill 4 to 6 inches from hot coals. Cook 20 to 25 minutes or until of desired doneness, turning on all sides and basting frequently with sauce.

   Tips: For extra dill pickle flavor, add 1 to 2 tablespoons pickle liquid to barbecue sauce, too.
   Steak rolls can be broiled as directed in oven.

TEXAS CHILI BEEF SLICES

5 to 6 servings

2 lbs. round or family steak, cut 2-inches
   thick
Instant meat tenderizer
¼ cup chopped onion or 2 tablespoons
   instant minced onion
2 cloves garlic, minced or ¼ teaspoon
   instant minced garlic
2 tablespoons vinegar
2 tablespoons cooking oil
2 tablespoons Worcestershire sauce
2 to 3 teaspoons chili powder or
   cayenne pepper
1 can (8 oz.) tomato sauce
1 lemon, sliced
2 tablespoons brown sugar
½ teaspoon ground mustard or
   1½ teaspoons prepared mustard
¼ teaspoon Tabasco sauce

BEFORE GRILLING: Sprinkle meat with meat tenderizer as directed on label. Combine onion, garlic, vinegar, cooking oil, Worcestershire sauce and chili powder to make marinade. Pour marinade over steak in shallow non-metallic container or plastic bag. Marinate 15 to 20 minutes at room temperature or 2 hours in refrigerator. Remove steak from marinade. Combine marinade with remaining ingredients in saucepan; simmer 10 minutes. Keep warm until serving time.

ON THE GRILL: Center steak on grill 4 to 6 inches from hot coals. Cook 30 to 40 minutes for medium rare or until of desired doneness, turning once. To serve, cut across grain into slices. Spoon sauce over steak.

   Tip: Steak can be broiled, as directed, in oven.

Pour on hickory smokehouse flavor. What better way to brighten a gray winter day! Cooked indoors or out, this savory steak will be a hit with baked beans and coleslaw.

SAVORY SMOKED STEAK

5 to 6 servings

2½ to 3 lbs. family or round steak, cut 2-inches thick
1 bottle (3 oz.) liquid smoke
1 teaspoon onion salt
1 teaspoon garlic salt
1 teaspoon celery salt
1 tablespoon Worcestershire sauce
Instant meat tenderizer, if desired

BEFORE GRILLING: Place steak in shallow non-metallic container or plastic bag. Pour liquid smoke over steak; sprinkle with onion, garlic and celery salts. Cover; marinate 12 to 24 hours in refrigerator. Remove steak from marinade; sprinkle with Worcestershire sauce. If desired, sprinkle with meat tenderizer as directed on label. Let steak stand at room temperature for 30 minutes before grilling.

ON THE GRILL: Center steak on grill 4 to 6 inches from hot coals. Cook 25 to 30 minutes for medium rare or until of desired doneness, turning once. To serve, cut across grain into slices. If desired, pour a favorite barbecue sauce over slices.

> **Tip:** Steak can be broiled, as directed, in oven.

Try other tomato based seasoning mixes to give this recipe international flavor. We liked enchilada sauce mix!

BARBECUED CHUCK STEAK

4 to 5 servings

2½ lbs. chuck (arm or blade) steak, cut 1½ to 2-inches thick
Meat tenderizer
1 cup catsup
½ cup water
¼ cup red wine vinegar or red wine
2 tablespoons barbecue seasoning blend*
2 tablespoons Worcestershire sauce

BEFORE GRILLING: Cut steak into serving size pieces; removing excess fat and bone from meat. Sprinkle with meat tenderizer as directed on label. Combine remaining ingredients in saucepan to make basting sauce; simmer 15 minutes and cool. Pour basting sauce over meat in shallow non-metallic container. Marinate at least two hours at room temperature or overnight in refrigerator. Remove meat from basting sauce; reserve basting sauce.

ON THE GRILL: Center steak on grill 4 to 6 inches from hot coals. Cook 30 to 45 minutes for medium rare or until of desired doneness, turning two or three times and brushing occasionally with basting sauce. Serve extra sauce along with steak.

> **Tips:** Steak can be broiled, as directed, in oven. The whole steak can be broiled. Remove bone and slice across grain to serve.
>
> *One pkg. Pillsbury Spaghetti, Chili or Sloppy Joe seasoning mix can be used for seasoning blend.

SHASLIK

4 to 6 servings

1 lb. round steak, ¼-inch thick, cut in strips
Russian dressing
1½ cups cherry tomatoes
½ cup (4 oz.) fresh mushroom caps
2 cups (1-lb. can) whole potatoes, drained
1 zucchini, cut in cubes

BEFORE GRILLING: In shallow non-metallic bowl or plastic bag, marinate meat overnight in enough dressing to cover. Alternately thread meat and vegetables on skewers accordion-style.

ON THE GRILL: Place skewers on grill 3 to 4 inches from coals. Cook for 10 minutes, brushing frequently with marinade.

> **Tips:** If round steak, cut ¼-inch thick is not available, just cut a thicker steak into strips ¼-inch thick.
>
> Kabobs can be broiled, as directed, in oven.

LEMON BARBECUED FLANK STEAK

4 servings

> 1 medium onion
> 1½ lbs. flank steak
> ½ cup lemon juice
> ⅓ cup cooking oil
> 1 package Pillsbury Sloppy Joe or
>   Spaghetti Seasoning Mix
> 2 tablespoons sugar
> 1 teaspoon grated lemon peel
> 1 tablespoon butter or margarine
> Salt or seasoned salt
> Pepper or seasoned pepper

BEFORE GRILLING: Slice onion; place half the slices in shallow non-metallic container or plastic bag. Place steak in container; top with remaining onions. Combine lemon juice, oil, seasoning mix, sugar and lemon peel to make marinade; pour over steak. Cover; marinate several hours at room temperature or overnight in refrigerator. Remove steak from marinade; drain onions. Cook onions in butter until tender. Keep warm while grilling steak.

ON THE GRILL: Center steak on grill 3 to 4 inches from hot coals. Cook 4 to 6 minutes on each side until medium rare. Season with salt and pepper. Cut on the diagonal, across grain into very thin slices. Top with onions and any remaining marinade that has been heated, if desired.

> **Tip:** Steak can be broiled, as directed, in oven.

Liver cooked over coals has unbeatable flavor. Add baked potatoes and Easy Caesar Salad, page 90.

CHARCOAL LIVER BROCHETTES

4 servings

> 12 bacon slices
> 1 lb. beef liver
> 1 teaspoon salt or seasoned salt
> ½ teaspoon celery salt

BEFORE GRILLING: Cook bacon in large fry pan until slightly crisp; drain on paper towel. Cut liver into 12 1-inch strips (strips may be cut in half if easier to handle). Place each liver strip on bacon strip; roll up. Thread on small skewers. Sprinkle with salt and celery salt.

ON THE GRILL: Place skewers on greased grill 4 to 6 inches from hot coals. Cook 8 to 10 minutes, turning once, until of desired doneness.

> **Tip:** Liver can be broiled as directed, in oven, or cook in large fry pan with 2 tablespoons butter or margarine about 10 to 15 minutes. When cooking in fry pan, precooking of bacon is not necessary.

STEAK STRIPS SAUTERNE

4 to 5 servings

> 1½ lbs. round or flank steak, cut less than 1-inch thick
> ¾ cup Sauterne
> 1 tablespoon soy sauce
> 1 clove garlic, minced or ¼ teaspoon instant minced garlic
> 2 tablespoons steak sauce
> 2 tablespoons butter or margarine
> 1 tablespoon brown sugar
> 2 teaspoons dry mustard or 1 tablespoon prepared mustard
> Instant meat tenderizer
> 2 cups whole mushrooms

BEFORE GRILLING: Cut steak into long strips, about ⅜-inch wide. Combine Sauterne and soy sauce to make marinade. Pour marinade over meat in non-metallic bowl or plastic bag. Marinate at least two hours at room temperature or overnight in refrigerator. Drain marinade from meat; reserve. Combine reserved marinade with garlic, steak sauce, butter, brown sugar and mustard in saucepan to make basting sauce. Heat just to boiling. Sprinkle with meat tenderizer as directed on label. Thread steak strips on 6 skewers accordion-style, with mushrooms.

ON THE GRILL: Place skewers on grill 3 to 4 inches from hot coals. Cook 15 to 20 minutes or until of desired doneness, brushing frequently with basting sauce.

> **Tip:** Steak can be broiled, as directed, in oven.

LEMON-LIME ROUND STEAK

5 to 6 servings

> 2 limes
> 1 lemon
> ½ cup cooking oil
> 1 clove garlic, minced or ¼ teaspoon
>   instant minced garlic
> 2 lbs. round or family steak, cut 2-inches
>   thick
> Salt or seasoned salt
> Pepper or seasoned pepper

BEFORE GRILLING: Cut limes and lemon into ½-inch slices. Heat oil in saucepan. Add limes, lemon and garlic. Cook over low heat about 5 minutes. Press fruit with back of a spoon as it heats. Pierce steak all over with a fork. Pour hot oil and fruit over steak in a shallow non-metallic container; cover. Marinate up to 4 hours at room temperature or longer in the refrigerator. Remove steak from marinade; if desired, reserve fruit slices for garnish.

ON THE GRILL: Center steak on grill 4 to 6 inches from hot coals. Cook 25 to 30 minutes for medium rare or until of desired doneness, turning once. To serve, cut across grain into slices; top with lemon and lime slices.

Tips: Steak can be broiled in oven or pan broiled in skillet, as directed.

Cut steak into serving size pieces before grilling, if desired.

Any extra sauce in this recipe gives a head start for the next barbecue. Try this one with ribs, chicken, other beef cuts or wieners.

PLANTATION SHORT RIBS

4 to 5 servings

> 3½ to 4 lbs. short ribs, cut into serving pieces

Plantation Barbecue Sauce:

> 1 (6 oz.) can tomato paste
> 1 cup water
> ½ cup bottled steak sauce
> ¼ cup (1 small) chopped onion or 1 tablespoon instant minced onion
> ¼ cup cooking oil
> ⅓ cup firmly packed brown sugar
> ⅓ cup lemon juice
> 1 clove garlic, minced or ⅛ teaspoon instant minced garlic
> ½ teaspoon bottled hot pepper sauce

BEFORE GRILLING: In large saucepan, cover ribs with water; salt to taste. Simmer, covered, over medium low heat for 1 hour; (meanwhile prepare Barbecue Sauce). Drain ribs; place in covered dish. Pour Barbecue Sauce over, coating each rib. Let cool; cover and refrigerate overnight.*

BARBECUE SAUCE: In saucepan, combine all ingredients; simmer 15 minutes. Use for basting sauce.

ON THE GRILL: Place ribs on the grill 4 to 6 inches from hot coals. Cook about 20 minutes until done, turning and brushing occasionally with additional sauce.

> **Tips:** By refrigerating the ribs in the sauce, there is more time for the flavors to penetrate into the meat; however, they can be grilled immediately by brushing with the sauce during cooking.
>
> Short ribs can be broiled, as directed, in oven.

SANDWICH SAUCE

1⅓ cups sauce

> ¼ cup chopped green pepper
> 1 tablespoon butter or margarine
> 1 can (10¾ oz.) beef gravy
> 2 teaspoons prepared mustard

In saucepan, cook green pepper in butter until tender. Add gravy and mustard. Heat, stirring occasionally.

RED PEPPER SAUCE

1 cup

> 1 package white sauce mix*
> ½ cup milk
> ¼ cup red pepper relish
> ¼ teaspoon Tabasco sauce

Prepare white sauce mix as directed, using ½ cup milk. Stir in relish and Tabasco sauce. Keep warm until serving. Spoon over beef slices.

> **Tips:** *May use a recipe for medium white sauce with 1 cup yield.
>
> For a thinner sauce, add more milk.

HERB BUTTER FOR STEAK

enough for 3 to 4 steaks

> ¼ cup butter or margarine, melted
> 1 tablespoon parsley flakes
> 1 to 2 teaspoons salad herbs or Italian seasoning*

In saucepan, melt butter. Add parsley and herbs; mix thoroughly. Brush on tender steaks before grilling.

> **Tip:** *Any favorite herb mixture totaling 1 teaspoon can be used for the salad herbs.

HORSERADISH CREAM SAUCE

½ cup

> ½ cup sour cream
> 2 to 4 tablespoons horseradish

Combine ingredients; mix well. Refrigerate until served.

> **Tip:** Softened butter or margarine, mayonnaise or salad dressing can be used for sour cream.

Lemon-Lime Round Steak; Basic Creamy Coleslaw, page 129; Molded Potato Salad, page 92; Brown-and-Serve Rolls, page 101.

Barbecued Ribs, opposite page.

Pork

When the phrase "Let's have a barbecue" is heard, pork comes next to beef in popularity. It's hard to surpass that deep smoky flavor with ribs, ham or chops.

Pork is a tender meat. Although it doesn't need tenderizing, it does require thorough cooking. Low to moderate temperatures, so that meats do not become dry before they're done, are the rule. Recipes on the following pages have been grouped according to meat cuts. A guide to choosing the method of cooking needed for barbecuing different pork cuts follows.

Cut	Cooking Method
Ribs — country ribs, spareribs	Grill easy to handle pieces; Rotisserie whole rib sections
Roasts — fresh or cured and smoked loin, shoulder or ham	Rotisserie or Covered Grill
Tenderloin	Grill
Chops and steaks	Grill — 4 to 6 inches from hot coals
Fully-cooked Ham, Canadian bacon	Grill slices; Rotisserie or use covered grill for whole hams and Canadian bacon pieces

PORK HINTS

• All pork takes well to smoking with wood chips.

• Chops, steaks and ham slices cut about one-inch thick will be more tender and juicy than thinner cuts. Treat pork cuts the same as similar beef cuts when preparing them for the grill.

• Check doneness by making a small cut in the meat near the bone in steaks and chops. Or use a meat thermometer in larger cuts.

• A wide variety of hams are available for the grill. Cured and smoked hams may be either "fully-cooked" or "cook-before-eating." Check the label since the cooking times are much different. We prefer the fully-cooked cured and smoked hams because of time, but fresh ham barbecued to doneness over the coals and smoking wood chips is an unforgettable treat even though it takes several hours.

• Boneless hams can be pre-sliced, then tied for roasting on a rotisserie. This saves slicing so is good to keep in mind for larger groups.

• Canned and picnic hams add to the array of ham choices for the grill. Their compact shapes make them ideal for the rotisserie.

BARBECUED RIBS

6 to 8 servings

    4 to 4½ lbs. country style ribs or spareribs, cut into serving pieces

Barbecue Sauce
- ½ cup catsup
- ½ cup chili sauce or tomato sauce
- 2 tablespoons brown sugar
- ¼ cup (1 small) chopped onion
- 1 teaspoon celery seed, if desired
- ½ teaspoon salt
- ⅛ teaspoon instant minced garlic or garlic powder or 1 clove garlic, minced
- 2 teaspoons prepared or dry mustard
- 1 tablespoon Worcestershire sauce
- Dash Tabasco sauce
- ½ lemon, sliced or 1 tablespoon lemon juice

BEFORE GRILLING: In large saucepan, cover ribs with water; salt to taste. Simmer, covered, over medium low heat for 1 hour; (meanwhile, prepare Barbecue Sauce). Drain ribs; place in covered dish. Pour Barbecue Sauce over, coating each rib. Let cool*; cover and refrigerate overnight.

BARBECUE SAUCE: Combine all ingredients; mix well.

ON THE GRILL: Place on grill 4 to 6 inches from hot coals. Cook about 20 minutes, until browned and heated through, brushing with sauce as necessary.

Tips: *By refrigerating the ribs in the sauce, there is more time for the flavors to penetrate into the meat, however they can be grilled immediately by brushing with the sauce during cooking.

Ribs can be broiled, as directed, in oven.

GUIDE FOR COOKING RIBS

There is more than one accepted way to cook spareribs. Like other pork cuts, they should be cooked until well done. One of these methods will become a favorite of yours; adapt it to other favorite recipes you have for ribs. Length of cooking time will vary with the meatiness of the ribs. Meat will shrink from the end of bones when done. Allow about 1 pound for each serving.

Cut ribs into 2 to 3 rib sections. In a large saucepan, cover ribs with water; salt to taste. Simmer over medium low heat for about 1 hour just until tender. Drain ribs; brush both sides with basting sauce. Place on grill. Cook 10 minutes on each side until ribs are crisp and nicely browned, basting often.

Wrap uncooked ribs securely in heavy duty foil. Grill 30 minutes, turning once, or heat in 350° oven. Unwrap; place ribs on grill. Cook 30 minutes until browned on all sides. Brush with basting sauce during last 15 minutes.

To cook ribs on the rotisserie, weave the spit rod in and out of the uncooked rack of ribs, forming accordion-like folds. Keep ribs in balance so they turn evenly while cooking. Cook 45 minutes to 1 hour, basting with barbecue sauce during last 5 minutes.

SWEET 'N SOUR RIBS POLYNESIA

4 to 6 servings

> 4 lbs. country style or spareribs, cut into serving pieces
> 2 beef bouillon cubes or 2 teaspoons instant beef bouillon
> ¼ cup firmly packed brown sugar
> 1 teaspoon dry mustard
> 1 teaspoon paprika
> 1 cup pineapple juice
> ¼ cup vinegar
> 2 tablespoons cornstarch
> ½ cup water

BEFORE GRILLING: If desired, precook ribs. In small saucepan, combine remaining ingredients except cornstarch and water. Cook over low heat, stirring until bouillon is dissolved. Combine cornstarch and water; stir into cooked mixture. Cook, stirring constantly, until mixture is thickened and clear.

ON THE GRILL: Place ribs on grill 6 to 8 inches from hot coals. Brush with sauce. Cook about 20 minutes, turning frequently and brushing with sauce until browned and heated through. Serve with any additional sauce.

> **Tip:** Ribs can be cooked by any of the methods given, or in the oven.

Hot chili peppers fire up these tasty ribs. The amount of chilis used depends on your taste; if not sure, better go lightly at first. Serve with Acapulco Pea Salad, page 95.

SOUTH OF THE BORDER RIBS

4 to 6 servings

> 4 lbs. country-style ribs or spareribs, cut into serving pieces
> ¼ cup firmly packed brown sugar
> 1 teaspoon salt
> ¼ teaspoon garlic powder
> 1 cup catsup
> ½ cup (1 med.) chopped onion
> ½ cup (4-oz. can) taco sauce
> ½ cup finely chopped green chilis
> ¼ cup cooking oil
> 2 tablespoons Worcestershire sauce

BEFORE GRILLING: Precook ribs. Combine remaining ingredients for basting sauce; set aside.

ON THE GRILL: Place ribs on grill 6 to 8 inches from hot coals. Brush with sauce. Cook about 20 minutes until browned and heated through, brushing occasionally with additional sauce.

> **Tip:** Ribs can be cooked according to any of the given methods, or in the oven.

Crispy barbecued ribs laced with bourbon. Ribs this easy never were so good!

KENTUCKY BARBECUED RIBS

3 to 4 servings

> ¼ cup firmly packed brown sugar
> ¼ cup bourbon
> ¼ cup soy sauce
> 1½ teaspoons salt
> 1 medium onion, sliced, if desired
> 3 to 4 lbs. spareribs or country style ribs

BEFORE GRILLING: Combine all ingredients except ribs to make marinade. Pour over ribs in shallow non-metallic container or plastic bag. Marinate at least 2 hours at room temperature or overnight in refrigerator. Remove ribs; reserve marinade for basting sauce.

ON THE GRILL: Place ribs on grill 6 to 8 inches from hot coals. Cook 45 to 60 minutes, turning and brushing frequently with basting sauce until ribs are browned and done.

> **Tip:** If desired, ribs can be roasted in oven at 350° for 1½ hours. Or, precook ribs before marinating, following either method given.

A garlic accent gives the marinade a special flavor.

LEMON-HERB PORK CHOPS

- 6 chops, cut ¾-inch thick
- ¼ cup lemon juice
- 2 tablespoons cooking oil
- 1 tablespoon instant minced onion or 4 cloves garlic, minced
- 1 teaspoon salt
- ¼ teaspoon powdered thyme
- ¼ teaspoon oregano
- ¼ teaspoon pepper or seasoned pepper

BEFORE GRILLING: Combine all ingredients except chops to make marinade. Pour marinade over chops in shallow non-metallic container or plastic bag. Cover; marinate at least 2 hours at room temperature or overnight in refrigerator. Remove chops; reserve marinade for basting sauce.

ON THE GRILL: Place chops 6 to 8 inches from hot coals. Cook 30 to 40 minutes, brushing with marinade and turning occasionally until done.

> **Tips:** Chops can be broiled, as directed, in oven.
>
> ½ teaspoon Italian herb seasoning or poultry seasoning can be used for thyme and oregano.

Soy flavor accents pork tenderloin. The longer it's marinated, the more flavor it has. See Tips for a quick grilling idea! Pork lends itself to smokey flavor, so why not add hickory chips for a special treat!

PORK TERIYAKI

3 to 4 servings

- ¼ cup soy sauce
- ¼ cup white wine, dry sherry or white wine vinegar
- 1 clove garlic, minced or ⅛ teaspoon instant minced garlic
- 2 tablespoons brown sugar
- 2 tablespoons Worcestershire sauce
- ½ teaspoon ground ginger
- 1 pork tenderloin
- 2 bananas, if desired

BEFORE GRILLING: Combine all ingredients except tenderloin and bananas to make marinade. Pour marinade over tenderloin in shallow non-metallic container or plastic bag. Marinate at least two hours at room temperature or overnight in refrigerator, turning several times to season. Remove tenderloin; reserve marinade for basting sauce.

ON THE GRILL: Place tenderloin on grill 6 to 8 inches from medium coals. Cook for 1 to 1½ hours until done, basting occasionally with marinade. If desired, cut bananas in half lengthwise and crosswise; brush with marinade. Place on grill about 5 minutes until heated through. Use bananas as garnish.

> **Tips:** For oven roasting, roast at 325° for 2 to 2½ hours until done.
>
> For quick Pork Teriyaki Slices, slice tenderloin into ½-inch slices; flatten by pounding with meat hammer or edge of saucer or use 4 to 6 pork tenderloin steaks. Marinate 1 to 2 hours. Cook 4 to 6 inches from coals for 15 to 20 minutes until browned, turning once. To serve, top meat slices with bananas.
>
> Prepared teriyaki marinade can be used for marinade ingredients.

CHRISTMAS PORK LOIN DINNER

Menu

*Festive Fruited Pork Loin

Parsley Boiled Potatoes

Broccoli

*Confetti Corn Relish

Homemade Bread

*Last of the Coals Fruit Jubilee

Pork loin that's enhanced by the smoky flavor from cooking over coals makes this a natural for a special holiday dinner. Plan a menu that combines your favorite traditional foods and some outdoor cooking favorites, too. The fruit dessert we feature makes use of the low heat from the last coals — and can be served flaming for a holiday masterpiece.

FESTIVE FRUITED PORK LOIN
8 to 12 servings

 2 cups (11-oz. pkg.) dried apricots
¼ cup firmly packed brown sugar
 1 teaspoon cinnamon
¼ teaspoon ground cloves
 2 cups dry sherry
 4 to 6 lbs. rolled pork loin roast

BEFORE GRILLING: Combine all ingredients except roast to make marinade. Pour marinade over roast in non-metallic bowl or plastic bag; turn to coat all sides. Cover; marinate overnight in refrigerator, turning several times. Remove roast from marinade. Drain apricots, reserving marinade for basting sauce. To stuff roast, cut strings, open between two loin portions or cut a pocket in center of roast. Insert fruit and tie roast again with string. Insert rotisserie rod, and meat thermometer, see page 19.

ON THE GRILL: Arrange coals for roasting meat; see method B, page 5. Center meat on grill 6 to 8 inches from coals; cover. Roast over slow fire to 170° for well done (2½ to 3½ hours), basting occasionally with marinade.

Tip: To roast in oven, roast at 325° to 170°, allowing 35 to 45 minutes per pound.

Planning Helps:

MEAT: Pork loin roasts that are rolled and tied are actually two loin pieces, so it's easy to stuff with apricots. Retie with heavy string.

VEGETABLES: Choose family favorites. The corn relish is an easy adaptation of a summer salad.

BREAD: Homemade or from the bakery, hot rolls and breads spell holidays. Look for regional bread specialties during the holiday season, too.

DESSERT: Purchase or make the pound cake — or use angel food or chiffon cake, if you prefer. Fruits for the dessert can be combined before dinner and heated. Avoid overcooking fruits as they will break apart.

Guests will love these attractive fruit glazed chops. Mix and match the fruit and liqueur flavors — such as plum and Burgundy or apricot and rum!

BRANDIED SMOKED PORK CHOPS

3 to 4 servings

⅓ cup peach preserves
⅓ cup brandy
½ to 1 teaspoon curry powder
4 smoked pork chops, cut 1-inch thick
Peach halves, if desired

BEFORE GRILLING: Combine peach preserves, brandy and curry powder to make marinade. Pour marinade over chops in shallow non-metallic container or plastic bag, turning several times to coat with glaze. Cover; marinate at least two hours at room temperature or overnight in refrigerator. Remove chops; reserve marinade for basting sauce.

ON THE GRILL: Place chops on grill 6 to 8 inches from hot coals. Cook 20 to 25 minutes, brushing with glaze and turning occasionally until done. During last 10 minutes, brush glaze on peach halves and cook along with chops. Move to side of grill to keep warm if done before chops.

> **Tips:** Chops can be broiled, as directed, in oven.
>
> Pineapple, plum or apricot preserves can be used. Omit curry powder, if desired.

CRANBERRY CANADIAN BACON BRUNCH

6 to 8 servings

3 to 4 lbs. whole Canadian bacon
Whole cloves
1 cup drained cranberry-orange relish
2 tablespoons honey
½ teaspoon cinnamon
⅛ teaspoon ground cloves

BEFORE GRILLING: Score Canadian bacon; insert whole cloves. Combine remaining ingredients for basting sauce; mix well and set aside.

ON THE GRILL: Arrange coals for roasting according to Method B, page 5. Place on grill 6 to 8 inches from coals; cover. Roast over slow fire for 1 to 1½ hours until heated through. Brush with basting sauce during last 30 minutes. Spoon on any remaining

basting sauce before serving.

> **Tips:** Canadian bacon can be roasted as directed in 325° oven.
>
> For rotisserie method, see page 5.

Pork chops can be pre-cooked for shorter cooking time on grill. Adapt this method to other pork chop and steak recipes you have.

FRUIT-GLAZED PORK CHOPS

6 servings

6 pork chops, cut 1-inch thick
½ cup apricot preserves
¼ cup light corn syrup
⅓ cup prepared smoke-flavored barbecue sauce
1 teaspoon prepared mustard
¼ teaspoon ground cloves

BEFORE GRILLING: Simmer pork chops, covered, in boiling salted water for 20 minutes, or until almost tender; drain. Combine remaining ingredients; mix well.

ON THE GRILL: Brush one side of chops with basting sauce. Place chops, sauce-side down, 6 to 8 inches from hot coals, brushing second side with more sauce. Cook about 20 minutes or until tender and done, turning and brushing chops several times. Brush on more sauce just before serving.

> **Tips:** Chops can be broiled, as directed, in oven.
>
> Try other fruit preserves for apricot.
>
> Regular barbecue sauce and liquid smoke can be used for smoke-flavored barbecue sauce.

BREAKFAST BUNWICHES

4 sandwiches

4 Canadian bacon slices
4 slices pasteurized process cheese
4 tomato slices
4 hamburger buns

ON THE GRILL: Place Canadian bacon slices on grill 3 to 4 inches from hot coals. Cook for 3 to 4 minutes on each side until heated through. Meanwhile, toast hamburger buns, turn; layer tomato slices and cheese on buns. Continue heating until cheese melts and buns are toasted. Place Canadian bacon in buns.

> **Tip:** Luncheon ham slices can be used for Canadian bacon.

GERMAN DINNER IN FOIL

4 servings

  2 cups (1-lb. jar) drained red cabbage
  1 tablespoon instant minced onion or
    ¼ cup chopped onion
  1 teaspoon caraway seed
  4 to 6 smoked pork chops

BEFORE GRILLING: Combine cabbage, onion and caraway seed. Divide cabbage mixture on 4 squares of heavy duty foil. Place 1 to 2 pork chops on cabbage. Seal securely.

ON THE GRILL: Place packets on grill 4 to 6 inches from hot coals. Cook 25 to 30 minutes until chops are done.

Tips: If desired, an 8 or 9-inch square metal baking pan, covered with foil can be used for foil packets.

Canadian bacon slices can be used for smoked pork chops.

Foil packets can be roasted, as directed, in 350° oven.

Basting sauce is excellent to use on smoked ham. Cook according to time table on opposite page and baste during last 30 minutes cooking time.

HAM 'N FRUIT KABOBS

    1 cup (10-oz. jar) orange marmalade or
      apricot preserves
    ½ cup orange juice
    ¼ cup firmly packed brown sugar
    2 tablespoons lemon juice
    1 teaspoon ground ginger, if desired
    1 lb. smoked cooked ham, cut into
      1-inch cubes
    3 large bananas, cut into cubes
    1 cup drained canned pineapple chunks

BEFORE GRILLING: Combine marmalade, orange juice, brown sugar, lemon juice and ginger to make basting sauce; mix well. Thread ham, bananas and pineapple on 4 large or 8 small skewers, beginning and ending with ham.

ON THE GRILL: Place skewers on grill 6 to 8 inches from hot coals. Cook 15 to 20 minutes, brushing frequently with basting sauce until ham and fruit are heated through.

> **Tip:** Kabobs can be broiled, as directed, in oven.

SWEET 'N SPICY HAM SLICE

    1 smoked ham slice, cut 1½-inches thick
    ½ cup currant or apple jelly
    1 tablespoon lemon juice
    1 teaspoon prepared mustard or
      ½ teaspoon dry mustard
    ⅛ teaspoon ground cinnamon
    ⅛ teaspoon ground cloves, if desired

BEFORE GRILLING: Cut slashes in fat edge of ham. Combine remaining ingredients in saucepan to make basting sauce. Heat over low heat, stirring occasionally, until jelly is melted.

ON THE GRILL: Brush ham with basting sauce. Center ham on grill 6 to 8 inches from hot coals. Cook 20 to 25 minutes until heated, turning two to three times and brushing occasionally with basting sauce.

> **Tips:** Ham can be broiled, as directed, in oven.
>
> Ham slices cut ¾ inch thick cook in about 10 minutes.

Men, especially, like this ham barbecue. Rosy barbecue sauce and onion rounds team up to make an easy and attractive dish. Serve with beans and cole slaw.

ONION BARBECUED HAM SLICE

4 to 6 servings

    1 smoked ham slice, cut 1½-inches thick
    1 cup prepared barbecue sauce
    2 tablespoons dry sherry, if desired
    1 teaspoon celery seed, if desired
    1 large onion, sliced ½-inch thick

BEFORE GRILLING: Cut slashes in fat edge of ham. Combine remaining ingredients except onion to make marinade; mix well. Pour marinade over ham in shallow non-metallic container or plastic bag; turn to coat both sides. Top with onion slices. Cover; marinate 1 to 2 hours at room temperature or several hours in refrigerator. Remove ham and onions; reserve marinade for basting sauce.

ON THE GRILL: Center ham and onion slices on grill 6 to 8 inches from hot coals. Cook 20 to 25 minutes until heated, turning two to three times and brushing occasionally with basting sauce. Brush with additional sauce before serving.

> **Tips:** Ham can be broiled, as directed, in oven.
>
> Thin slices of leftover ham make good sandwiches. Spoon on hot barbecue sauce and serve on rye buns.

CURRIED FRUIT

6 to 8 servings

    2 cups (1 lb. 13-oz. can) drained peach
      halves
    2 cups (1 lb. 13-oz. can) drained pear
      halves
    2 cups (1 lb. 4-oz. can) drained pineapple
      chunks
    5 maraschino cherries, sliced, if desired
    ⅓ cup butter or margarine
    ¾ cup firmly packed brown sugar
    2 to 4 teaspoons curry powder

Melt butter in heat proof casserole or skillet; add brown sugar and curry powder. Mix well. Add fruit; heat on range or grill for 10 to 15 minutes, stirring occasionally. Serve along with ham.

GLAZED HAM
8 to 12 servings

    1 boned, rolled ham, fully cooked
    1 cup Port wine or dry red wine
    ½ teaspoon cinnamon
    1½ cups (12-oz. can) apricot nectar

BEFORE GRILLING: Pierce ham deeply with a meat fork or ice pick. Combine remaining ingredients. Pour over ham in non-metallic bowl or plastic bag; cover. Marinate several hours at room temperature or overnight in refrigerator, turning several times to season. Remove ham from marinade; reserve marinade for basting sauce. Insert meat thermometer, see directions on page 19.

ON THE GRILL: Arrange coals for roasting meat; see method B, page 5. Center meat on grill 6 to 8 inches from coals; cover. Roast over slow fire to 130° (about 2 hours), turning and basting with marinade every 30 minutes.

> **Tips:** For rotisserie, see method B, page 5.
> For oven roasting, roast at 325° for 2 to 2½ hours until heated through.

HONEY GLAZED HAM
8 to 12 servings

    ½ cup butter or margarine
    ¼ cup honey
    ¼ cup lime juice
    2 teaspoons salt or seasoned salt
    1 boned and rolled ham, fully cooked

BEFORE GRILLING: Pierce ham deeply with a meat fork or ice pick. Combine remaining ingredients. Pour over ham in non-metallic bowl or plastic bag; cover. Marinate several hours at room temperature or overnight in refrigerator, turning several times to season. Remove from marinade; reserve marinade for basting sauce. Insert meat thermometer, see directions on page 19.

ON THE GRILL: Arrange coals for roasting meat; see method B, page 5. Center meat on grill 6 to 8 inches from coals; cover. Roast over slow fire to 130° (about 2 hours), turning and basting with marinade every 30 minutes.

> **Tips:** For rotisserie, see method B, page 5.
> For oven roasting, roast at 325° for 2 to 2½ hours until heated through.

MAPLE HAM DINNER
4 to 6 servings

    1 smoked ham slice, cut 1½-inches thick
    ¾ cup maple flavored syrup
    ¼ cup chopped candied ginger or
      1 teaspoon ground ginger, if desired
    2 tablespoons lemon juice
    1 tablespoon (3 teaspoons) dry or
      prepared mustard
    1½ to 2 cups (1-lb. can) drained sweet
      potatoes
    1½ to 2 cups (16 oz.) drained whole baby
      carrots

BEFORE GRILLING: Cut slashes in fat edge of ham. Combine syrup, ginger, lemon juice and mustard; mix well. Thread sweet potatoes and carrots on skewers.

ON THE GRILL: Brush ham and vegetables with basting sauce. Center ham steak and vegetables on grill, 6 to 8 inches from hot coals. Cook 20 to 25 minutes until heated, turning two to three times and brushing occasionally with basting sauce.

> **Tips:** Ham can be broiled, as directed, in oven.
> 2 large apples, cored and cut into ½ to ¾ inch slices can be cooked along-side ham. Brush with glaze during cooking.

TIMETABLE FOR ROASTING HAMS
(oven 325° or medium coals)

Ham	Average Weight	Meat Thermometer Reading	Approx. Time
(Cook before eating)			
Whole ham	10-14 lbs.	160°	3½-4½ hrs.
Half ham	5-7 lbs.	160°	1¾-2½ hrs.
(Fully cooked or canned)			
Whole ham	10-14 lbs.	130°	1¾-2½ hrs.
Half ham	5-7 lbs.	130°	1½-2¼ hrs.
(Cook before eating)			
Picnic shoulder	5-8 lbs.	170°	3-4¾ hrs.

Crispy Leg of Lamb, opposite page.

Lamb

Lamb is a tender, succulent meat with cuts similar to beef available for the grill or rotisserie. Some lamb recipes, such as the shish kabob, are among the oldest barbecue traditions.

Roasts — leg, shoulder	Rotisserie or Covered grill
Chops and steaks —	Grill
Lamb shanks	Precook simmered in liquid; Grill
Lamb spareribs	Grill

LAMB HINTS

• Lamb chops and steaks cut 1-inch or more thick can be cooked more easily to desired doneness than thinner cuts.

While popular preference seems to be for lamb that is medium to well done, lamb is perfectly safe when served underdone. Meat that is still slightly pink is especially juicy and flavorful.

• To prevent loss of meat juices, use tongs to turn chops and steaks rather than piercing with a fork. If a fork must be used, insert it in the fat at the edge of the chop.

• Marinating lamb in highly seasoned marinades flavored with garlic is popular and lends authenticity to the traditional shish kabob practice of marinating lamb cubes for many hours.

• This flavorful meat is also frequently served with glazes containing fruit juices and pungent herbs and flavorings of which mint is one of the most well known.

Flavorful basted lamb is basic for a Greek dinner. Serve the whole leg of lamb or see Tip for shish kabobs. The meal can be an at home dinner or as casual as our fisherman's picnic, opposite page.

CRISPY LEG OF LAMB
6 to 8 servings

¼ cup cooking oil
1 teaspoon salt
½ teaspoon garlic powder or instant minced garlic
¼ teaspoon pepper or seasoned pepper
¼ teaspoon rosemary, if desired
3½ to 4 lbs. boned and tied leg of lamb

BEFORE GRILLING: Combine all ingredients except lamb to make basting sauce. Insert meat thermometer; see directions on page 19.

ON THE GRILL: Arrange coals for roasting meat; see method B, page 5. Brush lamb with basting sauce. Center roast on grill 6 to 8 inches from coals. Cover; roast over slow fire to 175° for medium (180° for well done) — about 2½ hours. Turn three to four times during roasting.

> **Tips:** For oven roasting, roast at 325°, as directed.
>
> For rotisserie, see method B, page 5.
>
> Try this basting sauce to make lamb shish kabobs. Boned leg of lamb, cut into 1½ -inch cubes can be used, along with fresh mushrooms, tomato quarters, zucchini or Brussels sprouts.

FRUITED LAMB BURGERS
3 to 4 servings

1 lb. ground lamb
1 teaspoon salt
½ cup drained crushed pineapple
¼ cup any French dressing

BEFORE GRILLING: Combine lamb, salt, pineapple and 2 tablespoons of dressing. Shape into 3 to 4 patties.

ON THE GRILL: Place patties on grill 3 to 4 inches from hot coals. Cook for 10 to 15 minutes, brushing with additional dressing, until of desired doneness.

> **Tips:** If desired, use bottled sweet-sour sauce for French dressing.
>
> Burgers can be broiled, as directed, in oven.

*Pre-shaped lamb patties are sometimes
more available than ground lamb. Both will
work in this recipe, but check that patties
do not have seasoning added. Serve with
Tangy Cauliflower Make-Ahead, page 90,
and crispy rolls.*

ORANGE-GLAZED LAMB PATTIES

3 to 4 servings

> ¼ cup orange marmalade
> 2 tablespoons cooking sherry or
>   fruit juice
> 1 lb. ground lamb
> ½ teaspoon salt
> ½ teaspoon onion salt or ⅛ teaspoon
>   onion powder
> ½ teaspoon curry powder
> ⅛ teaspoon green pepper

BEFORE GRILLING: Combine orange
marmalade and sherry; set aside. Combine
remaining ingredients with 2 tablespoons of
marmalade mixture. Form into 3 to 4 patties.

ON THE GRILL: Place patties on grill 3 to
4 inches from hot coals. Cook for 10 to
15 minutes until of desired doneness, brushing
generously with marmalade mixture during last
5 minutes.

> **Tips:** For kabobs, form mixture into 1-inch
> meat balls. Thread on skewers, alternating
> if desired, with pineapple, banana or
> kumquats.
> Patties may be broiled, as directed,
> in oven.

*Cubes for kabobs can be cut from the leg or
shoulder of lamb. Allow extra when you buy
this form because these cuts contain bone
and excess fat.*

PICNIC KABOBS

4 to 6 servings

> ¼ cup molasses
> ¼ cup prepared mustard
> 3 tablespoons vinegar
> 2 tablespoons Worcestershire sauce
> 2 lbs. lamb, cut into 1½-inch cubes
> 1 green pepper, cut into 1-inch pieces
> 1 tomato, cut into wedges
> 2 cups (8 oz. or ½ pt.) mushrooms

BEFORE GRILLING: Combine molasses,
mustard, vinegar and Worcestershire sauce.

Pour over lamb in non-metallic bowl or
plastic bag, tossing to coat. Cover; marinate
1 to 2 hours at room temperature or overnight
in the refrigerator. Remove from marinade;
reserve marinade for basting sauce. Alternate
lamb with vegetables on four skewers.

ON THE GRILL: Place skewers on grill 3 to
4 inches from hot coals. Cook about 20 minutes,
turning once and brushing with marinade.

> **Tip:** If marinating is not convenient, just
> prepare sauce and brush liberally on
> kabobs while cooking.

*If rack of lamb ribs are not available, try with
6 to 8 lamb shoulder steaks. Precook for
about 30 minutes.*

BARBECUED ISLAND RIBS

4 to 6 servings

> 3 to 4 lbs. lamb ribs
> 1 cup (8-oz. can) undrained crushed
>   pineapple
> ¼ cup barbecue sauce
> 2 tablespoons brown sugar
> 1 tablespoon cornstarch
> 2 tablespoons vinegar
> 2 tablespoons soy sauce
> ½ teaspoon salt
> ½ teaspoon ground ginger

BEFORE GRILLING: Place ribs in large
saucepan. Combine remaining ingredients
and pour over ribs. Cover and simmer over
low heat until tender, about 1½ hours. If
desired, cool and refrigerate until ready
to grill.

ON THE GRILL: Place ribs on grill 6 to
8 inches from hot coals. Cook for 20 to
25 minutes, brushing with sauce and turning
occasionally until well browned and heated
through. (Mixture will be thick at first, but
becomes thinner as it cooks.) If desired,
heat remaining sauce and serve over ribs.

> **Tip:** Ribs in sauce can be covered and
> baked in 350° oven. If precooked, allow
> about 45 minutes to reheat; if uncooked,
> allow about 2 hours until tender.

CURRIED LAMB SHANKS

4 to 6 servings

>   4 to 6 lamb shanks
>   1 tablespoon cornstarch
>   1 teaspoon salt
>   1 teaspoon curry powder
>   ½ teaspoon ground ginger
>   ⅛ teaspoon instant minced garlic or
>   1 clove garlic, minced
>   2 tablespoons grated orange peel
>   ½ cup orange juice
>   ½ cup white wine*

BEFORE GRILLING: Place lamb shanks in large saucepan. Combine remaining ingredients; pour over shanks. Cover and simmer over low heat about 1½ hours until tender. (Mixture will be thick at first, but becomes thinner as it cooks.) If desired, cool and refrigerate until ready to grill.

ON THE GRILL: Place lamb shanks on grill 6 to 8 inches from hot coals. Cook for 20 to 25 minutes, brushing with sauce and turning occasionally until heated through.

> **Tips:** Lamb shanks can be broiled, as directed, in oven.
>
> If shanks are chilled before grilling, reheat in saucepan enough to liquify sauce.
>
> *Additional orange juice can be used for wine.

GINGER SHERRY LAMB CHOPS

4 servings

>   ¼ cup soy sauce
>   ¼ cup sherry
>   ⅛ teaspoon instant minced garlic or
>   1 clove garlic, minced
>   1 teaspoon dry or prepared mustard
>   ¼ teaspoon ground ginger
>   ¼ teaspoon ground thyme, if desired
>   4 lamb chops or steaks

BEFORE GRILLING: In non-metallic bowl or plastic bag, combine all ingredients except chops. Add chops, coating with marinade. Marinate 2 to 4 hours at room temperature or overnight in refrigerator.

ON THE GRILL: Place chops on grill 4 to 6 inches from hot coals. Cook about 10 minutes on each side, brushing occasionally with marinade, until of desired doneness.

> **Tip:** Chops can be broiled, as directed, in oven.

LAMB 'N MINTY PEARS

4 servings

>   ¼ cup mint jelly
>   1 tablespoon lemon juice
>   1-lb. can pear halves, drain and reserve
>   2 tablespoons syrup
>   6 lamb chops or steaks

BEFORE GRILLING: Combine mint jelly, lemon juice and 2 tablespoons pear syrup; mix well.

ON THE GRILL: Place lamb chops on grill 4 to 6 inches from hot coals. Cook about 10 minutes on each side, brushing with mint jelly glaze. During last few minutes, place pear halves, cut-side up on grill. Spoon any remaining mint jelly in each pear half and allow to heat through. If desired, serve with rice (the leftover pear syrup can be used for part of cooking liquid).

> **Tips:** Chops can be broiled, as directed, in oven.
>
> To prevent fruit from slipping through widely spaced grids, cover grill with a piece of foil before heating pears.

APRICOT GLAZED LAMB CHOPS

4 to 6 servings

>   ⅓ cup apricot preserves*
>   1 teaspoon salt
>   ½ teaspoon nutmeg
>   ¼ teaspoon ground ginger
>   2 tablespoons lemon juice
>   6 lamb chops (rib, loin or shoulder)

BEFORE GRILLING: Combine all ingredients except chops to make basting sauce; mix well.

ON THE GRILL: Place chops on grill 4 to 6 inches from hot coals. Cook for about 20 minutes, turning and brushing often with apricot mixture, until done. Brush with any remaining glaze just before serving.

> **Tips:** Chops can be broiled, as directed, in oven.
>
> *Peach, pineapple or other light-colored preserves can be used for apricot.

Poultry

Chicken has been on the barbecue scene for years. It's readily available, inexpensive, easy to cook and good to eat.

With a few easy guidelines, the barbecue beginner can select and prepare poultry for the grill so the finished birds have crisp skin with moist, tender meat.

Long, slow cooking ends the disappointment of birds overcooked outside and underdone inside. A meat thermometer thrust into breast of larger birds when barbecuing will tell you when it's done. Meat is also done when it pulls away from the bones, especially at the ends of the legs; or when the drumstick and thigh joints move easily.

Poultry should be kept under refrigeration until cooking time.

Poultry Buying Guide

Chicken: Select 2 to 3-pound well-meated birds of uniform size. Chickens can be cut into pieces for grililng, or into portion-sized halves or quarters. The larger pieces will take longer to cook, but will generally be juicier.

Cornish Game Hens and Cornish Capons: Prepared and barbecued the same as chicken. Select game hens that weigh about ¾ to 1-pound each; capons that weigh between 5 to 7-pounds.

Turkey: An 8 to 12-pound young hen turkey is a good choice to barbecue, leaving plenty of leftovers. Owner's manuals that accompany grills give specific weights of birds that can be barbecued on either rotisseries or covered grills.

Rolled boneless turkey roasts make excellent roasting choices, especially to rotisserie, since the shape of the roast allows even cooking.

Turkey pieces, available in some supermarkets, are an economical buy. Because of their size and shape, we recommend precooking these in foil first.

Duckling: Younger waterfowl weighing 4 to 5-pounds are a deliciously different barbecue treat.

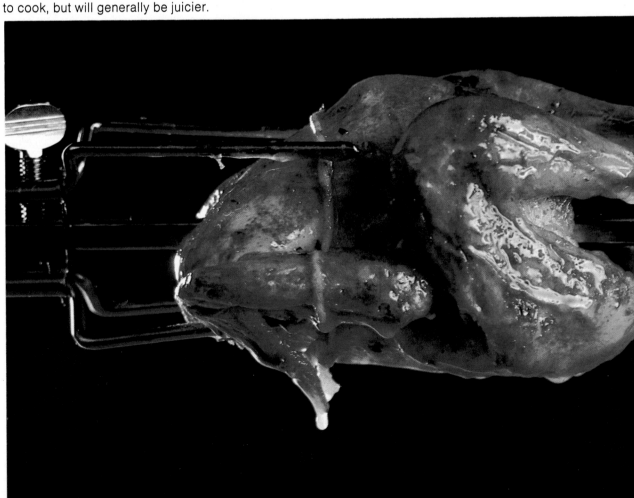

CHICKEN ON THE SPIT

3 to 4 servings

> 1 whole roasting chicken, 3 to 4 lbs.
> 1 teaspoon salt
> Dash pepper
> ½ cup cooking oil
> 1 teaspoon celery seed, oregano or basil, if desired

BEFORE GRILLING: Season inside of chicken with salt and pepper. Skewer neck skin to back. Wrap string around wings and breast to fasten securely. Insert spit from tail end of chicken toward front. Insert skewers or spit forks firmly in place in chicken and secure, making sure chicken is evenly balanced on spit. Tie legs to spit. Combine cooking oil and seasoning for basting sauce.

ON THE GRILL: Arrange coals for roasting, see page 5. Insert rotisserie 4 to 6 inches from coals; brush with oil. Cover; roast according to timetable, adding 4 to 6 pieces of charcoal and brushing with cooking oil every 30 minutes.

> **Tip:** Chicken can be stuffed with Savory Apple or Cornbread Stuffing, page 76.
>
> Chicken can be roasted, as directed, in oven.

GOLDEN GLAZED CORNISH HENS

4 servings

> 2 tablespoons melted butter
> ⅓ cup soy sauce
> ¼ cup light corn syrup
> ⅛ teaspoon instant minced garlic or 1 clove garlic, minced
> 4 Rock Cornish game hens

BEFORE GRILLING: Thaw hens, if frozen. In saucepan, melt butter; blend in soy sauce, corn syrup and garlic for basting sauce. Season body cavity with salt. Tie legs to tails and wings to bodies. Insert spit rod, alternating front to back, either lengthwise or crosswise through hens.

ON THE GRILL: Arrange coals for rotisserie roasting, see page 5. Brush hens with basting sauce. Insert rotisserie 6 to 8 inches from coals. Roast 1¼ to 1½ hours, brushing frequently with basting sauce during last 30 minutes.

> **Tips:** Hens can be roasted in 325° oven for about 1 hour.
>
> Split halves of Rock Cornish game hens can be placed directly on grill 6 to 8 inches from hot coals, skin-side up. Cook 20 to 25 minutes; turn and cook 20 to 25 minutes more, basting frequently.

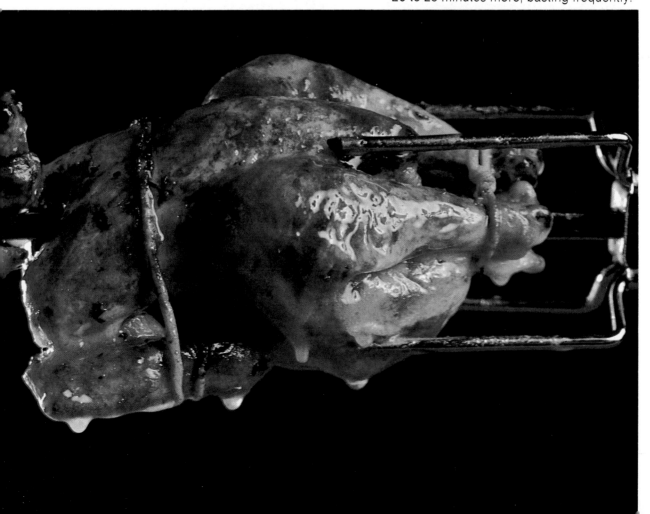

CORNISH HENS WITH WILD RICE STUFFING

4 servings

> 4 Rock Cornish game hens, about 1 lb. each
> ¼ cup butter or margarine
> 2 tablespoons chopped onion or
>   1½ teaspoons instant minced onion
> 1 tablespoon chopped green pepper, if desired
> 1 cup cooked wild rice or white and wild rice mixture
> ¾ cup (8½-oz. can) crushed pineapple; drain and reserve syrup
> ¼ cup diced roasted almonds
> 2 tablespoons currants or chopped raisins, if desired
> ¼ teaspoon salt

Glaze:

> ¼ cup reserved pineapple syrup
> ¼ cup honey
> ¼ cup melted butter or margarine
> ½ teaspoon mace, if desired

BEFORE GRILLING: In small saucepan, melt butter; add onion and green pepper and cook until tender. In mixing bowl, combine rice, pineapple, roasted almonds, currants, salt, onion and green pepper; mix well. Spoon mixture into body cavity. Fasten with skewers or lace shut. Insert rotisserie rod through hens; secure by tying legs and wings to bird and rotisserie rod. (See directions on page 77.) Meanwhile prepare Glaze.

GLAZE: Combine ingredients; mix well.

ON THE GRILL: Place on grill about 4 inches from hot coals. Cook on rotisserie 60 to 70 minutes or until tender, basting occasionally with Glaze.

> **Tip:** Game hens can be roasted, as directed, in 325° oven about 1 hour.

Get acquainted with this brother of the Rock Cornish hen. Weights of these birds are about 5 to 7 lbs., so they can be used like roasting chickens or small turkeys.

CORNISH CAPON WITH ORANGE RICE

4 to 6 servings

> 7 lbs. Rock Cornish capon
> 2½ cups cooked wild rice or white rice
> ¼ cup chopped celery
> ¼ cup chopped pecans
> 2 tablespoons melted butter
> 1 tablespoon grated orange peel
> ½ teaspoon salt

Ginger Orange Glaze:

> ⅓ cup (½ 6-oz. can) frozen orange juice concentrate
> 2 tablespoons cooking oil
> 1 tablespoon wine vinegar or white wine
> ½ teaspoon ground ginger
> ½ teaspoon mace, if desired

BEFORE GRILLING: Remove any excess fat from inside capon. In large bowl, combine remaining ingredients for stuffing; toss lightly. Loosely stuff body cavity with rice mixture. Truss as you would for stuffed turkey or chicken, see page 77. Meanwhile, prepare Ginger Orange Glaze.

GINGER ORANGE GLAZE: Combine all ingredients; mix well. Spoon any remaining glaze over capon just before serving.

ON THE GRILL: Arrange coals for rotisserie roasting with drip pan in place, see page 5. Roast capon slowly 2 to 3 hours until internal temperature reaches 195°, brushing with glaze during last 30 minutes.

> **Tips:** Capon can be roasted as directed in 325° oven.
>
> For added orange flavor, add ⅓ cup frozen orange juice concentrate to water when cooking rice.

CITRUS HONEY BARBECUED CHICKEN

4 to 6 servings

> 2 frying chickens, quartered or halved
> ½ cup lemon juice
> ½ cup orange juice
> ⅓ cup honey
> 1 cup cooking oil
> 2 tablespoons prepared mustard
> ½ teaspoon dried thyme
> ½ teaspoon dried marjoram

BEFORE GRILLING: Place chicken pieces in shallow non-metallic container or plastic bag. Combine remaining ingredients to make marinade. Pour over chicken; marinate in refrigerator for at least two hours, turning several times to season. Drain chicken; reserve marinade for basting sauce.

ON THE GRILL: Place chicken, skin-side up, on grill 6 to 8 inches from hot coals. Cook for 20 to 25 minutes on each side, turning once and brushing occasionally with reserved marinade until chicken is done.

> **Tip:** Chicken can be broiled, beginning with skin-side down, as directed, in oven.

LEMON GRILLED CHICKEN

6 large servings

> 2 teaspoons MSG (monosodium
> glutamate), if desired
> 2 teaspoons salt
> 2 teaspoons pepper
> 2 teaspoons paprika
> 3 frying chickens, halved or quartered
> ¼ cup lemon juice
> 2 tablespoons cooking oil
> 2 teaspoons tarragon, if desired

BEFORE GRILLING: Combine MSG, salt, pepper and paprika; sprinkle over all sides of chicken. Combine lemon juice, cooking oil and tarragon; reserve for basting sauce.

ON THE GRILL: Brush chicken with basting sauce. Place on grill skin-side up 6 to 8 inches from hot coals. Cook for 25 to 30 minutes on each side, turning and brushing occasionally with basting sauce until done.

> **Tips:** Chicken can be broiled, as directed, in oven.
> Try this sauce with turkey or duckling pieces, or Cornish hens.

Glazes high in sugar are best used during the last minutes of barbecuing to prevent burning. This one gives chicken pieces a rich golden glaze. Cardinal Coleslaw, page 93, rice pilaf and cake for dessert complete the meal.

CHICKEN WITH PINEAPPLE GLAZE

6 to 8 large servings

> 2 frying chickens, quartered
> ⅛ cup softened butter or margarine
> Salt
> Pepper
> Paprika
> ¾ cup (9-oz. can) undrained crushed
> pineapple
> 1 cup firmly packed brown sugar
> 2 tablespoons lemon juice
> 2 tablespoons prepared mustard or
> 1 teaspoon dry mustard
> Dash salt

BEFORE GRILLING: Rub chicken with butter; sprinkle with salt, pepper and paprika. Meanwhile, combine remaining ingredients for basting sauce; mix well.

ON THE GRILL: Place chicken on grill, skin-side up, 6 to 8 inches from hot coals. Cook for 30 to 45 minutes, turning once to brown both sides. Brush with basting sauce during last 10 to 15 minutes. If desired, heat any remaining sauce and serve with chicken.

> **Tip:** Chicken can be broiled, as directed, in oven.

CHOW HOUND CHICKEN

4 to 5 servings

> ⅓ cup cooking oil
> 1 can (8 oz.) tomato sauce
> ⅓ cup lemon juice
> 2 tablespoons Worcestershire sauce
> 1 tablespoon prepared mustard
> 1 garlic clove, minced or ⅛ teaspoon
> instant minced garlic
> 1 frying chicken, cut up

BEFORE GRILLING: Combine all ingredients except chicken in saucepan; simmer 5 minutes. Use for basting sauce.

ON THE GRILL: Place chicken on grill, skin-side up 6 to 8 inches from hot coals. Cook for 25 to 30 minutes on each side, turning and brushing occasionally with basting sauce until done.

> **Tip:** Chicken can be broiled beginning with skin-side down, as directed, in oven.

CHILI BARBECUED CHICKEN

4 to 5 servings

  1 frying chicken, cut up
  1 cup catsup or chili sauce
  ¼ cup chopped onion or 2 tablespoons
    instant minced onion
  ¼ cup firmly packed brown sugar
  1 clove garlic, crushed
  1 tablespoon grated lemon peel, if desired
  2 tablespoons lemon juice
  1 tablespoon Worcestershire sauce
  1 teaspoon chili powder
  1 teaspoon paprika

BEFORE GRILLING: Preheat oven to 350°. Place chicken on large square of heavy duty foil; wrap tightly. Roast in foil for 30 minutes. Meanwhile, in small mixing bowl, combine all ingredients.

ON THE GRILL: Place chicken skin-side up on grill 4 to 6 inches from hot coals. Cook for about 20 minutes, until done, turning and brushing often with basting sauce.

> **Tip:** Chicken can be broiled, as directed, beginning skin-side down in oven.

ONION BARBECUED CHICKEN

4 large servings

  1 chicken, quartered
  Salt
  Pepper
  ½ cup (1 envelope) dry onion soup mix
  ½ cup cooking oil
  ½ cup Sauterne or white wine
  1 tablespoon lemon juice
  1 tablespoon Worcestershire sauce

BEFORE GRILLING: Preheat oven to 350°. Place chicken on large square of heavy duty foil; season with salt and pepper. Roast in foil 45 minutes. In small bowl, combine remaining ingredients for basting sauce.

ON THE GRILL: Place chicken on the grill 4 to 6 inches from hot coals. Cook about 30 minutes until done, turning and brushing often with basting sauce. Pour any remaining sauce over chicken before serving.

> **Tips:** Chicken can be broiled, as directed, in oven.
>
> If desired, apple juice can be used for Sauterne.

Precook chicken for this easy recipe by roasting in foil first in the oven or on the grill. Twenty minutes later, these golden chicken pieces are ready without as much chance of burning. Adapt this method to other favorite recipes.

EASY BUTTER BASTED CHICKEN

4 to 5 servings

  1 frying chicken, cut up
  ½ cup butter or margarine
  ½ teaspoon salt
  ½ teaspoon lemon pepper marinade*
  ¼ teaspoon leaf basil, crushed,
    if desired

BEFORE GRILLING: Preheat oven to 350°. Place chicken on large square of heavy duty foil; wrap tightly. Roast in foil for 30 minutes. Meanwhile, melt butter in saucepan; add lemon pepper marinade and basil to make basting sauce.

ON THE GRILL: Place chicken, skin-side up on grill 4 to 6 inches from hot coals. Cook about 20 minutes, until done, turning and brushing often with basting sauce.

> **Tip:** Chicken can be broiled, as directed, in oven.
>
> *Another favorite seasoned salt blend can be used for lemon pepper marinade.

Cooking Methods for Poultry

Type of Poultry	Cooking Method
Whole Chicken	Rotisserie or Covered Grill
Chicken halves, quarters, or pieces	Grill
Whole Turkey	Rotisserie or Covered Grill
Turkey pieces	Grill
Whole Cornish Game Hens	Rotisserie
Split Cornish Game Hens	Grill
Duckling	Rotisserie

Chili Barbecued Chicken, opposite page; Biscuit Tortillas, page 105; Old-Fashioned Lemonade, page 111.

TOMATO BARBECUED CHICKEN

4 servings

½ cup catsup
2 tablespoons chopped onion
2 tablespoons brown sugar
1 tablespoon lemon juice
1 tablespoon Worcestershire sauce
½ teaspoon celery seed
⅛ teaspoon garlic powder or salt
1 frying chicken, cut up

BEFORE GRILLING: In small mixing bowl, combine all ingredients except chicken to make barbecue sauce.

ON THE GRILL: Place chicken pieces, skin-side up on grill 6 to 8 inches from hot coals. Cook 45 to 60 minutes, turning and basting frequently, until tender and well done.

> **Tips:** Chicken can be broiled, as directed, in oven.
> Barbecue sauce is also good on Cornish hens that have been split in half. Cook as directed.

GOURMET CHICKEN GRILL

4 servings

4 boned chicken breasts
Salt
Pepper
¼ cup butter or margarine
2 tablespoons sliced green onion
1 tablespoon chopped green pepper, if desired
¼ cup canned or fresh sliced mushrooms
Melted butter, margarine or cooking oil

Wine Butter Sauce:

¼ cup butter or margarine
2 tablespoons sliced green onion
1 tablespoon chopped green pepper, if desired
1 teaspoon parsley flakes or 1 tablespoon chopped parsley
2 tablespoons Sauterne or white wine

BEFORE GRILLING: Bone chicken breasts. Sprinkle with salt and pepper. In small saucepan, melt butter; cook onion, pepper and mushrooms until tender. Spoon about 2 tablespoons of vegetable mixture on inside of each chicken breast. Roll up; tie with cord. Meanwhile, prepare Wine Butter Sauce.

WINE BUTTER SAUCE: In small saucepan, melt butter; cook onion and green pepper until tender. Add parsley and wine. Heat to boiling. Keep warm until serving time.

ON THE GRILL: Place chicken on grill 6 to 8 inches from hot coals. Cook for 45 to 60 minutes, turning frequently and brushing occasionally with melted butter. To serve, spoon Wine Butter Sauce over chicken.

> **Tip:** Chicken can be broiled or roasted, as directed, in oven.

Rich tasting peanut glaze fits into a southern style meal plan. Serve with Vegetable Patch Salad, page 90, corn muffins and an easy fruit dessert.

PEANUT GLAZED CHICKEN

4 to 5 servings

¼ cup butter or margarine
¼ cup peanut butter
¼ cup dry sherry or white wine
¼ cup lime juice or 2 tablespoons lemon juice
¼ cup soy sauce
2 tablespoons honey or brown sugar
1 frying chicken, cut up

BEFORE GRILLING: Melt butter in saucepan; add remaining ingredients except chicken for marinade; mix well. Pour marinade over chicken in non-metallic bowl or plastic bag; cover. Marinate at least 2 hours at room temperature or overnight in the refrigerator. Remove chicken pieces from marinade; reserve marinade for basting sauce.

ON THE GRILL: Place chicken on grill, skin-side up, 6 to 8 inches from hot coals. Cook for 20 to 25 minutes on each side, turning and brushing occasionally with basting sauce until done.

> **Tips:** Chicken can be broiled beginning with skin-side down, as directed, in oven.
> When in a hurry, just coat chicken with marinade and grill as directed.

CHICKEN MADRAS

4 to 5 servings

>   1 frying chicken, cut up
>   Cooking oil
>   Salt or seasoned salt
>   Pepper or seasoned pepper
>   1 can (8 oz.) tomato sauce
>   ¼ cup cinnamon-flavored apple jelly*
>   1 clove garlic, crushed
>   ½ teaspoon oregano

BEFORE GRILLING: Brush chicken pieces with oil; sprinkle with salt and pepper. Combine remaining ingredients in saucepan; heat over low heat, stirring until smooth. Reserve for basting sauce.

ON THE GRILL: Place chicken on grill, skin-side up, 6 to 8 inches from hot coals. Cook for 20 to 25 minutes on each side, brushing each side with sauce during last 5 minutes until done. Serve with any remaining sauce.

> **Tips:** Chicken can be broiled, beginning with skin-side down, as directed, in oven.
>
> * ¼ cup apple jelly and ⅛ teaspoon cinnamon can be used for cinnamon-flavored apple jelly.
>
> Try Madras Sauce with pork, turkey or spareribs.

COUNTRY CHICKEN DINNER

4 servings

>   1 can (10½ oz.) condensed cream of
>   chicken soup
>   1 frying chicken, cut up
>   2 cups (1-lb. can) drained sliced potatoes
>   2 cups (1-lb. can) drained whole carrots
>   2 cups (1-lb. can) drained whole onions
>   1 package frozen peas
>   1 teaspoon parsley flakes, if desired
>   ½ teaspoon salt
>   Dash pepper

BEFORE GRILLING: Grease a 13x9-inch metal or foil pan with butter or margarine. Spread undiluted soup evenly over bottom. Place chicken in pan. Arrange potatoes, carrots and peas, compartment-style around chicken in pan. Scatter whole onions over vegetables. Season chicken with parsley flakes, salt and pepper. Cover pan with foil.

ON THE GRILL: Place pan on grill on another sheet of foil 4 inches from hot coals. (This prevents pan from darkening.) Cover with hood or foil tent, see page 5. Cook about 1 hour or until chicken is tender. Spoon the chicken gravy over chicken and vegetables before serving. Chicken can be served from pan, or place on platter and pour gravy into a separate bowl.

> **Tip:** Chicken can be prepared, as directed, in 350° oven.

CURRIED CHICKEN WITH SWEET POTATOES

6 servings

>   1 frying chicken, cut up
>   4 cups (two 1 lb. cans) sweet potatoes,
>   drained
> 3½ cups (29-oz. can) peach halves; drain
>   and reserve ¼ cup juice
> 1¼ cups (10-oz. jar) peach preserves
>   2 tablespoons chopped chutney, if desired
>   2 tablespoons wine vinegar or vinegar
>   1 teaspoon curry powder
> 1½ tablespoons cornstarch, if desired

BEFORE GRILLING: Grease a 13x9-inch metal or foil pan with butter or margarine. Arrange chicken pieces in center with sweet potatoes and peach halves around chicken. In small mixing bowl, combine peach preserves, chutney, vinegar, reserved peach juice and curry powder. Spoon curry mixture over chicken, sweet potatoes and peaches. Cover with foil.

ON THE GRILL: Place pan on grill on another sheet of foil 4 inches from hot coals. (This prevents pan from darkening.) Cover with hood or foil tent, see page 156. Cook 1 hour or until chicken is tender. To serve, place chicken, potatoes and peaches on heated platter. If desired, combine cornstarch and ¼ cup water and thicken juices in pan with cornstarch mixture.

> **Tips:** Chicken can be prepared, as directed, in 350° oven.
>
> For 3 to 4 servings, use 1 chicken but halve remaining ingredients.

CHICKEN LIVER WRAP-UPS

12 appetizers

¼ cup dry sherry
¼ cup soy sauce
1 tablespoon sugar
⅛ teaspoon garlic powder
½ lb. (8-oz. pkg.) chicken livers
6 strips bacon, cut in half
Water chestnuts, if desired
Stuffed green olives, if desired

BEFORE GRILLING: Combine soy sauce, sherry, sugar and garlic powder to make marinade. Cut livers in half. Pour marinade over livers in shallow non-metallic bowl or plastic bag. Marinate at room temperature for 1 hour. Remove from marinade. To make appetizer, wrap chicken liver around water chestnut or olive, then wrap bacon around both. Secure with toothpicks. Thread on bamboo or small skewers.

ON THE GRILL: Place skewers on grill 4 to 6 inches from hot coals. Cook, turning frequently, until bacon is crisp.

Tips: Appetizers can be broiled, as directed, in oven.

If desired, water chestnuts can be marinated in soy mixture along with chicken livers.

Duck roasted on a spit is the best way to cook this bird. All fat drains away, leaving the skin crisp and the meat tender.

ROAST DUCK ON A SPIT

4 servings

One 5 lb. duckling
1 stalk celery with leaves, cut into pieces
2 or 3 sprigs parsley
1 small onion, quartered
½ orange with peel, cut into quarters
Salt
Pepper

Orange Barbecue Sauce:

2 oranges or ½ to ⅔ cup orange juice
  and 2 tablespoons peel
½ cup tarragon vinegar or ½ cup white
  vinegar and ½ teaspoon dried tarragon
½ teaspoon dried rosemary
¼ cup firmly packed brown sugar
1 tablespoon prepared mustard

BEFORE GRILLING: Remove excess fat from duck. Rinse; drain and dry bird. Salt and pepper body cavity; place celery, parsley, onion and orange inside. Close cavity with skewers. Insert spit rod through center of duck, lengthwise. Secure it firmly by inserting the holding prongs into the duck at either end; tie legs and wings securely to bird and rotisserie rod with string. (See directions on page 77.) If desired, insert meat thermometer; see page 19. Meanwhile, prepare Orange Barbecue Sauce.

ORANGE BARBECUE SAUCE: Remove a thin layer of peel from 1 orange. Squeeze juice from both oranges. Add peel and juice to remaining ingredients in small saucepan. Heat just to boiling, but do not boil. Keep hot for 10 minutes; then strain and use for basting sauce.

ON THE GRILL: Arrange coals for rotisserie roasting with drip pan in place, see page 5. Roast duck slowly 2 to 3 hours until internal temperature reaches 195°, brushing with sauce every 15 minutes. (Drippings may need to be removed from drip pan, if excessive, to avoid flare-up.)

> **Tip:** Duckling can be roasted as directed in 350° oven.

This traditional duckling is full of flavorful sauerkraut and apple stuffing. Potato pancakes are good with this meal. Fry them at the table on an electric griddle.

DUCKLING WITH SAUERKRAUT

One 4 to 5 lb. duckling
Salt
4 cups (29-oz. can or 2 qts.) drained
  sauerkraut
1 finely chopped unpared apple
½ cup chopped onion
1 teaspoon caraway seed
½ cup honey
2 tablespoons wine vinegar or vinegar

BEFORE GRILLING: Remove excess fat from duck. Rinse; drain and dry bird. Salt and pepper body cavity. Combine remaining ingredients except honey and vinegar to make stuffing. Loosely stuff body cavity with sauerkraut mixture. Close cavity with skewers. Insert spit rod through center of duck, lengthwise. Secure it firmly by inserting the holding prongs into the duck at either end; tie legs and wings securely to bird and rotisserie rod with string. (See directions on page 77.) Prick skin of duckling on breast and back with tines of fork. (This allows excess fat to drip from duckling while cooking.) Combine honey and vinegar to make basting sauce. If desired, insert meat thermometer; see page 19.

ON THE GRILL: Arrange coals for rotisserie roasting with drip pan in place; see page 5. Roast duck slowly 2 to 3 hours until internal temperature reaches 195°, brushing with glaze during last 30 minutes. (Drippings may need to be removed from drip pan, if excessive, to avoid flare-up.)

> **Tip:** Duckling can be roasted as directed in 350° oven.

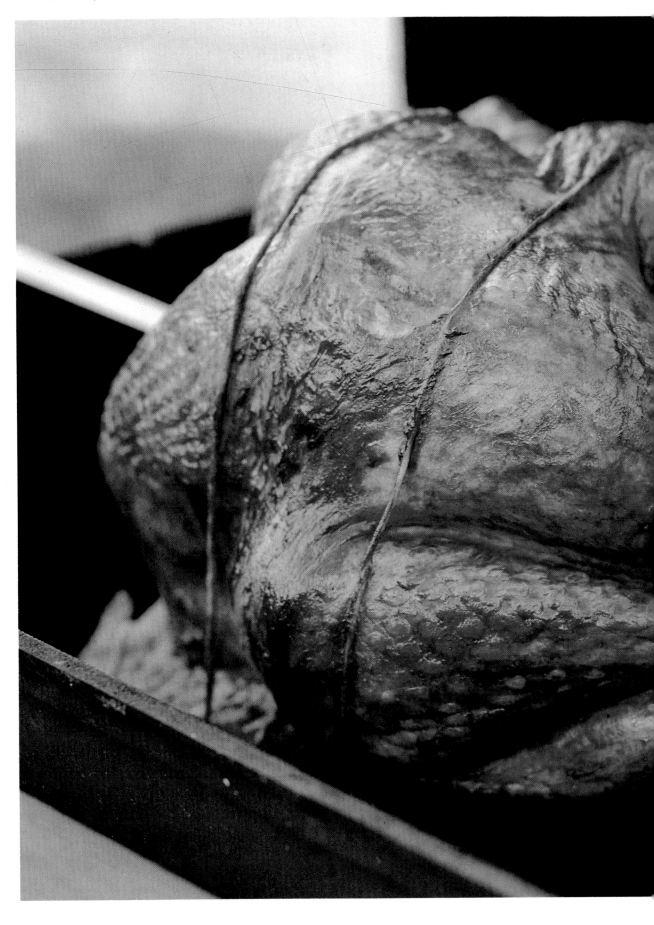

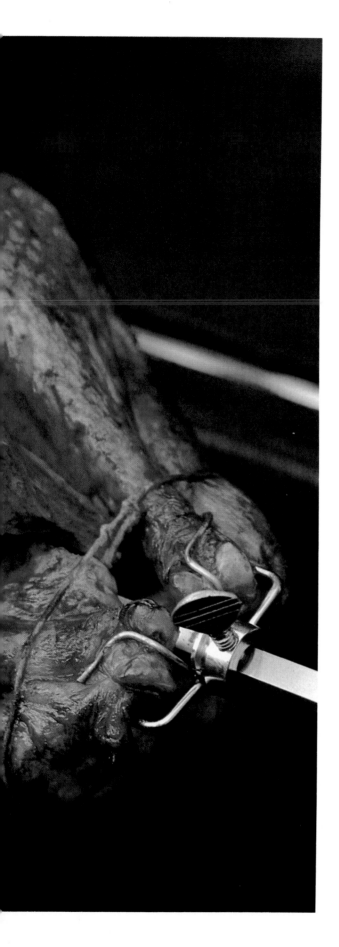

HICKORY SMOKED TURKEY

1 turkey
1 tablespoon salt
Cooking oil for basting

BEFORE GRILLING: Rinse turkey; pat dry. Rub inside with salt. Skewer neck skin to back. Wrap string around wings and breast to fasten securely. Insert spit from tail end of bird toward front. Insert skewers or spit forks firmly in place in bird and secure, making sure turkey is evenly balanced on spit. Tie drumsticks to spit. For moisture, place a small pan of water behind bed of coals. Sprinkle a large handful of dampened hickory chips over coals.

ON THE GRILL: Arrange coals for roasting, see page 5. Insert rotisserie 4 to 6 inches from coals; brush with oil. Cover; roast according to timetable, adding 4 to 6 pieces of charcoal and brushing with cooking oil every 30 minutes. Add hickory chips at beginning and 2 or 3 times during roasting. For easier slicing, allow roast to stand 15 to 20 minutes.

Tips: To check temperature, insert meat thermometer in thickest part of breast, or test doneness by raising drumstick up and down — leg should move easily. Thermometer should register 170°-175°.

Use hot pads to protect your fingers when checking doneness.

APPROXIMATE TIMETABLE FOR ROASTING WHOLE TURKEYS

(Oven 325° or Medium Coals)

Ready-to-Cook Weight	Approximate Time	Approximate Servings
4 to 6 lbs.	2 to 3 hrs.	6 to 8
6 to 8 lbs.	3 to 3½ hrs.	8 to 10
8 to 10 lbs.	3½ to 4 hrs.	10 to 14
10 to 12 lbs.	4 to 5 hrs.	14 to 18

TIMETABLE FOR ROASTING BONELESS TURKEY ROASTS

(Oven 350° or Medium Coals)

Ready-to-Cook Weight	Total Cooking Time	Approximate Servings
2 to 5 lbs.	1½ to 2 hrs.	6 to 12
5 to 7 lbs.	2 to 3 hrs.	12 to 16
7 to 9 lbs.	3 to 3½ hrs.	16 to 24

GLAZED BONELESS TURKEY

BEFORE GRILLING: Arrange coals for rotisserie roasting with drip pan in place, see page 5. Insert spit through center of thawed roast. Tie roast securely several times around and once lengthwise. Insert skewers and screw tightly. Test balance and readjust if necessary.

ON THE GRILL: Place spit in rotisserie 6 to 8 inches from coals and brush with glaze*; roast following timetable. Brush generously with glaze during last 30 to 45 minutes of cooking. If desired, insert meat thermometer in center of roll, being careful not to touch spit. Thermometer should register 170 to 175°.

*Curry Pineapple Glaze

Combine ½ cup pineapple preserves with ¼ cup melted butter or margarine and 1 teaspoon curry powder.

Ginger Peach Glaze

Combine ½ cup peach preserves with ¼ cup melted butter or margarine and 1 teaspoon ground ginger or ¼ cup chopped candied ginger.

Frozen turkey pieces are usually an economical buy. Prepared according to this method, the meat stays flavorful and moist. Use any leftovers for hot turkey sandwiches or salad.

BARBECUED TURKEY QUARTERS

3 to 4 servings

> 1 quartered turkey portion, thawed, about
>   4 to 5 lbs.
> 1 teaspoon salt
> Dash pepper
> Sauce from Golden Glazed Cornish Hens,
>   page 65*

BEFORE GRILLING: Place turkey portion on large square of heavy duty foil. Season with salt and pepper; seal securely.

ON THE GRILL: Place on grill 3 to 4 inches from hot coals. Cook 1½ hours. Meanwhile, prepare sauce, as directed. Remove turkey from foil. Return to grill; brush with sauce. Continue cooking about 15 minutes on each side, brushing frequently with sauce.

> **Tips:** *Sauces from the following recipes would also be good: Chicken Madras, page 71, Onion Barbecued Chicken, page 68, or a favorite prepared sauce.
> Turkey can be roasted, as directed, in 325° oven. See table on page 75 for roasting time.

STUFFINGS FOR TURKEYS OR CHICKENS

SAVORY APPLE STUFFING

1 quart stuffing

> ¼ cup butter or margarine
> ¼ cup (½ med.) chopped onion
> ¼ cup chopped celery
> 2 tablespoons raisins, if desired
> 4 cups dry bread cubes
> ¾ cup (1 small) coarsely chopped apple
> ½ teaspoon ground thyme
> ¼ teaspoon ground sage
> ¼ teaspoon salt

In large fry pan, melt butter. Cook onion and celery in butter until tender. Add remaining ingredients. Toss lightly. Loosely stuff turkey.

CORNBREAD STUFFING

1 quart stuffing

> ½ lb. pork sausage
> ¼ cup (1 med.) chopped onion
> ¼ cup chopped celery
> 2 cups dry bread cubes
> 2 cups crumbled corn bread
> ¼ cup chopped pecans, if desired
> 1 teaspoon poultry seasoning
> ½ teaspoon salt

In large fry pan, cook sausage, onion and celery until sausage is browned. Add remaining ingredients except water. If desired, add 2 to 3 tablespoons water for a more moist stuffing. Loosely stuff turkey.

HOT TURKEY SALAD BUNS

4 sandwiches

> 2 cups cubed cooked turkey
> 1 cup shredded Cheddar cheese
> ½ cup mayonnaise or salad dressing
> ¼ cup chopped celery
> ¼ cup diced roasted almonds, if desired
> 1 chopped sweet pickle
> ¼ teaspoon salt
> 4 hamburger buns

BEFORE GRILLING: In large mixing bowl, combine all ingredients except buns; mix well. Spoon about ½ cup turkey on bottom half of bun; top with remaining bun to make sandwich. Wrap each sandwich in heavy duty foil.

ON THE GRILL: Place packets on grill 6 to 8 inches from hot coals. Heat about 15 to 20 minutes.

> **Tip:** Sandwiches can be heated in 350° oven about 20 to 30 minutes.

TURKEY SALAD POLYNESIAN

4 to 6 main dish servings

> 3 cups cubed, cooked turkey
> 1¼ cups (13¼ oz. can) drained pineapple chunks
> ¾ cup thinly sliced celery
> ¾ cup salad dressing or mayonnaise
> 2 tablespoons chopped chutney
> 1 teaspoon curry powder
> 1 banana
> ½ cup salted peanuts
> ½ cup flaked coconut, if desired
> 1 cup (11-oz. can) mandarin oranges

In large bowl, combine turkey, pineapple, celery, salad dressing, chutney and curry powder; toss lightly. Cover and refrigerate at least 2 hours. Just before serving, slice banana. Add to turkey mixture along with peanuts. Serve on lettuce and garnish with coconut and oranges.

STUFFING

Never stuff turkey until ready to cook. But you may prepare dressing ahead, cover and refrigerate. Allow about 1 hour to prepare bird and stuffing and to stuff.

Allow 1 cup of stuffing for each pound of ready-to-cook poultry.

Loosely pack stuffing into bird; too tight packing makes it soggy and heavy.

Use herb seasoned stuffing cubes or 2 to 4 day-old bread, torn into ¼ to ½-inch pieces or cut into cubes. A 1 lb. loaf of bread makes 8 cups (2 qts.) loosely packed crumbs or cubes.

STUFFING GUIDE

	Average Wt. (lbs.)	Amt. of Stuffing (quarts)
Turkey — Whole	4 to 6	1 to 1½
	6 to 8	1½ to 2
	8 to 12	2 to 3
	12 to 16	3 to 4
Chicken — Broilers, Fryers	1½ to 2½	¼ to ½
	2½ to 4½	½ to 1¼
	4 to 8	1¼ to 1¾

Seafood

Lucky you if you live where seafood abound. A whole world of good eating awaits those who try fish enhanced with smokey barbecue flavor. Frozen fish and seafood are appearing in greater quantities all across the country as people become familiar with this economical and low calorie food source.

Special Helps for Fish and Seafood

When choosing Fresh Fish look for:

- fresh, mild odor
- bright, clear convex eyes
- red gills
- firm, springy flesh
- bright and tight scales

• Store dry, dressed fish in a dish, loosely wrapped with foil or plastic wrap in the coldest part of your refrigerator. Use within one day.

When choosing Shellfish look for:

- in-shell oysters and clams with tightly closed shells
- scallops that are creamy pink
- firm, meaty shrimp and lobster tails with mild odor
- keep fresh shellfish in cracked ice in the refrigerator
- to prevent sogginess and flavor loss, frozen fish fillets need only partial thawing before grilling.

GRILLING GUIDE FOR SHELLFISH

LOBSTER — Either frozen lobster, thawed, fresh split whole lobster or lobster tails can be used. Frozen lobster that you buy may or may not be cooked (you can tell by the bright red or orange color of the cooked shell). If cooked, reheating on the grill will take a very short time. If uncooked, you can either pre-cook them by boiling in salted water before preparing them — 1 tablespoon per quart for about 5 minutes or, cook them completely on the grill. To prepare lobster tails, cut along the underside of the tail with scissors; clip off fins along edges. Peel back soft undershell; discard. To prevent curling, bend tail back to crack shell or insert skewers between meat and shell.

Buying Guide — Allow 1 lb. per person for live or cooked in the shell whole lobster; ½ lb. for lobster tails.

How to Barbecue — Place on grill 6 to 8 inches from hot coals. Cooked lobster need only reheat about 5 minutes. *Do not overcook.* For uncooked lobster, begin with meat-side down; cook for 5 minutes; turn and continue cooking with shell-side down for about 10 minutes until meat is opaque. Brush with melted butter or lemon butter — 1 teaspoon lemon juice for ¼ cup butter, while cooking.

How to Serve — Add herbs and spices to butter; see page 21. Sprinkle with paprika or Parmesan cheese before serving; serve with Drawn Butter Sauce, page 84. Alternate chunks of lobster meat with sirloin beef cubes for kabobs.

SHRIMP — Either thawed frozen or fresh shrimp can be used. Fresh shrimp can be cooked in the shell or shelled before cooking. To devein shrimp in the shell, insert a small sharp skewer or pick beneath the vein in the middle of the back; carefully pull out vein. Repeat as necessary. Split along underside before cooking to make shelling easier; if desired, clip off fins. Shelled shrimp can be deveined in the same manner. Or, cut through the shell down the center of the back, then pull out vein. If desired, leave tail intact when shelling for easy handling when eating.

Buying Guide — 1¼ lbs. shrimp in the shell will yield 1 lb. shelled shrimp. Allow about ¼ lb. shelled shrimp per serving.

How to Barbecue — Place on grill 4 to 6 inches from hot coals. Cook about 15 to 20 minutes, turning and brushing occasionally with melted butter until shell is reddish and meat is opaque.

How to Serve — Add herbs and spices to butter; serve with Seafood Cocktail Sauce, Creamy Herb Dipper or Tartar Sauce, page 84. Alternate shrimp with sirloin beef cubes to make kabobs.

OYSTERS — Live in the shell oysters can be placed directly on the grill for cooking. Wash first to remove any mud or sand, then rinse.

Buying Guide — Oysters in the shell are usually sold by the dozen. When alive, they have tightly closed shells. Any with an opened shell are dead and therefore no longer usable. Allow about 6 oysters per serving. When using with other appetizers, fewer oysters will be needed.

How to Barbecue — Place whole oysters on the grill 4 to 6 inches from hot coals. Cook for 10 to 15 minutes. When shells pop open, oysters are done. Drain any juice. Shells will be hot; use hod pads when removing top shell.

How to Serve — Brush with melted butter; season with salt and pepper. Serve hot with Seafood Cocktail Sauce, page 84. Grilled oysters can be used as the base for such oyster specialties as Oysters Rockefeller.

CLAMS — See OYSTERS. However, when using clams that are to be eaten from the shell, first cover with clean salt water — ⅓ cup salt to 1 gallon tap water — and allow to stand 15 to 20 minutes; change the water two or three times. Clams will open and cleanse themselves of sand.

SCALLOPS — Fresh or frozen shelled scallops can be barbecued. Thaw frozen scallops; remove any shell particles and wash before using. Scallops are always shelled before being sold.

Buying Guide — Allow about ⅓ lb. per serving.

How to Barbecue — See SHRIMP.

How to Serve — Brush with seasoned butter or barbecue sauce while cooking. Here are two easy kabob ideas: alternate with squares of bacon, whole mushrooms and green pepper squares; brush with thyme flavored butter; or, alternate scallops with pineapple chunks, brush with sweet 'n sour sauce.

SHRIMP IN GARLIC BUTTER

4 to 6 servings

- ½ cup butter or margarine
- 3 cloves garlic, minced
- 1 tablespoon parsley flakes
- 2 tablespoons lemon juice
- ¼ teaspoon salt or seasoned salt
- 1½ to 2 lbs. cleaned and shelled fresh shrimp*

BEFORE GRILLING: Melt butter in small fry pan. Add garlic, parsley, lemon juice and salt; reserve for basting sauce. Thread shrimp on 4 to 6 skewers.

ON THE GRILL: Place shrimp on greased grill, 4 to 6 inches from hot coals. Cook 15 to 20 minutes, turning and brushing occasionally with garlic butter until done.

> **Tips:** *2 packages (12-oz. each) frozen large shrimp, thawed, can be used for fresh.
>
> Shrimp can be broiled, as directed, in oven.

ITALIAN STYLE FISH STEAK

4 to 6 servings

- 2 lbs. fresh or frozen fish steaks, 1-inch thick*
- 2 cups Italian dressing
- 2 tablespoons lemon juice
- 2 teaspoons salt
- ¼ teaspoon pepper
- Paprika

BEFORE GRILLING: Thaw frozen fish. Cut into serving-size portions and place in a single layer in a shallow non-metallic container or plastic bag. Combine remaining ingredients except paprika to make marinade. Pour marinade over fish; marinate for 30 minutes, turning once. Remove fish, reserving marinade for basting sauce.

ON THE GRILL: Place fish on greased grill 3 to 4 inches from hot coals. Sprinkle with paprika. Cook 5 to 8 minutes. Brush with sauce and sprinkle with paprika. Turn and cook 5 to 8 minutes longer or until fish flakes.

> **Tips:** Fish can be broiled, as directed, in oven.
>
> For more highly seasoned fish, marinate several hours or overnight in refrigerator.
>
> *Haddock, cod, sole or halibut can be used.

Whole trout look and taste great when barbecued. Try larger trout with stuffing, see page 82. If you barbecue fish often, a wire fish basket found with gourmet cooking equipment in dept. stores would be a good investment.

TROUT ON THE GRILL

4 servings

- 4 dressed brook trout, about ½ lb. each
- ⅓ cup melted butter or margarine
- Salt or seasoned salt
- Pepper or seasoned pepper

BEFORE GRILLING: Brush trout inside and out with butter. Season with salt and pepper.

ON THE GRILL: Place trout on greased grill 3 to 4 inches from hot coals. Cook 15 to 20 minutes until fish flakes, turning once and brushing occasionally with butter.

> **Tip:** Fish can be broiled, as directed, in oven.

Choose this tasty fish for a calorie counter's barbecue. Add a mixed green salad and foil cooked vegetables.

BAYOU FISH

4 servings

- 2 to 4 fish steaks or fillets (about 1 to 1½ lbs.)*
- 2 tablespoons butter or margarine
- ¼ cup chopped green pepper
- ¼ cup (1 small) chopped or sliced onion
- 1 teaspoon celery seed, if desired
- 1 can (8 oz.) tomato sauce
- 1 teaspoon salt
- ¼ teaspoon pepper

BEFORE GRILLING: Divide fish into 4 portions or leave whole. Place fish on squares of heavy duty foil. In fry pan, melt butter; cook green pepper, onion and celery seed until tender. Add tomato sauce, salt and pepper; mix well. Pour sauce over fish in foil. Seal securely.

ON THE GRILL: Place packets on grill 4 to 6 inches from hot coals. Cook for 20 to 25 minutes, turning once. Serve with sauce spooned over fish.

> **Tips:** *Halibut, haddock, cod, sole or flounder can be used.
>
> Fish can be prepared, as directed, in 350° oven.

Whole fish for grilling include trout, salmon, red snapper, cod, bass and haddock. Your particular area of the country will determine the species of whole fish available to you. The size fish you choose will depend upon your grill and the number of people to be served. Generally, allow about ½ lb. of whole fish per serving.

BARBECUED WHOLE FISH

Dressed whole fish
Mushroom Stuffing or Savory Bacon
  Stuffing, next column
Melted butter or margarine

BEFORE GRILLING: Fill the cavity of the fish with stuffing. Fasten edges together with metal skewers or sew opening closed with heavy thread.

ON THE GRILL: Brush both sides of fish with melted butter. Place on grill on a piece of heavy duty foil 6 to 8 inches from hot coals; cover. Allow 15 to 20 minutes per lb. of fish, turning several times during cooking. Brush occasionally with melted butter.

> **Tips:** For oven roasting, roast, uncovered, in 350° oven for 45 to 60 minutes until fish flakes.
>
> If grill does not have cover, wrap fish in foil before grilling.

BREAD STUFFING

2 cups Stuffing

¼ cup butter or margarine
2 tablespoons chopped onion
¼ cup chopped celery
2 cups (2 slices) soft bread cubes
¼ teaspoon salt
¼ teaspoon powdered thyme
⅛ teaspoon pepper

In fry pan, cook onion and celery in butter until tender. Stir in remaining ingredients.

> **Tips:** For LEMON STUFFING, add 2 teaspoons grated lemon peel and 2 tablespoons lemon juice with bread.
>
> For DILL STUFFING, add ¼ chopped dill pickle with bread.
>
> For MUSHROOM STUFFING, cook ½ cup sliced mushrooms with onion and celery.
>
> For SHRIMP or CRAB STUFFING, add ½ cup cooked shrimp or crab meat with bread.

MUSHROOM STUFFING

2 cups stuffing

2 tablespoons butter or margarine
¼ cup chopped celery
2 to 4 tablespoons chopped onion
1 can (4 oz.) mushroom stems and pieces, drained
2 cups soft bread cubes
1 tablespoon parsley flakes
½ teaspoon salt
Dash pepper

In large fry pan, melt butter; cook onion and celery until tender. Add remaining ingredients; toss lightly.

SAVORY BACON STUFFING

2 cups stuffing

4 strips bacon
¼ cup chopped onion
1 tablespoon chopped green pepper
2 cups fresh bread cubes
¼ teaspoon powdered thyme
½ teaspoon salt
⅛ teaspoon pepper

In large fry pan, cook bacon until crisp. Remove; drain on paper towel. Cook onion and green pepper in bacon drippings until tender. Remove from heat. Add remaining ingredients; crumble bacon. Toss lightly.

Rich, distinctive flavor of salmon is a natural with dill. Salmon is readily available all year in the frozen variety. It's the colorful member of the fish family.

DILL MARINATED SALMON STEAKS

4 servings

    4 fresh or frozen salmon steaks,
      cut 1-inch thick
    2 tablespoons lemon juice
    1 tablespoon cooking oil
    ¾ teaspoon dill weed
    Salt or seasoned salt
    Pepper or seasoned pepper

BEFORE GRILLING: Thaw frozen steaks. Combine remaining ingredients to make marinade. Pour marinade over salmon in shallow non-metallic container or plastic bag, turning to coat both sides. Cover; marinate 1 hour at room temperature or several hours in refrigerator. Remove salmon; reserve marinade for basting sauce.

ON THE GRILL: Place salmon on greased grill 4 to 6 inches from hot coals. Cook 10 to 15 minutes, turning once and brushing occasionally with marinade, until fish flakes. Serve with Creamy Herb Dipper, page 84, if desired.

> **Tip:** Salmon can be broiled, as directed, in oven.

SAUCY FOILED FILLETS

4 servings

    1½ to 2 lbs. fish fillets or steaks
       Salt and pepper
     1 small green pepper, cut into squares
     1 small onion, sliced
     4 tablespoons barbecue sauce, catsup or
       tomato sauce
     2 tablespoons butter or margarine
       Parmesan cheese

BEFORE GRILLING: Divide fish into 4 equal portions. Place each portion on a square of heavy duty foil. Season with salt and pepper. Top each with green pepper, onion and a tablespoon of barbecue sauce. Dot each with butter; sprinkle with Parmesan cheese. Seal each packet securely.
ON THE GRILL: Place 4 inches from hot coals. Cook 15 to 20 minutes or until fish flakes, turning packet once.

> **Tip:** Any lean fish can be used — red snapper, halibut, bass, walleye, pike or sole.

LEMON BARBECUED SWORDFISH STEAKS

8 servings

    ¾ cup lemon juice
    ¾ cup salad oil
    2 tablespoons prepared horseradish
    1 tablespoon grated lemon peel
    1½ teaspoons salt
    ½ teaspoon crushed basil
    ½ teaspoon oregano
    ¼ to ½ teaspoon pepper
    3 lbs. swordfish steaks, sliced 1-inch thick

BEFORE GRILLING: Combine all ingredients except fish for marinade; mix well. Pour marinade over fish in shallow non-metallic container or plastic bag; turn to coat both sides. Chill, covered, several hours or overnight. Remove fish, reserving marinade for basting sauce.

ON THE GRILL: Place fish on greased grill 3 to 4 inches from hot coals. Cook 10 to 15 minutes, turning once and brushing occasionally with marinade until fish flakes.

> **Tip:** Fish can be broiled, as directed, in oven.

CREAMY HERB DIPPER

1 cup sauce

- ½ cup mayonnaise or salad dressing
- ¼ cup dairy or imitation sour cream
- 2 tablespoons chopped parsley
- 1 tablespoon lemon juice
- 1 clove garlic, crushed or ⅛ teaspoon garlic powder
- ½ teaspoon salt
- ¼ teaspoon leaf tarragon, crushed, if desired
- Dash pepper

Combine all ingredients; mix well. Chill before using.

> **Tip:** Sauce is good with most grilled fish and seafood, except clams, oysters and lobster.

SAVORY FISH IN FOIL

4 servings

- 2 lbs. fish fillets*
- 1 package sour cream sauce mix
- ¼ cup (1 small bunch) sliced green onions
- 2 teaspoons chopped parsley or parsley flakes, if desired
- Salt or seasoned salt
- Pepper or seasoned pepper

BEFORE GRILLING: Divide fish into serving portions or leave whole. Place fish on square of heavy duty foil. Sprinkle evenly with remaining ingredients. Seal securely.

ON THE GRILL: Place on grill 4 to 6 inches from hot coals. Cook 20 to 25 minutes, until fish flakes.

> **Tips:** *Halibut, haddock, walleye, cod, red snapper, sole or flounder fillets can be used.
>
> 1 package cheese sauce mix can be used for sour cream sauce mix.
>
> Fish can be prepared, as directed, in a 350° oven.

SEAFOOD COCKTAIL SAUCE

1½ cups sauce

- 1 cup chili sauce
- ¼ cup lemon juice
- 2 to 3 teaspoons horseradish, if desired
- 1 teaspoon celery seed
- 1 teaspoon Worcestershire sauce

Combine all ingredients; mix well. Chill before using.

FISH FILLETS AU GRATIN

6 to 8 servings

- ½ cup dry bread crumbs
- ½ cup shredded Cheddar cheese
- 1 teaspoon paprika
- ½ teaspoon onion salt
- ¼ teaspoon salt
- ¼ teaspoon pepper
- 2 lbs. fish fillets*

BEFORE GRILLING: Combine all ingredients except fish. Place fish on squares of heavy duty foil. Spoon crumb mixture over fish. Seal securely.

ON THE GRILL: Place packets on grill 3 to 4 inches from hot coals. Cook 20 to 25 minutes until fish flakes.

> **Tips:** *Walleye, trout, halibut, haddock, cod, red snapper, sole or flounder can be used.
>
> Fish can be prepared, as directed, in 350° oven.

TARTAR SAUCE

1⅓ cups sauce

- 1 cup mayonnaise
- ¼ cup finely chopped dill pickle
- 1 tablespoon parsley flakes
- 1 tablespoon lemon juice
- 1 tablespoon chopped pimiento, if desired
- ½ teaspoon grated onion, if desired
- ¼ teaspoon Worcestershire sauce

Combine all ingredients in small bowl; mix well. Chill before serving. Store, covered, in refrigerator after using.

> **Tip:** If desired, use ¼ cup chopped sweet pickle or pickle relish for dill pickle.

DRAWN BUTTER SAUCE

- ¼ cup butter or margarine
- 2 tablespoons flour
- ½ teaspoon salt
- ⅛ teaspoon paprika
- Dash cayenne pepper
- 1 cup water

In small saucepan, melt butter. Stir in flour, salt, paprika and cayenne pepper. Add water and cook, stirring constantly, until thickened. Serve along with lobster.

> **Tip:** If desired, 1 tablespoon lemon juice and 1 tablespoon chopped parsley can be added.

GRILLING GUIDE FOR FISH

One important clue when choosing fish for barbecuing is the fat content of different species. Fatter fish tend to be best for outdoor grilling. Not only are they easier to handle, but the smoke enhances their stronger flavor. Leaner fish need special treatment. This might include cooking in a hinged wire broiler or wrapping them in foil. Watch carefully because lean fish tend to fall apart if overcooked. The following chart includes a variety of fish that can be cooked on the grill. If you can buy fresh fish, it also serves as a guide to what may be available in local markets.

ATLANTIC COAST
Fat: Shad;
Lean: Flounder, Swordfish

GREAT LAKES, NORTHERN INLAND RIVERS
Fat: Lake Trout, Salmon, Whitefish;
Lean: Catfish

NEW ENGLAND
Fat: Mackerel;
Lean: Cod, Haddock, Halibut, Sole, Swordfish

NORTHWEST
Fat: Lake Trout, Salmon;
Lean: Flounder, Halibut, Rainbow Trout

PACIFIC COAST
Fat: Shad;
Lean: Flounder, Halibut, Sole, Swordfish

SOUTHERN ATLANTIC, GULF
Fat: Mackerel;
Lean: Flounder, Red Snapper

FISH BUYING GUIDE

Whole or serving-size pieces of fish can be barbecued. The following chart will help you in buying fresh fish. Thick steaks, fillets and smaller whole fish (8 to 10 inches long) are best for placing directly on the grill. A hinged wire broiler will aid in turning smaller pieces and a large fish rack will help when turning large whole fish.

Market Form	Description	Amount to buy per serving
Whole or Round	As it comes from the water. Must be scaled, cleaned; head, tail, fins must be removed.	1 pound
Drawn	Cleaned only. Scales, head, tail and fins must be removed.	1 pound
Dressed	Scaled, cleaned, usually with heads, tail and fins removed. Ready for cooking.	½ pound
Steaks	Cross-section slices of large dressed fish, with a section of backbone.	⅓ pound or 1 steak
Fillets	Sides of fish, cut lengthwise from the backbone, boneless.	⅓ pound

Meal Accompaniments

While meat takes the number one spot in a barbecue, it can't stand alone. No good barbecue meal is ever a solo performance. This chapter contains the foods that go along with whichever meat you choose.

Salads — refreshing fruit combinations, tossed salads galore, jiffy vegetable salads.

Vegetables — guide to cooking corn, squash and other summer vegetables right on the grill, inventive frozen vegetables cooked in foil.

Breads, Potatoes, Rice and Beans — breads to bake or heat with seasoned spreads, potato and rice favorites, new ideas for baked beans.

Snacks and Beverages — party starters, thirst quenching drinks.

Desserts — homemade ice cream, desserts for picnic toting or flaming desserts that heat over the last coals of the barbecue.

Casual summer meals still need to follow guidelines for good nutrition, appetite and taste appeal. Even when the menu is simple, delicious ideas in eating can be combined using the season's bounty of ingredients.

Variety in your barbecue meals is possible when you think of different ways to fix your family's favorite foods. Even corn-on-the-cob or French bread can take on exciting new flavor sensations. Just remember to keep a balance between the flavors of all foods in the menu — tart or sweet, mild or highly seasoned, light or heavy.

Whether the meal is eaten indoors or out, climate and season of the year affect both food and people. Tips on the recipes in this chapter will help you decide which foods are best for your particular barbecue occasion. The activity, age and food habits of your family and friends are considerations too.

Salads

Crispy tossed salad and creamy coleslaw are perfect complements of the hearty barbecue meal. The following pages offer you many ideas for tossed salad combinations plus variations to many interesting vegetable salads. On the hearty side are potato, macaroni and rice salads.

Fruits — fresh, canned or frozen — provide pretty-as-a-picture salads. Whether simple combinations or creative molded gelatin salads, these complement spicy barbecue flavors, too. Many fruit salads can double as dessert. Serve them any time, anywhere!

MINTY MELON BOWL

6 servings

> 1 cup watermelon balls
> 1 cup cantaloupe balls
> 1 cup green grapes
> 1 cup (8¾ oz. can) pineapple tidbits, drained
> 1 cup (8½ oz. can) pear halves, drained and cubed
> 1¼ cups (10 oz. jar) apple-mint jelly

In salad bowl, combine all ingredients except jelly. Melt jelly or stir with fork; pour over fruit. Toss lightly. Chill before serving. If desired, garnish with fresh mint leaves.

OVERNIGHT FRUIT SALAD

8 to 10 servings

> 2 cups (about 1 lb.) Tokay grapes, seeded
> 2 cans (8¾ oz. each) pineapple tidbits, drain and reserve ½ cup syrup
> 1 can (1 lb.) pear halves, drained and cubed
> ½ cup sliced maraschino cherries
> 3 tablespoons lemon juice
> 1 egg, slightly beaten
> 1½ tablespoons sugar
> Reserved ½ cup pineapple syrup
> 3 to 4 cups miniature marshmallows
> 2 cups whipped topping or whipped cream*

In large mixing bowl, combine all fruits; sprinkle with lemon juice. In small saucepan, combine egg and sugar; stir until smooth. Gradually add reserved ½ cup pineapple syrup; stir until smooth. Cook over medium heat, stirring constantly, until thickened and clear. Remove from heat; cool slightly. Pour over fruit; toss lightly. Fold in whipped topping. Cover and chill overnight. If desired, garnish with orange peel.

> **Tips:** *Use 1 cup whipping cream, whipped and sweetened, 1 pt. frozen whipped topping, thawed, or 1 package whipped topping mix, prepared as directed on package.

> Green seedless grapes may be used for the Tokay grapes and a 1-lb. can peach slices, drained and cubed, for the pear halves.

VEGETABLE PATCH SALAD

Canned or leftover cooked vegetables make good salad additions. Try this combination for a start. Drain a 1-lb. can cut green beans; toss with sliced carrots, celery and onion rings. Lettuce for this salad bowl can be cut into 1-inch chunks for a change. Serve with a creamy Russian dressing.

SALAD REFRESHER

Spinach and lettuce torn into bite-size pieces, then tossed with canned drained julienne beets and cauliflowerettes makes a good and different salad combination. A creamy dressing like Russian is good with these ingredients.

CHINESE VEGETABLE SALAD

Here's the salad for those teriyaki marinated meats. It will give meals an added Oriental flair. Choose greens with Far Eastern flavor like endive and Chinese cabbage to combine with leaf or iceberg lettuce. Sliced green onions, cherry tomatoes, celery and carrots can be added. To be really authentic, do all your slicing on the diagonal! Peanuts, water chestnuts or sliced mushrooms add crunch. Now, add either 1 package (6 oz.) frozen thawed snow peas (cooking isn't necessary) or 1 can (16 oz.) drained mixed Chinese vegetables. For dressing, try prepared oil and vinegar mixed with some soy sauce. Or, for a sweeter dressing, use prepared sweet and sour sauce or dressing.

GREEK COUNTRY SALAD

Greek tradition combines salad ingredients with an olive oil-vinegar dressing. Whether you make your own dressing or use a prepared dressing you'll want to toss it with these salad ingredients. Crisp leaf and Romaine lettuce, lots of tomatoes, cucumbers or zucchini, whole olives and Feta cheese are usually used. Feta cheese is salty, soft white cheese made from goat's milk that's found in many Greek dishes. If it isn't available, Roquefort can be used.

TANGY CAULIFLOWER MAKE-AHEAD

Make this salad a day or hours ahead, so the French or Italian dressing blends with the other ingredients. Marinate 1 small head fresh cauliflower, separated into small pieces, ½ cup sliced stuffed or ripe olives and ½ cup crumbled roquefort of blue cheese in ½ cup French or Italian dressing. Just before serving, toss with salad greens. One small head is enough, but a combination of different varieties for contrast is good, too. Add more salad dressing as needed.

WESTERN ORANGE SALAD BOWL

Toss another fruit and salad green combination with peeled and chopped oranges — or cut them into slices to make bright cartwheels. Add chopped green onions and a fruit dressing like our Honey Celery Seed Dressing, page 93. Good proportions for 2 quarts of greens would be two to three oranges and ½ cup chopped onions. Other dressings to try would be Russian and Roquefort.

EASY CAESAR SALAD

A favorite with steaks, make this Caesar salad easily with prepared Caesar dressing. Romaine's the lettuce most often used. Two to 3 heads torn into bite-size pieces will be enough, or a combination of spinach and leaf lettuce is good. Toss with 2 cups dry seasoned bread cubes* and dressing, then sprinkle on a generous amount of Parmesan cheese. No wonder this salad is so popular!

Tip: *Or, prepare soft bread cubes: use 2 cups soft bread cubes; marinate ⅛ teaspoon instant minced garlic or 1 clove garlic, halved, in ½ cup cooking oil for about 30 minutes. In 2 tablespoons of the oil, brown bread cubes.

MARINATED ARTICHOKE SALAD

Artichokes make any tossed salad super! This one combines marinade and dressing all in one. Cook 1 package (9 oz.) frozen artichoke hearts and 3 to 4 slices onion as directed on package, using 1 cup prepared Italian dressing and 2 tablespoons water for liquid. Chill. Just before serving, toss artichoke mixture lightly with salad greens, 1 or 2 tomatoes, cut into wedges, and a sprinkle of salt and coarsely ground pepper or lemon pepper marinade. A variety of greens is good for this salad. We like to combine romaine, iceberg and fresh spinach.

> **Tip:** Marinated artichokes can be stored, covered, in refrigerator. Use as needed for smaller salad bowls.

ROQUEFORT TOSSED FRUIT SALAD

Romaine and Boston or Bibb lettuce are good choices to combine with fruit. Outer leaves can line the bowl, while inner leaves can be torn and tossed with fresh fruits. Bananas, plums and peaches can be sprinkled with lemon juice to prevent darkening before tossing with lettuce. Strawberries and other berries along with clusters of grapes look pretty as garnishes as well as being good to eat. To serve, toss prepared fruit and greens with Roquefort or Blue Cheese dressing until well coated. Turn into lettuce-lined bowl; garnish, if desired.

GRAPEFRUIT SPINACH TOSS

Lots of good eating in this citrus salad combination. Start with 4 cups lettuce and add 2 to 3 cups fresh spinach. Dark green spinach is a color, flavor and nutrition booster for salads. Two peeled and sectioned grapefruit add citrus tanginess (save 2 to 3 tablespoons grapefruit juice to add with salad dressing). Salted cashews add crunch to this salad. Other nuts, water chestnuts or sliced fresh mushrooms can be used. Toss with Green Goddess, French or a fruit salad dressing and the reserved grapefruit juice.

SALAD TOSS-UPS

Any combination of vegetables and greens can be tossed in a salad. The recipes on these two pages are only a few of the possibilities. So, use your imagination along with ingredients that you have on hand and create your own salad!

Crisp, chilled greens are the first commandment in the art of salad making. They add variety in color and flavor, as well as texture.

The following descriptions serve as a guide to choosing one kind or a combination of greens to accompany your meal:

Iceberg or head: rather watery taste and very crisp leaves.

Curly Endive or Chicory: bitter flavor with wiry, feathered leaves.

Bibb: rather sweet flavor, velvety texture and very small, pliable dark leaves.

Boston or Butter: resembles Bibb lettuce in flavor and texture; usually larger.

Romaine: rather strong flavor; fibrous, deep green, straight leaves.

Escarole: bitter flavor, rough texture and broad curling leaves.

Leaf (red or green): delicate in flavor with crisp, flat, ruffly leaves.

Watercress: slightly bitter flavor with extremely fragile leaves. Makes a nice garnish.

Crispness and color can also be added to vegetable salads with celery, green onions, fresh spinach, parsley, fresh chives, mustard greens or celery and beet tops.

To store wash greens carefully in cold water, discarding wilted outer leaves. Dry thoroughly (placing on paper towels will help), and store in refrigerator until serving time.

To prepare in advance, salad greens can be torn into bite-size pieces and placed on a tray or in a plastic bag with a wet towel for a few hours before serving.

Toss the salad with your choice of dressing just before serving to keep the greens fresh and crisp.

Cheese in this salad makes it just a little different. With or without melon slices, try it for dessert, too.

PINEAPPLE MELON TOPPER

4 to 6 servings

 1 can (8½ oz.) crushed pineapple, drained
 1 jar (6 oz.) pimiento cheese spread
 1 cup whipped topping or whipped cream*
 ¼ cup mayonnaise or salad dressing
 3 cups miniature marshmallows
 1 small cantaloupe, honeydew, crenshaw or casaba melon, peeled and cut into slices or wedges

In medium mixing bowl, combine all ingredients; mix well. Refrigerate at least 2 hours. If desired, garnish with maraschino cherries. Spoon pineapple mixture onto melon slices to make individual salads.

> **Tip:** *Use 1 cup whipping cream, whipped and sweetened, 1 pint frozen whipped topping, thawed, or 1 package whipped topping mix, prepared as directed.

MOLDED POTATO SALAD

8 servings

 1 envelope unflavored gelatin
 ¼ cup cold water
 ¾ cup sweet pickle juice
 1 cup mayonnaise or salad dressing
 4 cups (4 med.) cubed cooked potatoes
 1 cup (2 stalks) chopped celery
 ½ cup (1 small) chopped onion
 ½ cup chopped sweet pickles
 ½ teaspoon salt
 Sliced pitted ripe olives, if desired
 Sliced stuffed green olives, if desired

In small saucepan, soften gelatin in cold water; add pickle juice. Heat over low heat, stirring until dissolved. In large bowl, add gelatin to mayonnaise; mix well. Combine with remaining ingredients except olives; mix lightly. Spoon into oiled 1½-quart mold or 8 individual molds. Chill until firm, about 2 hours. Unmold on lettuce. Garnish with olives, if desired.

GERMAN POTATO SALAD

6 to 8 servings

 6 cups cubed cooked potatoes*
 5 slices bacon
 ½ cup (1 small) chopped onion
 ¼ cup sugar
 2 tablespoons flour
 1 teaspoon salt
 Dash pepper
 1⅓ cups hot water
 ⅔ cup white vinegar

In medium skillet, fry bacon until crisp. Drain on paper toweling, reserving 3 tablespoons drippings. In reserved 3 tablespoons bacon drippings, sauté onion until tender. Add sugar, flour, salt and pepper; stir until smooth. Gradually add water and vinegar. Cook over medium heat, stirring constantly, until mixture boils and thickens. In large mixing bowl, combine potatoes and crumbled bacon. Pour hot vinegar mixture over potatoes; toss lightly. Serve hot. If desired, garnish with chopped chives.

> **Tips:** *6 medium potatoes, cooked and cubed, will give the 6 cups needed for this recipe.

Plain potatoes never had this much color. Make this the night before, so potatoes have a chance to absorb lots of red color. Picture on page 8.

RED PICKLED POTATO SALAD

4 servings

 2 cups (1-lb. can) sliced cooked potatoes
 1 cup sliced pickled beets, drain and reserve ½ cup liquid
 ¼ cup Italian salad dressing
 ½ teaspoon salt

In bowl, combine all ingredients and reserved liquid. Cover; refrigerate at least 4 hours or overnight.

CELERY SEED COLESLAW

4 servings

1 small head cabbage, shredded

Honey-Celery Seed Dressing
$\frac{1}{3}$ cup sugar
$\frac{1}{2}$ teaspoon dry mustard
$\frac{1}{2}$ teaspoon celery seed
$\frac{1}{2}$ teaspoon paprika, if desired
$\frac{1}{8}$ teaspoon salt
$2\frac{1}{2}$ tablespoons vinegar
$2\frac{1}{2}$ tablespoons honey
2 tablespoons cold water
$\frac{1}{2}$ cup cooking oil

In large bowl, combine cabbage and Dressing; gently toss. Serve immediately.

Honey-Celery Seed Dressing: In small mixing bowl, combine all ingredients except oil. Gradually add oil, beating constantly with rotary beater, until thoroughly combined. Store, covered, in refrigerator. Mix well before using.

Tip: To make in blender, combine all ingredients except oil; process on low speed until smooth. Gradually add oil through small opening in lid, continuing to process on medium speed until thick and thoroughly combined.

PICNIC MACARONI BEAN SALAD

6 to 8 servings

1 cup macaroni
2 cups (1-lb. can) red kidney beans, drained
3 chopped hard cooked eggs
1 medium red onion, cut into rings
1 chopped green pepper
1 cup (8 oz.) prepared creamy salad dressing*

Cook macaroni as directed on package; drain. In large bowl, gently toss with remaining ingredients. Chill at least 2 hours before serving.

Tip: *We like Creamy Onion, Creamy Russian, Green Goddess and Thousand Island dressings.

COTTAGE STUFFED TOMATOES

5 to 6 salads

5 to 6 medium tomatoes
2 cups (1 pt. or 16 oz.) cottage cheese
2 tablespoons chopped green pepper
2 tablespoons (1 to 2 small) chopped green onions
$\frac{1}{4}$ to $\frac{1}{2}$ teaspoon Worcestershire sauce
Salt
Pepper

Cut small slice from top of each tomato. Carefully remove pulp, using a paring knife or a spoon. (Reserve $\frac{1}{4}$ cup pulp; use any remaining for tomatoes in soups, casseroles or meat sauces.) Cut up reserved tomato pulp; combine with remaining ingredients. Season to taste. Spoon cottage cheese mixture into tomato shells. To serve, arrange on lettuce leaves; if desired, garnish with additional chopped green pepper and onion.

CARDINAL COLESLAW

4 servings

4 cups (2 heads) shredded cabbage
1 cup (1 med.) cubed unpeeled apple
$\frac{1}{2}$ cup raisins
$\frac{1}{4}$ cup peanuts
Salad dressing or mayonnaise

Combine cabbage, apple, raisins, nuts and enough salad dressing to moisten; toss lightly.

SUMMERTIME BEAN SALAD

6 servings

> 1½ cups (1-lb. can) drained kidney beans
> 1 medium cucumber, chopped
> 1 cup (2 stalks) sliced celery
> 1 cup sliced radishes
> 1 teaspoon salt
> ½ cup prepared Thousand Island dressing

In medium bowl, combine all ingredients; mix well. Chill 2 to 3 hours before serving.

> **Tip:** Creamy French or Russian dressings can be used for Thousand Island.

SALAD ON A STICK

Take along this lunch-time treat as a change from carrot and celery sticks! Cut chunks of iceberg lettuce to thread on a bamboo skewer with cherry tomatoes, cucumber wedges, radishes, fresh mushrooms and cheese cubes. Let your imagination — and refrigerator's contents — be your guide. Add a small container of your favorite dressing as a salad dipper.

RICE 'N FRUIT TOSS

5 to 6 servings

> 2½ cups (29 oz. can) peach slices, drain and reserve syrup*
> 2 to 2½ cups cooked rice, cooled
> 1 cup sliced celery
> ½ to ¾ cup Honey-Celery Seed Dressing, page 93

In large bowl, combine all ingredients; toss. Cover and chill at least 2 hours before serving. Serve in lettuce lined salad bowl.

> **Tips:** *If desired, use part or all of syrup as cooking liquid for rice.
> Fresh or drained canned fruits such as peaches, pears, apricots or fresh tropical fruits such as papaya or mangoes can be used. Coat fruits that darken with lemon juice or ascorbic acid mixture before combining with other ingredients.
> Try this salad served hot as an accompaniment to chicken or lamb.
> Prepared fruit salad dressing can be used for Honey-Celery Seed Dressing.

So easy — guests will wonder how you made these colorful wedges of melon and gelatin. See picture, page 88.

SOUTHERN PLANTATION CANTALOUPE

8 servings

> 1 package (3 oz.) strawberry or orange flavored gelatin
> 2 cups (16 oz. can) pineapple juice
> 2 cantaloupes
> Salad dressing

Dissolve strawberry gelatin in 1 cup boiling pineapple juice. Add remaining juice; chill until slightly thickened. Cut cantaloupes in half; remove seeds. Remove fruit, leaving ½-inch shell; chop fruit. Fold in gelatin mixture. Pour into cantaloupe shells; chill until firm, at least 4 hours. Cut into wedges; serve with salad dressing.

> **Tips:** Individual bowls work nicely to hold cantaloupe halves steady until gelatin is set.
> If desired, water or other fruit juice can be used for part of pineapple juice.

Beans are delightfully coated with a smooth and tangy dressing. Chill them while you prepare the rest of the meal.

CREAMY LIMA SALAD

4 servings

> 2 cups (1-lb. can) drained lima beans
> 1 onion, sliced
> ⅓ cup dairy or imitation sour cream
> 1 tablespoon wine or cider vinegar
> 1 tablespoon sugar
> ½ teaspoon cream-style horseradish
> 1 teaspoon salt
> Dash pepper
> Dash parsley

In mixing bowl, combine all ingredients except lima beans. Gently stir in limas. Chill in refrigerator 20 minutes or until ready to serve. Serve on lettuce leaves. If desired, garnish with parsley or pimiento strips.

*A distinctive wine-flavored gelatin salad —
certain to please when served with Savory
Smoked Steak, see our menu on page
13. Sauterne or other sweet white wines can be
used to make this salad when serving pork or
chicken.*

CREAMY BURGUNDY CHERRIES

8 servings

> 2 packages (3 oz. each) cherry flavored
>   gelatin
> 1 cup boiling water
> 1 package (8 oz.) regular or low calorie
>   cream cheese, softened
> 1 can (1 lb. 5 oz.) cherry pie filling
> ½ cup Burgundy or red wine

Dissolve gelatin in boiling water. In large bowl,
cream cheese; add gelatin slowly and continue
beating until well blended. Add pie filling and
Burgundy. Pour into oiled 1½-quart mold or
8-inch square pan. Chill until firm, about
2 hours.

> **Tip:** If desired, water can be used for part
> or all of the wine.

CONFETTI CORN QUICKIE

3 to 4 servings

> 1½ cups (16 oz. can) drained whole
>   kernel corn
> 1 tomato, cut-up
> ¼ cup red pepper relish
> 1 teaspoon salt
> ¼ cup prepared oil and vinegar salad
>   dressing

In medium bowl, combine all ingredients. Toss
lightly. Refrigerate until serving time. If desired,
garnish with red or green pepper rings and
serve on lettuce.

> **Tip:** For Confetti Corn Relish, omit tomato.
> If desired, add chopped green pepper or
> onion.

*Accompany fish or pork with this tart frozen
salad. Good for dessert, too, with a spoonful of
whipped cream and citrus peel garnish.*

DAIQUIRI FRUIT SALAD

4 to 5 servings

> 1½ cups (13¼-oz. can) pineapple tidbits,
>   drain and reserve 1 cup syrup
>   (adding water if necessary)
> 1 package (3 oz.) lime flavored gelatin
> ½ cup (3 oz.) frozen daiquiri mix, thawed
> ⅓ cup salad dressing or mayonnaise
> 2 cups whipped topping or whipped
>   cream*
> 2 medium bananas, sliced

Bring reserved syrup to boil. Dissolve gelatin in
hot syrup. Add daiquiri mix and salad dressing,
stir until well blended. Chill until slightly
thickened, but not set; about 45 minutes. Fold
in pineapple and remaining ingredients. Pour
into oiled 1½-quart mold or 8-inch square pan.
Freeze until firm, about 2 hours.

> **Tip:** *Use 1 cup whipping cream,
> whipped and sweetened, 1 pint frozen
> whipped topping, thawed, or 1 package
> whipped topping mix, prepared as
> directed on package.

ACAPULCO PEA SALAD

3 to 4 servings

> 1 package (10 oz.) frozen peas
> ½ cup (1 small) cucumber, diced
> 2 tablespoons (2 med.) chopped green
>   onions
> ½ cup (4 oz.) dairy sour cream or plain
>   yogurt
> ¼ teaspoon salt
> ¼ teaspoon sugar
> ¼ teaspoon chili powder

Cook peas as directed on package; drain well.
In medium bowl, combine all ingredients; mix
well. Chill before serving. If desired, garnish
with cucumber slices.

Top, clockwise — Creamy Peas and Onions, page 98; Corn Cob Curry, page 99; Summer Squash and Zucchini; Grilled Cheesy Crunch Tomatoes, page 99; French Style Green Beans, page 98.

Vegetables

Many vegetables are delicious cooked on an outdoor grill. Some like corn or squash, can cook directly on the grill; others need a foil wrapping. Vegetables tucked around meat while it cooks take advantage of the heat from the coals and keep the cook out of the kitchen.

Herbs and spices added to your vegetables as they cook give a delightful flavor. Since most vegetables need seasoning with butter or margarine, the herbs and spices can be added at the same time whether they're tucked inside a foil packet or brushed on during cooking.

Here are some herbs you might like to try next time you have vegetables at your barbecue. The amounts to use will vary with your own preferences, however a few sprigs of fresh herbs or about ¼ teaspoon dried herbs for 4 servings is good as a starter.

- Chives: cauliflower, zucchini, green beans, carrots, corn.

- Dill: squash, carrots, sweet potatoes.

- Marjoram: carrots, onions, peas, zucchini.

- Oregano: peas, mushrooms, corn, onions, tomatoes, eggplant, green beans.

- Parsley: green beans, carrots, turnips, yellow squash, onions.

- Rosemary: mushrooms, peas, zucchini.

- Tarragon: corn, green beans, lima beans, mushrooms, tomatoes.

- Thyme: beans, carrots, mushrooms, tomatoes, zucchini.

VEGETABLES TO ROAST OVER THE COALS

Although the list is not long, firm meaty vegetables such as squash, mushrooms, eggplant, and corn-on-the-cob can be cooked right on the grill. Many times these vegetables are combined with meats or with each other on skewers for kabobs. Similar cooking times are necessary to assure quality — or the vegetables can be cooked on separate skewers.

Preparation and cooking times for these vegetables are given below:

Summer Squash: Small whole yellow zucchini or patty pan squash can be placed on skewers before grilling or directly on the grill. One to 2-inch slices or quartered patty pan squash can be placed on skewers. These are fun to combine as we did for the picture, opposite page. Allow about 1 small squash per serving. Brush with seasoned butter or prepared French or Italian dressing before grilling. Cook over coals 20 to 30 minutes until tender, brushing occasionally with butter.

Mushrooms: Large mushroom caps can be placed on skewers either alone or combined with meat. Allow about 5 to 6 mushrooms per serving if used as a vegetable, less if combined with meat. To prevent splitting, mushrooms can be cooked in a small amount of boiling water for about 5 minutes before placing them on skewers. Brush with seasoned butters, meat marinades or basting sauces before grilling. Cook over coals for about 10 minutes, brushing occasionally with butter.

Eggplant: A medium eggplant serves 4 to 5 people. No need to peel, just cut into 1-inch slices. See Summer Squash for cooking directions.

Tomatoes: Tomatoes cook more quickly than firmer vegetables. Both cherry tomatoes and larger tomatoes can be used. Allow 1 large tomato or 5 to 6 cherry tomatoes per person. No need to baste; just place small tomatoes on skewers or cut halves on the grill or on a sheet of aluminum foil to prevent skin from breaking. Small tomatoes cook in about 5 minutes; larger ones take about 10 minutes.

Corn-on-the-Cob: Corn will cook to a caramelly goodness when placed directly over the coals. Husk the corn; then place directly over the coals. Cook about 10 minutes, turning frequently until tender. Check doneness by pressing a kernel with your thumbnail. It should be tender, but juicy.

Corn Roasted in the Husk: Pull husks back on ears of corn and remove silks. Replace husks; soak in cold water about 30 minutes. Remove from water; place about 4 inches from hot coals for about 20 minutes, until tender. Turn frequently to roast evenly.

To Heat Canned Vegetables: Remove lid and label from can. Place can on grill along with other foods being cooked. Heat until liquid bubbles and vegetables are hot. If desired, drain. Season with butter, salt, pepper, or see the Herb Guide for other seasoning suggestions.

Vegetables for Picnic Toting: Heat frozen vegetables that come in cooking pouches just before you leave home. Carry to the picnic in an insulated bag to keep them hot. Just open and serve. What could be easier!

Any frozen vegetables, plain or with sauces, or vegetable casseroles need only a foil wrapping for heating on the grill. If the vegetables come in cooking pouches, remove them before wrapping. Place vegetables in sauces away from *hot* coals; allow a little extra cooking time. Frozen corn on the cob takes about an hour. To serve, place the foil package in a wicker basket. Leave the package closed until just before serving so the vegetables stay piping hot.

FOIL COOKING DIRECTIONS

Remove frozen vegetables from freezer package. Place in center of a square of heavy duty foil. Season with two pats butter, salt, pepper or herb seasonings. Bring up sides of foil; fold down onto vegetables in tight double fold; fold ends up in tight double folds. Place package on grill over hot coals; grill 20 to 30 minutes, turning frequently.

FRENCH STYLE GREEN BEANS

3 to 4 servings

  1 package (10 oz.) frozen French style
     green beans
½ teaspoon salt
  1 tablespoon chopped onion or
     ½ teaspoon instant minced onion
  1 tablespoon butter
  2 tablespoons slivered almonds
½ cup (4-oz. can) drained mushroom
     stems and pieces, if desired

ON THE GRILL: Place frozen beans on square of heavy duty foil. Add remaining ingredients. Prepare according to foil cooking directions.

PEANUTTY CARROT STRIPS

4 servings

  6 medium carrots, cut into strips
  2 tablespoons butter or margarine
  2 tablespoons honey
  2 tablespoons chunky peanut butter

ON THE GRILL: Prepare carrots according to foil cooking directions. Open packet during last 5 minutes. Add remaining ingredients; reclose. Toss lightly; serve hot.

> **Tips:** Carrots can be cooked as directed in oven or according to package directions in saucepan.
>
> 1 can (1 lb.) sweet potatoes can be used for carrots. Heat 10 to 15 minutes.

CREAMY PEAS AND ONION

4 servings

1½ cups (10-oz. pkg.) frozen peas
¼ cup (1 med.) sliced green onion
¼ cup dairy or imitation sour cream
¼ teaspoon salt
  Dash pepper

ON THE GRILL: Prepare peas according to foil cooking directions. Drain. Toss with remaining ingredients. Serve hot.

> **Tip:** Peas can be cooked as directed, in oven, or according to package directions in saucepan.

SWEET BUTTERY BEANS

4 to 5 servings

  3 cups (two 10-oz. pkgs.) frozen green
     beans
  2 tablespoons butter or margarine
  2 tablespoons brown sugar
  1 tablespoon lemon juice
½ teaspoon salt

ON THE GRILL: Prepare beans according to foil cooking directions. Drain. Add remaining ingredients; mix well. Serve hot.

> **Tip:** Beans can be cooked as directed in oven, or according to package directions in saucepan.

ARTICHOKE KABOBS

6 servings

>   2 packages (10 oz. each) frozen artichoke
        hearts
     2 cups (½ lb. or 1 pt.) fresh mushrooms
     ¾ cup prepared Italian or Russian
        dressing
     Cherry tomatoes
     Salt
     Pepper

BEFORE GRILLING: Cook artichoke hearts as directed on package; drain well. Combine artichoke hearts, mushrooms and dressing. Cover and let stand about 4 hours at room temperature or overnight in refrigerator. Alternate artichoke hearts and mushrooms on skewers with cherry tomatoes.

ON THE GRILL: Place kabobs over hot coals for about 5 minutes, turning and basting occasionally. Season with salt and pepper. Serve hot with additional dressing.

>   **Tips:** Kabobs can be prepared, as directed, under broiler in oven.
>
>   If desired, other vegetables can be used, such as green pepper pieces and small onions.

GRILLED CHEESY CRUMB TOMATOES

6 servings

>   ½ cup bread crumbs
     2 tablespoons Parmesan cheese
     ½ teaspoon salt
     ⅛ teaspoon pepper
     2 tablespoons butter or margarine
     6 tomatoes, halved

BEFORE GRILLING: In small bowl, combine bread crumbs, cheese, salt and pepper; mix well. Sprinkle several tablespoons crumb mixture over each tomato half. Dot each half with 1 teaspoon butter (or drizzle with melted butter).

ON THE GRILL: Place cut-side up on sheet of aluminum foil on greased grill over hot coals. Cook for about 10 minutes or until heated through. Serve hot.

ONION CORN ON THE COB

8 servings

>   1 envelope (1⅜ oz.) dry onion soup mix
     ½ cup butter or margarine, softened
     ½ teaspoon salt
     8 ears corn

BEFORE GRILLING: Combine onion soup mix, butter and salt. Spread each ear of corn with 1 tablespoon butter mixture. Wrap each tightly in foil.

ON THE GRILL: Place wrapped ears of corn on grill over hot coals. Cook for 30 to 35 minutes until tender. Serve with additional butter.

>   **Tip:** Wrapped ears of corn can be baked in 425° oven, as directed.

Try this tasty sauce as a topper for corn on the cob. Few ingredients make it speedy.

CORN COB CURRY

6 to 8 servings

>   6 to 8 ears of corn

Curry Sauce:

>   1 cup dairy or imitation sour cream
     1 teaspoon curry powder
     ¼ teaspoon salt
     Dash Tabasco sauce

Prepare corn according to one of the given methods. Top with Curry Sauce to serve.

Curry Sauce: Combine all ingredients; mix well.

CORN COOKING TIPS

For grill cooking directions, see page 97 or opposite page. To cook in boiling water, place corn on cob in large saucepan with water. Cover tightly, bring to a boil and cook 3 to 5 minutes, depending on the maturity of the corn. Serve steaming with plenty of butter!

Having melted butter available so that guests can simply dip ears of corn in it is thoughtful, especially for buffet dinners. A tall paper hot-drink cup works perfectly as a container for the butter!

Top, clockwise — Charcoal Grilled Biscuits, page 105; Pork and Beans Luau, page 107; Cheesy Garlic Hot Roll Braid, page 102; Spud 'n Onions, page 106; Toasted Cheese Slices, opposite page.

Breads, Potatoes and Beans

Barbecue traditionals these — the breads, potatoes or beans that accompany every grill-cooked meal.

Bread choices are many. See this page for easy "fix-ups" for baked or brown-and-serve breads. Breads and rolls with cheese, spices, herbs — even liquid smoke added — make great meal accompaniments. These use convenience products or streamlined yeast-rising methods, so even the inexperienced cook can enjoy making them.

To make breads ahead, prepare and bake as directed. Cool; wrap in foil for reheating later. When using refrigerated fresh dough products, breads or rolls can be shaped, covered and refrigerated *up to 2 hours before* baking. Then, bake as directed.

To reheat breads, wrap in foil. Place on grill, away from hottest coals, or in 350° oven, 10 to 15 minutes for rolls; 15 to 20 minutes for loaves.

To grill brown-and-serve rolls, thread rolls on skewers or, place small loaves right on grill. Brush rolls with melted butter; bake about 10 minutes turning to brown all sides. If rolls are frozen, thaw first.

High Altitude Adjustments are given with some recipes in this section. All recipes that contain baking powder or soda as leavening were tested at high altitude with necessary adjustments made.

Rice goes well with the flavors of many kabobs. Our recipe for cooking precooked rice in foil is found on page 105.

To heat frozen rice dishes on the grill, remove from cooking pouch. Wrap securely in foil; heat away from hottest coals, 20 to 25 minutes, turning once or twice.

Fluffy foil roasted potatoes are nearly everyone's favorite. Other frozen potato products can heat in foil on the grill, as a change from baked potatoes.

To grill frozen French fries or potato balls, first thaw; then place in foil pan. Heat, stirring frequently, until hot. A popcorn popper that you use over the open fire works even better. Add potatoes and just shake the basket over hot coals until potatoes are hot! Sprinkle with salt before serving.

People have preferences for baked beans: dark baked with molasses, spicy tomato sauced or, the heat and eat variety from a can.

To heat beans right in the can, remove lid and label. Place on grill; heat until liquid bubbles and beans are hot.

When baking beans for a crowd, see Cooking For Crowds chapter for additional recipes.

TOASTED FRENCH BREAD
6 to 8 servings

    1 loaf French bread or other unsliced loaves
    Butter or flavored spreads, see below

Cut bread almost through to bottom crust. Spread every other slice with butter. Wrap in heavy duty foil. Place on grill along with meat. Heat 30 to 45 minutes until loaf is hot.

    Tip: Loaf can be heated in 350° oven.

ADDITIONS TO TOASTED FRENCH BREAD

• Three tablespoons dry onion soup mix, added to ½ cup softened butter or margarine. Good with fish and beef.

• Brush with melted butter or margarine; sprinkle with garlic salt or Parmesan cheese.

• Rye bread with Swiss or Provolone cheese slices inserted between thick slices makes a hit served with ham.

• Softened cheese spreads layered in sliced French bread or hard rolls.

• To make Toasted Cheese Slices, see photograph; cut unsliced French loaves into 2-inch slices. Make slashes in each slice just to bottom crust. Insert small cheese slices; brush bread slices with melted butter. Toast on grill until bread is golden brown and cheese just begins to melt.

ONE-STEP SUPPER ROLLS

12 to 15 large rolls

> 1 cup dairy sour cream
> 2 egg yolks*
> 2 cups Pillsbury Hungry Jack Buttermilk
>   Pancake and Waffle Mix**
> Poppy seed or sesame seed

Preheat oven to 375°. In large mixing bowl, combine sour cream and egg yolks. Add pancake mix (measure by lightly spooning into cup and leveling off); blend until dry ingredients are well moistened. Drop by tablespoonfuls onto greased cookie sheet. Sprinkle with poppy seed. Bake at 375° for 10 to 15 minutes until lightly browned. Serve warm.

> **Tips:** *One whole egg may be used for the 2 egg yolks.
>
> Also good, baked as directed, in 12 greased muffin cups.
>
> **Pillsbury Extra Light Pancake and Waffle Mix can be used for the buttermilk pancake and waffle mix.
>
> Reheat, wrapped loosely in foil, at 350° for about 10 minutes.

CHEESY GARLIC HOT ROLL BRAID

1 braid

> 1 package Pillsbury Hot Roll Mix
> ⅔ cup warm water
> 1 egg, separated
> ¾ cup dairy sour cream
> ¼ cup butter or margarine, softened
> 1 tablespoon cold water
> 1 tablespoon sesame seed

Filling

> ½ cup grated Parmesan cheese
> 1 tablespoon garlic salt
> ¼ cup chopped onion or 1 tablespoon
>   instant minced onion
> 1 teaspoon Italian seasoning
> 1 teaspoon paprika

Preheat oven to 375°. Prepare Filling; set aside. In large mixing bowl, sprinkle yeast (from mix) into warm water; stir until dissolved. Add egg yolk (reserve white) and sour cream. Blend well. Stir in flour mixture to form a soft dough. Toss on well-floured surface until no longer sticky. Roll out on well-floured surface to a 13x11-inch rectangle. Spread with softened butter. Sprinkle evenly with Filling. Fold 13-inch sides to center overlapping about 1 inch. Press to seal center and ends. Place on greased cookie sheet, seam-side up. Make diagonal cuts 1 inch apart on each side of rectangle to within 1 inch of center. Do not cut through center. Fold opposite strips of dough at an angle, alternating from side to side to give a crisscross appearance. Pinch ends to seal. Beat egg white with cold water and brush over top of loaf. Sprinkle with sesame seed. Let rise in warm place until light and doubled in size, 30 to 45 minutes. Bake at 375° for 25 to 30 minutes until golden brown. Serve warm or cold.

Filling: Combine all ingredients; mix well.

> **Tip:** Reheat, wrapped in foil, at 325° for 10 to 15 minutes.

SMOKY BARBECUE BUNS

12 rolls

    3½ to 4 cups Pillsbury's Best All Purpose
        Flour*
    1 tablespoon sugar
    1 teaspoon salt
    1 package active dry yeast
 1¼ cups warm water
    1 tablespoon butter or margarine, softened
    2 teaspoons barbecue seasoning
 ¼ teaspoon liquid smoke
    2 egg whites (reserve 1 tablespoon for
        glaze)
    3 tablespoons sesame seeds
    1 tablespoon butter or margarine, melted

Glaze

    Reserved 1 tablespoon egg white
    1 tablespoon water
    1 teaspoon liquid smoke

Preheat oven to 400°. In large mixer bowl, combine 2 cups of flour, sugar, salt and dry yeast. Add warm water, butter, barbecue seasoning, liquid smoke and egg whites. Blend at low speed until moistened; beat 3 minutes at medium speed. By hand, stir in remaining flour to form a stiff dough. Knead on floured surface until smooth, about 5 minutes. Place in greased bowl, turning to grease top. Cover; let rise in warm place until light and doubled in size, about 1 hour. Prepare Glaze.

Divide dough in half. On floured surface, roll out each portion to a 16x9-inch rectangle. Cut dough lengthwise into three 16x3-inch strips. Cut strips in half, crosswise. Roll up jelly-roll fashion, starting with the 3-inch ends. Pinch edges to seal. Place, seam-side down, on greased cookie sheets. With scissors or sharp knife, make a diagonal cut across top of each bun. Brush tops with Glaze. Sprinkle generously with sesame seeds. Let rise in warm place until light and doubled in size, about 45 minutes. Bake at 400° for 20 to 25 minutes until golden brown. Brush with melted butter. Serve warm or cold.

Glaze: In small mixing bowl, combine reserved egg white, water and liquid smoke.

*For use with Pillsbury's Best Self-Rising Flour, omit salt.

CHEESE POPOVER PUFFS

6 to 8 popovers

    1 cup Pillsbury's Best All Purpose Flour*
 ½ teaspoon salt
    1 cup milk
    1 tablespoon butter or margarine, melted
    2 eggs
 ¼ cup shredded Cheddar cheese

Preheat oven to 425°. In small mixing bowl, combine flour, salt, milk, butter and eggs. Beat with rotary beater until smooth. Stir in cheese. Pour into greased popover pan or muffin cups, filling two-thirds full. Bake at 425° for 15 minutes, then reduce oven temperature to 350° and bake 35 minutes longer until golden brown. Prick with a sharp knife during last 5 minutes of baking to allow for escape of steam. Serve immediately.

*Pillsbury's Best Self-Rising Flour is not recommended for use in this recipe.

    HIGH ALTITUDE ADJUSTMENT —
    5,200 feet. Bake at 450° for 15 minutes,
    then reduce oven temperature to
    350° for 25 minutes.

CHEESE 'N CHILI CORNBREAD

    1 egg
    1 package (9½ oz.) cornbread mix
 ½ cup milk
 ½ cup creamed corn
 ½ cup shredded Cheddar cheese
 ¼ cup chopped green chilies
 ¼ cup chopped onions

Preheat oven to 425°. Grease bottom only of 8x4 or 9x5-inch loaf pan. In large mixing bowl, slightly beat egg. Add cornbread mix, milk and corn; stir until moistened. Stir in remaining ingredients. Pour into prepared pan. Bake in 425° oven for 25 to 30 minutes until toothpick inserted in center comes out clean. Cool 5 minutes, then remove from pan. Serve warm, cut into thick slices.

BUTTERFLAKE HERB LOAF

2 loaves

- 4½ to 5½ cups Pillsbury's Best All Purpose Flour*
- ¼ cup sugar
- 3 teaspoons salt
- 1 package active dry yeast
- 1¼ cups milk
- ⅓ cup shortening
- 2 eggs

Herb Butter

- ½ cup butter or margarine, softened
- ½ teaspoon caraway seed
- ½ teaspoon sweet basil
- ½ teaspoon grated onion
- ¼ teaspoon leaf oregano
- ⅛ teaspoon cayenne pepper
- 1 clove garlic, minced or ¼ teaspoon garlic powder

Preheat oven to 350°. In large mixer bowl, combine 2 cups of flour, sugar, salt and dry yeast. In saucepan, heat milk and shortening until milk is warm. (Shortening does not need to melt.) Add eggs and warm milk to flour mixture. Blend at lowest speed until moistened; beat 3 minutes at medium speed. By hand, stir in remaining flour to form a stiff dough. Knead on floured surface until smooth and elastic, about 3 minutes. Place in greased bowl, turning to grease top. Cover; let rise in warm place until light and doubled in size, 1 to 1½ hours.

Punch down dough. Divide dough in half. Roll out one portion of dough on lightly floured surface to a 15x9-inch rectangle. Spread on half of the Herb Butter. Roll up towards you from 9-inch edge to shape a loaf. Seal ends; place, seam-side down, in greased 9x5-inch loaf pan. Repeat with remaining dough. Cover; let rise in warm place until dough reaches top of pan and corners are filled, 1 to 1½ hours. Bake at 350° for 30 to 35 minutes until golden brown.

Herb Butter: In small mixing bowl, combine all ingredients and mix until well blended.

*For use with Pillsbury's Best Self-Rising Flour, omit salt.

TATO-FLAKE CHEESE BUNS

24 rolls

- 3 to 3¼ cups Pillsbury's Best All Purpose Flour*
- 1 tablespoon sugar
- 2 teaspoons salt
- ⅛ teaspoon cayenne pepper
- 1 package active dry yeast
- ½ cup Pillsbury Hungry Jack Mashed Potato Flakes
- 1 cup boiling water
- ¾ cup evaporated milk
- ¼ cup shortening
- 1 egg
- 1 cup shredded Cheddar cheese

Preheat oven to 425°. In large mixer bowl, combine 2 cups of flour, sugar, salt, cayenne pepper, dry yeast and dry potato flakes. Combine boiling water, evaporated milk and shortening; cool to lukewarm. Add egg and warm liquid to flour mixture. Blend at lowest speed until moistened; beat 3 minutes at medium speed. By hand, stir in remaining flour and cheese to form a stiff batter. Cover; let rise in warm place until light and doubled in size, 1 to 1½ hours.

Stir down batter. Spoon batter into 24 well-greased muffin cups. Cover; let rise in warm place until light and doubled in size, 45 to 60 minutes. Bake at 375° for 20 to 25 minutes, until golden brown. Remove from pans immediately.

*For use with Pillsbury's Best Self-Rising Flour, omit salt.

BISCUIT TORTILLAS

BEFORE GRILLING: Sprinkle cornmeal on work surface. Separate 1 can (8 oz.) Pillsbury Refrigerated Buttermilk or Country Style Biscuits into 10 biscuits. Coat both sides of biscuits with cornmeal; roll or pat out to 4-inch circles.

ON THE GRILL: Place biscuits on greased grill. Bake until lightly browned on the bottom and bubbles form on the top. Turn; continue baking until bottom is light brown. Serve with butter.

> **Tips:** For plain grilled biscuits, omit cornmeal.
>
> Biscuits can be baked in oven as directed on package.

ONION BUNS

10 rolls

>   2 tablespoons butter or margarine
> ½ cup (1 med.) chopped onion
>   1 tablespoon shredded Cheddar or grated Parmesan cheese
>   1 tablespoon sesame seed
>   1 teaspoon garlic salt
> ¾ teaspoon paprika
>   1 can (8 oz.) Pillsbury Refrigerated Buttermilk or Country Style Biscuits
>   1 slightly beaten egg, if desired
> Sesame seed, if desired

Preheat oven to 400°. Grease cookie sheet. In small saucepan, melt butter. Add remaining ingredients except biscuits; mix well.
Separate biscuit dough into 10 biscuits. Roll or pat each biscuit into a 5-inch circle. Place about one tablespoon of onion mixture in the center of each biscuit; fold in half, pressing edges to seal. Place on prepared cookie sheet. If desired, brush with egg and sprinkle with sesame seed. Bake at 400° for 12 to 15 minutes until golden brown.

> HIGH ALTITUDE ADJUSTMENT —
> 5200 feet. No adjustment necessary.

BISCUIT FRENCH BREAD

1 loaf

>   2 cans (8 oz. each) Pillsbury Refrigerated Country Style or Buttermilk Biscuits
>   1 egg white, beaten
> Sesame seeds

Preheat oven to 350°. Stand biscuits on edge on ungreased cookie sheet; lightly press together and shape ends to form a long loaf. Brush with egg white. Sprinkle with sesame seeds. Bake at 350° for 30 to 40 minutes until deep golden brown. Slice; serve hot.

RICE IN FOIL

In foil packet, combine quick-cooking rice and water as directed on package. Dot with butter; season with salt and pepper.
Seal securely. Place about 6 inches from coals for about 10 minutes.
For seasoned rices, add any of the following before sealing in the foil packet:

> Thyme
> Oregano
> Italian seasoning
> Dill weed
> Seasoned salt (omit regular salt)
> Basil
> Rosemary leaves
> Bay leaf
> Dry mustard
> Parmesan cheese

Or, use any of the following for half of the water:

> Beef or chicken bouillon
> Barbecue sauce

BAKED POTATO

BEFORE GRILLING: Scrub potatoes; oil skin lightly and pierce with fork. Wrap each potato securely in squares of heavy duty foil.

ON THE GRILL: Place potatoes on grill 4 to 6 inches from hot coals. Roast, turning several times, about 1 hour until tender. Unwrap potatoes; slit top of each lengthwise; serve with butter or sour cream.

WHIPPED LEMON BUTTER

   ½ cup butter or margarine, softened
   2 tablespoons lemon juice
   1 teaspoon salt
   2 tablespoons chopped parsley,
     if desired

In small bowl, cream butter and lemon juice until fluffy. Add remaining ingredients; mix well. Store any remaining butter in refrigerator, but serve at room temperature. Enough for 4 potatoes.

GARLIC SOUR CREAM

   1 cup dairy or imitation sour cream
   1 teaspoon dry garlic flavored salad
     dressing mix

Combine sour cream and mix. Cover. Refrigerate at least 1 hour to allow flavors to blend. Enough for 4 potatoes.

GOLDEN ONION BUTTER

   ½ cup butter or margarine
   ½ cup (1 med.) chopped onion

In saucepan, melt 2 tablespoons butter. Cook onions in butter until golden brown. Add remaining butter; heat until melted. Serve warm. Enough for 4 potatoes.

SPUD N' ONIONS

4 servings

   4 medium baking potatoes
   ½ cup butter or margarine, softened
   2 medium, mild onions, sliced
   Salt
   Pepper
   Paprika, if desired

BEFORE GRILLING: Peel potatoes; cut into four or five crosswise slices. Spread butter generously between slices. Place one onion slice between each potato slice; reassemble; secure slices with toothpick or skewer. Spread tops with butter; sprinkle with salt, pepper and paprika. Place each potato on large square of heavy duty foil; seal securely.

ON THE GRILL: Place over medium coals; cook for 45 to 50 minutes until soft. Serve in opened packages.

CHEESE POTATOES

3 to 4 servings

   2 tablespoons butter or margarine
   1 lb. frozen French fries, thawed
   Salt
   Pepper
   1 cup grated cheese
   3 tablespoons cream or milk

BEFORE GRILLING: Place butter on large square of double thickness heavy duty foil, spreading to grease foil. Add potatoes, salt, pepper, cheese and cream. Seal package securely.

ON THE GRILL: Heat along with meat over coals at least 20 to 25 minutes until cheese melts.

BAKED STUFFED POTATOES

6 servings

   6 medium baking potatoes
   1 teaspoon salt
   ⅛ teaspoon pepper
   ¼ cup butter or margarine
   ¼ cup hot milk
   1 cup (4 oz.) shredded American or
     Cheddar cheese

ON THE GRILL: Bake potatoes as directed above. Cut potatoes in half lengthwise. Scoop out potato; mash. Add salt, pepper, butter and hot milk. Beat until light and fluffy. Spoon into shells; top with cheese. Continue heating on the grill until cheese is melted.

   Tip: Potatoes can be baked, as directed, in oven.

PORK AND BEANS LUAU

2 to 3 servings

2 tablespoons butter or margarine
1 cup (1 med.) green pepper, cut in 1-inch squares
¼ cup (1 bunch) diagonally sliced green onions
1 clove garlic, minced or ⅛ teaspoon instant minced garlic
1 can (1 lb.) pork and beans with tomato sauce
½ cup drained pineapple tidbits or crushed pineapple
¼ cup sliced water chestnuts, if desired
1 teaspoon soy sauce

In saucepan, melt butter; add pepper, onion and garlic. Cook until vegetables are tender. Add remaining ingredients. Heat, stirring occasionally, until heated through.

A fun new taste for pork and beans begins with a bottle of soda pop. Heat in oven or on the grill.

ZIPPY BAKED BEANS

3 to 4 servings

2 cups (1-lb. can) pork and beans with tomato sauce
¼ cup (2-oz. can) drained mushrooms
¼ cup (1 small) chopped onion or 1 tablespoon instant minced onion
¼ cup lemon-lime carbonated beverage
2 tablespoons hickory flavored barbecue sauce*

In saucepan, combine all ingredients; mix well. Heat, uncovered, on stove or grill until heated through.

Tips: *Regular barbecue sauce or catsup and 1 to 2 drops liquid smoke can be used for hickory flavored barbecue sauce.

If desired, place beans in 1-quart casserole and heat for 35 to 45 minutes in 350° oven.

Recipe can be doubled.

CHEESE 'N BOSTON BEAN BAKE

6 servings

4 cups (two 1-lb. cans) molasses baked beans
1 cup cubed American or Cheddar cheese
¼ cup chopped onion or 1 tablespoon instant minced onion
¼ cup barbecue sauce or catsup
¼ cup red wine, if desired
6 slices crisp cooked bacon

Preheat oven to 350°. In 1½-quart casserole, combine all ingredients except bacon; mix well. Crumble bacon over beans. Bake in 350° oven for 20 to 30 minutes until bubbly and cheese melts.

INDIVIDUAL BEAN 'N APPLE POTS

5 to 6 servings

4 to 8 slices diced bacon
½ cup (1 med.) chopped onion or 2 tbsp. instant minced onion
2 cans (1 lb. each) pork and beans with tomato sauce
2 tablespoons brown sugar
1 teaspoon dry or prepared mustard
1 apple, cut into 16 thin wedges

BEFORE GRILLING: Partially cook bacon; pour off all but 2 tablespoons drippings. Add onion; cook until tender. Stir in remaining ingredients except apple. Spoon individual servings on squares of heavy duty foil. Top with apple wedges. Seal securely. Wrap again in another square of foil.

ON THE GRILL: Place 4 to 6 inches from hot coals. Heat 30 to 45 minutes, turning every 15 minutes.

Tips: To heat in oven, place bean mixture in 1½ or 2-quart casserole. Top with apple slices. Bake at 350° for 35 to 45 minutes until heated through.

To heat in saucepan, add all ingredients to fry pan; cover and simmer on stove or grill until heated through.

Top, clockwise — Seasoned Chipper Snacks, Grapefruit Cider Mist, Tomato Noggins, Scotch Frost, Plantation Almond Tea, Coconut Snacks, Snack Sticks, Sour Cream Dip and Vegetable Dippers, Tasty Braunschweiger Cheese Ball.

Snacks and Beverages

Snacks fill the empty spaces while everyone's waiting for a meal to cook. Sometimes the snacks easiest to make, are the most popular. Then the hostess can relax with an icy cold glass of punch and take a moment before the meal to enjoy the sounds and smell of a barbecue happening. Mmm!

CAESARETTES

32 appetizers

>   1 egg
> ¼ cup Caesar salad dressing
> ½ teaspoon onion salt
>   1 can (8 oz.) Pillsbury Refrigerated Quick Crescent Dinner Rolls
>   2 cups herb seasoned stuffing, coarsely crushed
> ⅓ cup grated Parmesan cheese

Preheat oven to 375°. In small mixing bowl, combine egg, salad dressing and onion salt; mix well. Unroll crescent dough and separate into 8 triangles. Dip each triangle into salad dressing mixture, then pat in crushed stuffing, coating both sides. Cut each triangle into 4 pieces making 32 in all. Place 1 inch apart on ungreased cookie sheets. Sprinkle with Parmesan cheese. Bake at 375° for 8 to 10 minutes until golden brown. Serve warm or cold.

> **Tips:** Other creamy salad dressings such as Green Goddess, Creamy Onion or Creamy French may be used for Caesar salad dressing.
>
> To rewarm, loosely cover appetizers on cookie sheet; heat at 375° for 2 to 3 minutes.
>
> To make ahead, prepare, cover and refrigerate up to 1 to 2 hours; bake as directed.

Strips of fresh coconut toasted golden brown liven any snack table. One coconut goes a long way, but will disappear quickly.

COCONUT SNACKS

3 to 4 cups

To remove meat from fresh coconut, punch in eyes and drain milk. Place in 350° oven 15 minutes; cool. Crack; remove coconut meat from shell, keeping pieces as large as possible. Remove brown outer covering from coconut meat with a vegetable peeler; then cut coconut pieces into long, thin strips.

Preheat oven to 300°. Place strips on cookie sheet or jelly roll pan. Sprinkle with salt. Toast in oven until light golden brown, turning several times for even browning. (Once coconut begins to brown, watch closely as it will brown quickly.)

SEASONED CHIPPER SNACKS

Sauce mixes add flavor to plain potato chips. Give them fun new flavors — that you can't buy — by adding a few teaspoons sauce mix to a bag of potato chips. We've used sour cream, cheese, taco, spaghetti, chili and sloppy joe seasoning. Try our's or find others you like as well. One teaspoon sauce mix for 2 cups potato chips is a good level of seasoning for a starter; add more as you choose.

SNACK STICKS

> Pasteurized process American cheese spread, sharp
> Pasteurized Neufchatel cheese spread with olives and pimiento
> Assorted cold cuts
> Bread or snack sticks

For each snack, spread cheese on slice of meat. Wrap around bread stick, pressing gently to secure edge. Serve with your favorite beverage.

> **Tip:** To make ahead, prepare, cover and refrigerate until serving time.

This tangy seafood dip adds a party-special flavor to fish or seafood that's dipped in it. See Tip for other dipper ideas.

FISH STICK DIPPERS

24 appetizers

1 package (8 oz.) frozen fish sticks

Seafood Dip:

1 cup (8-oz. can) tomato sauce
¼ cup (½ stalk) finely chopped celery
2 teaspoons lemon juice
2 teaspoons cream-style horseradish
2 teaspoons Worcestershire sauce
½ teaspoon onion salt
¼ teaspoon salt
Dash Tabasco sauce

Prepare fish sticks as directed on package. Meanwhile, prepare Seafood Dip. When fish sticks are cooked, cut into 1 to 2-inch pieces. Arrange on hot tray for serving. Serve on toothpicks with Seafood Dip for dunking.

Seafood Dip: In small mixing bowl, combine all ingredients; mix well.*

Tips: *Seafood Dip can be made in blender. Process on medium speed for 30 seconds.

Seafood Dip is a great sauce for cocktail shrimp, breaded scallops and other seafood.

POPCORN

ON THE GRILL: Place kernels in popper or a large heavy duty foil packet with enough room for expansion. (A green stick or roasting fork can be tied to foil packet for a handle.) Hold container over hot coals; shake until kernels have popped. Salt; toss with melted butter or margarine.

Tips: To prepare on the range, use heavy pan or skillet. Heat ¼ cup cooking oil and use enough kernels to cover the bottom of the pan.

BEEFED-UP POPCORN: Cook 1 package (3 oz.) cut-up smoked, sliced beef in ½ cup butter or margarine; toss with about 3 quarts popped corn. Serve immediately.

A very mild braunschweiger flavor plus easy seasonings provide great taste inuendos in this spread.

TASTY BRAUNSCHWEIGER CHEESE BALL

1 package (8 oz.) cream cheese, softened
⅓ cup (2 oz.) braunschweiger or liver sausage
1 to 2 tablespoons sweet pickle relish
½ to 1 teaspoon Worcestershire sauce
¼ teaspoon garlic salt
½ cup (3 oz.) chopped peanuts or pecans

In medium mixing bowl, combine all ingredients except peanuts; blend thoroughly. Place cheese mixture in refrigerator about 15 minutes to harden slightly for easier handling. Shape cheese mixture into ball. Roll in chopped nuts to coat well. Return to refrigerator; chill 15 to 20 minutes or until serving time. Serve with assorted crackers or chips.

Tips: For Onion-Flavored Braunschweiger Spread, mix 1 package (.56 oz.) dry onion dip mix with ¼ cup sour cream; add to cheese mixture. Prepare as directed.

If desired, cheese mixture can be thinned with sour cream or milk to serve as a dip. Use nuts as a garnish.

PARTY POPPERS CORN

Serve hot buttered corn to easily feed a crowd. It's easy and inexpensive to pop a large quantity, to serve right away or reheat later in a 250° oven. Served with your favorite beverage, it's good plain or sprinkled with one of these:

Garlic salt or seasoned salt blends
Curry or chili powder
Grated American or Parmesan cheese
Salted nuts

GRAPEFRUIT CIDER MIST

4 to 6 (8 oz.) servings

2 cups (16 oz. can) grapefruit juice
½ cup apple cider
2 tablespoons lime juice
1½ cups (12 oz.) ginger ale

Combine grapefruit juice, cider and lime juice. Just before serving, add ginger ale. Serve over ice cubes.

Nothing matches fresh lemon flavor or says summertime refreshment quicker than lemonade. Lemon slices fill the pitcher with color!

OLD FASHIONED LEMONADE

4 to 6 (8 oz.) servings

4 lemons
¾ cup sugar
1 quart (4 cups) water

Cut lemons into thin slices; remove any seeds. Place in a bowl; sprinkle with sugar. Let stand about 10 minutes, then press fruit with a potato masher to extract juice. Add water, pressing fruit until well flavored. Serve over ice cubes; garnish with lemon slices, if desired.

> **Tips:** If desired, add more sugar to chilled lemonade; stir to dissolve.
>
> Two limes can be used for two lemons. Prepare as directed, increasing sugar to 1 cup.
>
> Two oranges can be used for one lemon. Prepare as directed, decreasing sugar to ½ cup.

TOMATO NOGGINS

8 (8 oz.) servings

5½ cups (46 oz. can) tomato juice
2½ cups (two 10½ oz. cans) beef broth
1 to 2 lemons, sliced

In large saucepan, combine ingredients. Heat over low heat until hot. Serve in mugs; garnish with lemon slices.

> **Tips:** 3 beef bouillon cubes or 3 teaspoons instant beef bouillon and 2½ cups water can be used for beef broth.
>
> For spicier Tomato Noggins, use tomato juice cocktail or mixed vegetable juice.
>
> Tomato Noggins may be spiked with 1 cup vodka just before serving. Or, allow 2 tablespoons (1 jigger) vodka for each serving.

A very smooth cooler. Serve as a beverage or as a dessert.

SCOTCH FROST

1 serving

1 cup vanilla ice cream
2 tablespoons (1 jigger) scotch

Combine all ingredients in blender. Process on high speed for 15 seconds until well blended. Serve in glass with cherry.

> **Tip:** Multiply amount of ingredients by number of servings desired.

PLANTATION ALMOND TEA

1 quart

2 tea bags or 2 teaspoons tea leaves
¾ cup sugar
¼ cup lemon juice*
2 cups boiling water
2 cups water
½ teaspoon almond extract
½ teaspoon vanilla

Place tea bags, sugar and lemon juice in teapot. Pour boiling water over tea mixture. Cover; let stand about 10 minutes. Pour tea and remaining ingredients over ice; stir to combine. If desired, garnish with lemon slices.

> **Tip:** *If fresh lemon juice is used, add whole peel when making tea for stronger lemon flavor.

POLYNESIAN FRUIT PUNCH

24 (4 oz.) servings

¾ cup (6 oz. can) frozen grapefruit juice
¾ cup (6 oz. can) frozen orange juice
¾ cup (6 oz. can) frozen lemonade
3 quarts chilled gingerale
2 tablespoons grenadine
Orange slices

In large punchbowl or pitcher, combine grapefruit, orange juice, frozen lemonade, gingerale and genadine. Pour over an ice mold or serve in tall glasses filled with ice. Garnish with orange slices.

> **Tip:** For an alcoholic punch, add 1 pint rum, vodka or gin.

Top, clockwise — Strawberry Social, page 118; Fruit Shortcake Spoon-up, page 116; Doughnut S'mores, opposite page; Almond Brittle Sticks, opposite page; Dessert Apples, page 119; Bananas Foster, page 119.

Desserts

Desserts at a barbecue can be as simple as marshmallows roasted on a stick or as spectacular as flaming fruit served in the French tradition. Both are equally at home — and appreciated.

In addition to the recipes given in this section, ideas are offered in the Salads and Snacks and Beverages Chapters. You will find refreshing desserts that are compatible with the spicy flavors predominating in barbecued meals.

Ice cream is summer's favorite dessert. Make some with an old fashioned freezer you crank yourself. Guests will want to lend a hand, too, when they see how much fun it is. Even if you sit back and listen to the hum of an electric freezer, no one will dispute the pleasure of eating good homemade ice cream.

High Altitude Adjustments are given with some recipes in this section. All recipes that contain baking powder or soda as leavening were tested at high altitude with necessary adjustments made.

SPICY SUGAR CRISPS
60 cookies

> 1 egg white, slightly beaten
> 2 tablespoons water
> ½ cup sugar
> 1½ teaspoons cinnamon
> 1½ teaspoons nutmeg
> 1 roll Pillsbury Refrigerated Sugar or Butterscotch Nut Cookies
> ½ cup sliced almonds

Preheat oven to 375°. Beat together egg white and water. In small bowl, combine sugar, cinnamon and nutmeg. Slice cookie dough into ⅛-inch slices. Roll into balls. Brush with egg white mixture. Roll in sugar-spice mixture. Place on ungreased cookie sheet. Bake at 375° for 8 to 10 minutes until golden brown. (Cookies will be puffy when removed from oven.) Press a few sliced almonds into top of each warm cookie. Cool; loosen with spatula.

Use leftover doughnuts in this fun recipe that children love. They'll enjoy making it, too.

DOUGHNUT S'MORES

> Cake doughnuts
> Chocolate candy bars
> Miniature marshmallows

Before grilling: Cut doughnuts in half. Place chocolate candy on one half, marshmallows on the other. On the grill: Place doughnut halves on grill 3 to 4 inches from coals. Heat for several minutes, until marshmallows are softened. Place 2 halves together and serve.

Buttery spritz flavor in a quick and easy cookie bar. These can be ready in about an hour.

ALMOND BRITTLE STICKS
36 bars

> 1 roll Butterscotch Nut, Chewy Almond, Sugar or Peanut Butter Slice 'N Bake Cookies
> 1 cup (6-oz. pkg.) butterscotch pieces
> ¼ cup light corn syrup
> 2 tablespoons butter or margarine
> ¼ teaspoon salt
> Sliced or slivered almonds

Preheat oven to 375°. Grease a 13x9-inch baking pan. Slice cookie dough in ¼-inch slices; place in prepared pan. Bake at 375° for 15 to 20 minutes until golden brown. (Cookies will be puffy when removed from oven.) Cool slightly. In medium saucepan, over low heat, melt butterscotch pieces with remaining ingredients except almonds; stir mixture until smooth. Spread butterscotch mixture evenly over baked cookies. Sprinkle with almonds. Chill until firm; cut into bars.

ONE STEP MERINGUE SQUARES

36 bars

 1 roll Pillsbury Refrigerated Slice 'N Bake Cookies
 1 package Pillsbury Coconut-Almond or Coconut-Pecan Frosting Mix
 1 cup (6-oz. pkg.) semi-sweet or milk chocolate pieces
 3 egg whites
 1 cup firmly packed brown sugar

Preheat oven to 350°. Slice cookie dough into ¼-inch slices; place in ungreased 13x9-inch baking pan. Sprinkle frosting mix and chocolate pieces evenly over cookie dough. Beat egg whites until foamy. Gradually add brown sugar; beat until stiff peaks form, about 5 minutes. Spread meringue on frosting mix-chocolate layer. Bake at 350° for 30 to 35 minutes until meringue is browned and firm to touch. Cool; cut into bars.

CHOCO-NUT PINWHEELS

48 cookies

 1 package Pillsbury Coconut-Pecan or Coconut-Almond Frosting Mix
 ⅓ cup milk
 3 tablespoons butter or margarine
 1 roll Pillsbury Refrigerated Fudge Nut or Swiss Style Chocolate Chunk Slice 'N Bake Cookies

Preheat oven to 350°. In medium saucepan, combine frosting mix and milk; add butter. Cook over medium heat, stirring constantly, until butter is melted. Cool. Cut cookie roll in half; roll out each half between sheets of waxed paper to form two 8x11-inch rectangles. (For ease in rolling, allow cookie dough to soften to room temperature.) Remove top sheets of waxed paper. Spread each rectangle with half the frosting mixture. Roll up each from longer side; remove all waxed paper. Wrap cookie rolls and chill 2 hours or until firm enough to slice. Cut into ¼-inch slices; place on ungreased cookie sheets 2 inches apart. Bake at 350° for 10 to 12 minutes. Remove cookies from oven when they are moist, soft and puffy. Cool 2 minutes before removing from cookie sheet.

FRUIT CRACK-UP SUNDAE

4 to 5 servings

Prepare 1 package (3 oz.) any flavor gelatin as directed on package, using 1½ cups water. Pour into 8 or 9-inch square pan. Chill at least 2 hours until firm. Using a fork, break gelatin into pieces. Lightly spoon into individual serving dishes; mound ice cream or sherbet in center. Serve immediately.

A convenient homemade ice cream that cuts calories by not using whipping cream.

KITCHEN CUPBOARD ICE CREAM

1 gallon

 3 eggs
 1 cup sugar
 1 tablespoon vanilla
 3 cups (two 13-oz. cans) evaporated milk
 1 quart (4 cups) milk

In large mixer bowl, beat eggs with sugar. Add vanilla and evaporated milk; mix until well blended. Pour into ice cream freezer container. Add remaining milk. Freeze according to manufacturer's directions.

EASY ICE CREAM DESSERTS

For a Hawaiian touch, serve vanilla ice cream on a pineapple ring and sprinkle with chopped macadamia nuts.

Serve ice cream with cantaloupe and honey dew melon balls. Garnish with fresh strawberries or raspberries.

Serve vanilla ice cream with chocolate or hot fudge sauce. Top with Spanish peanuts.

Serve cinnamon ice cream over warm apple sauce, apple pie or apple crisp.

Spoon warm *or* cold prepared cherry pie filling over chocolate ice cream and sprinkle with slivered almonds.

Spoon vanilla or strawberry ice cream over brownies. Add marshmallow topping and chopped pecans.

The base of this ice cream is traditional cooked custard. What seems like a little extra time at the start pays off in rich creamy mounds of extra good eating!

PEACH RUMBA ICE CREAM

1 gallon

>   3 cups (two 13-oz. cans) evaporated milk
>   2 cups water
>   1 cup sugar
>   6 eggs
>   ½ cup flour
>   1 pint (2 cups) whipping cream
>   1 cup sugar
>   1 to 2 teaspoons rum extract or ¼ cup rum
>   2 cups sliced peaches*
>   ½ cup chopped macadamia nuts or toasted almonds

In large saucepan, heat milk and water. Meanwhile, in large mixing bowl, beat eggs and 1 cup sugar until well blended. Add flour; mix until smooth. Add egg mixture to heated milk. Cook, stirring constantly, until slightly thickened. Cool. Add whipping cream, 1 cup sugar and rum extract. Freeze according to manufacturer's directions. When almost frozen, add peaches and nuts.

> **Tips:** *2 to 3 fresh peaches, peeled and sliced, 2 packages (10 oz. each) frozen peach slices or 1 can (29 oz.) drained peach slices can be used for peaches in this recipe.
>   For vanilla ice cream, omit peaches and nuts. Use vanilla for rum extract.

QUICK ICE CREAM PIE

Bake Pillsbury Refrigerated Slice 'N Bake Cookies as directed on package; cool. Line ice cube tray, loaf pan or pie pan with cookies. Scoop in your favorite flavors of ice cream, pressing ice cream gently into cookies. Freeze until serving time. To serve, cut into pie shape wedges; drizzle on ice cream topping. If desired, garnish with fruit or a chocolate curl.

Remarkably smooth textured ice cream that's easy to vary with favorite pudding flavors. We especially liked chocolate with marshmallows.

PUDDIN' ICE CREAM

1 gallon

>   2 packages (4½ oz. each) chocolate instant pudding
>   1 quart (4 cups) milk
>   4 eggs
>   1 pint (2 cups) whipping cream
>   ½ cup sugar
>   1 teaspoon vanilla
>   2 cups miniature marshmallows

Prepare pudding as directed on package; chill until set. In large bowl, beat eggs until fluffy. Add sugar, whipping cream, vanilla and pudding; beat until well blended. Stir in marshmallows. Freeze according to manufacturer's directions.

> **Tip:** Use vanilla or lemon instant pudding with 4 cups (1 qt.) fresh or 4 packages (10 oz. each) frozen drained peach slices, strawberries or raspberries for delicious fruit flavored ice cream.

ICE CREAM PARFAITS

One quart ice cream makes 6 parfaits.

Combine any of the following in chilled glasses. Alternate the ice cream or sherbet with the fruit or nuts to form layers of different colors. Freeze until serving time.

Vanilla ice cream and fresh or partially thawed frozen raspberries, strawberries *or* peaches.

Peppermint ice cream and blueberry preserves.

Orange sherbet and cashew nuts.

Raspberry sherbet, vanilla ice cream and fresh raspberries.

Peppermint ice cream, vanilla ice cream, chocolate topping and chopped nuts.

Vanilla ice cream and whipped black raspberry jelly.

Vanilla ice cream, thawed frozen orange juice and crushed pineapple.

Great change from traditional shortcake. This one makes entertaining easy since guests can serve themselves. Add a pitcher of cream or a bowl of sour cream sweetened with brown sugar to spoon on shortcakes.

FRUIT SHORTCAKE SPOON-UP

5 to 6 servings

1⅔ cups biscuit mix
2 tablespoons sugar
2 tablespoons melted butter or margarine
⅓ cup milk
2 cups fresh strawberries or raspberries
1 cup fresh blueberries
1 cup (10-oz. pkg.) frozen sliced peaches
½ to 1 cup sugar

Preheat oven to 475°. Grease a cookie sheet. In mixing bowl, combine biscuit mix and sugar. Cut in melted butter. Stir in milk until moistened. Turn onto floured board or pastry cloth. Knead 5 or 6 times. Roll out ½-inch thick, cut shortcakes with round scalloped or flower shaped cutter. If desired, sprinkle with additional sugar. Place on prepared cookie sheet. Bake at 475° for 10 to 12 minutes until golden brown. Meanwhile, combine fruits and sugar in large bowl or compote. Top with hot shortcakes; serve while warm.

> **Tips:** To make ahead, combine fruits with sugar. Refrigerate until serving time. Berries frozen without syrup can be used for fresh. These are best served slightly frozen so fruits retain their shape.

STRAWBERRY CHEESE PIE

9-inch pie

1⅔ cups sifted powdered sugar
2 packages (8 oz. each) cream cheese, softened
1 cup (10 oz. pkg.) frozen strawberries, drain and reserve ½ cup syrup*
1 cup (½ pt.) whipping cream, whipped and sweetened**
Baked pie shell or graham cracker crust
Whole strawberries

In large mixer bowl, combine powdered sugar, cream cheese and reserved strawberry syrup. Blend at low speed until thoroughly combined; beat 2 minutes at medium speed until smooth. By hand, fold in strawberries and whipped cream. Pour mixture into crust. If desired, garnish with whole strawberries. Freeze at least 4 hours or until served. Remove from freezer 15 minutes before serving.

> **Tips:** *If desired, 1 pint fresh strawberries, sliced, can be used, omitting strawberry syrup. Or, use a 10-oz. package frozen raspberries or peaches.
>
> **If desired, use 2 cups (4½-oz. carton) frozen whipped topping, thawed or 1 envelope whipped topping mix, prepared as directed on package.

MINCEY PEACH PIE

9-inch pie

1 package Pillsbury Pie Crust Mix or 2 pie crust sticks
1½ cups prepared mincemeat
1 can (1 lb. 5 oz.) prepared peach pie filling
2 teaspoons grated orange peel
Cream or milk
Sugar, if desired

Preheat oven to 375°. Prepare pie crust mix according to package directions for double crust pie. In large mixing bowl, combine mincemeat, pie filling and orange peel. Pour into pastry-lined 9-inch pie pan. Roll out remaining dough; cut slits for steam to escape. Moisten rim of bottom crust. Place top crust over filling. Fold edge under bottom crust, pressing to seal. Flute edge. Brush top crust with cream; sprinkle with sugar, if desired. Bake at 375° for 40 to 45 minutes until golden brown.

CHEDDAR APPLE DANDY

6 servings

- 6 medium cooking apples, peeled and sliced
- 1 cup (4 oz.) shredded Cheddar cheese
- ¾ cup Pillsbury All Purpose Flour*
- ½ cup firmly packed brown sugar
- ½ teaspoon cinnamon
- ¼ teaspoon salt
- ½ cup butter or margarine

BEFORE GRILLING: Slice each apple onto a 12-inch square of foil. Top with cheese. Combine flour, brown sugar, cinnamon and salt; cut in butter until crumbly. Spoon equally over tops of apples. Bring foil up and seal well. Place in another square of foil.

ON THE GRILL: Place packets 4 to 6 inches from coals. Cook 45 to 55 minutes, turning packets every 15 minutes, until apples are tender. Serve warm.

> **Tips:** To make in oven, place apples in 9-inch square pan, top with cheese and then crumb mixture. Bake at 375° for 30 to 35 minutes until apples are tender.
>
> *For use with Pillsbury Self-Rising Flour, omit salt.

MACAROON CRUNCH PIE

9-inch pie

- 1 baked 9-inch pastry shell
- ½ cup toasted coconut
- 1 pint lime sherbet, softened
- 2 cups whipped cream*
- ⅓ cup powdered sugar
- 1 cup crushed crisp macaroon cookies
- ½ cup chopped pecans

Sprinkle 6 tablespoons coconut in bottom of baked pastry shell (reserve remaining for garnish); cover with softened sherbet. In mixing bowl, fold crushed cookies and pecans into whipped cream; spoon over sherbet, sealing to edge. Garnish with reserved coconut. Freeze 6 hours or overnight before serving.

> **Tip:** 2 cups frozen whipped topping, thawed, 1 cup whipping cream, whipped and sweetened, or 1 packet (½ cup) whipped topping mix, prepared as directed on package, can be used for whipped cream.

APRICOT-BANANA BARS

- ½ cup butter or margarine
- 1 cup firmly packed brown sugar
- ¾ cup (10-oz. jar) apricot preserves
- 2 eggs
- 1 teaspoon vanilla
- 1¾ cups Pillsbury All Purpose Flour*
- 1 teaspoon baking powder
- ½ teaspoon soda
- ¼ teaspoon salt
- ¾ cup (1 large) mashed ripe banana
- ½ cup chopped pecans or walnuts

Lemon Glaze

- 1½ cups sifted powdered sugar
- 1 tablespoon lemon juice
- 1 tablespoon water

Preheat oven to 350°. Grease and flour 15x10x1-inch jelly roll pan. In large mixing bowl, cream butter and sugar until fluffy. Blend in preserves, eggs and vanilla. Add dry ingredients. (No need to sift flour. Measure by lightly spooning into cup and leveling off.) Stir in bananas and nuts. Pour into prepared pan. Bake at 350° for 25 to 30 minutes until toothpick inserted in center comes out clean. Cool. Glaze with Lemon Glaze or sprinkle with powdered sugar.

LEMON GLAZE: Combine ingredients; mix well.

> **Tips:** For cake-like bars, pour batter into prepared 13x9-inch baking pan; bake at 350° for 30 to 35 minutes.
>
> *For use with Pillsbury Self-Rising Flour, omit baking powder, soda and salt.

LAST OF THE COALS FRUIT JUBILEE

8 to 10 servings

>   2 teaspoons grated orange peel
>   3 or 4 oranges
>   1½ cups (1-lb. can) pear halves, drain and
>   reserve ½ cup syrup
>   2 cups (1 lb. 5-oz. can) cherry pie filling
>   ⅓ cup sugar
>   2 tablespoons butter or margarine
>   2 to 3 tablespoons brandy, if desired
>   Angel food or pound cake

BEFORE GRILLING: Cut oranges into bite-size pieces; cut pears into slices. In large fry pan, combine orange peel, oranges, pears and pie filling. Carefully stir in ½ cup reserved pear syrup and sugar. Top with butter.

ON THE GRILL: Place on grill 8 to 10 inches from coals. Warm, stirring occasionally, while eating main course. If desired, just before serving, add brandy and flame. To serve, spoon over cake slices.

FLAMING DESSERTS

For a spectacular finish to an evening meal, set fruit desserts aflame.

You can flame any fruits which have been cooked or heated in a rich butter sauce along with a pinch of spice and appropriate fruit-flavored or dry brandy, rum or wine.

Brandy, rum and liqueurs . . . at least 50% alcohol liquor . . . are favorites for flaming because of the pleasant flavor they add to fruits.

To flame desserts: Heat the required amount of liquor in a small, long-handled saucepan or ladle. Warm just until the first bubble forms — if liquor gets too hot, the alcohol will evaporate and there will be nothing to flame!

Now, flame the liquor — a long fireplace match or candle takes some of the risk away. Pour it over the fruit until the fire dies out, then serve.

It doesn't take a lot of liquor to have a nice flame, however the flame doesn't last more than a few seconds. Have the scene set just as you want it — ice cream served, lights dimmed — before you heat the liquor. *Avoid* adding any more liquid once the fire is lit. A lid kept nearby to suffocate the flame, should it get out of hand, is a good precaution.

APRICOT SPECTACULAR

4 to 6 servings

>   2 tablespoons butter or margarine
>   ¼ cup firmly packed brown sugar
>   ¼ teaspoon nutmeg
>   2½ cups (29-oz. can) drained apricot
>   halves
>   Pound cake
>   Vanilla ice cream
>   ¼ cup rum

ON THE GRILL: In shallow fry pan or heat-proof casserole, melt butter 6 to 8 inches from coals or over low heat. Add brown sugar and nutmeg. Stir until bubbly. Add apricots; spoon sauce over apricots; heat just until heated through. (Apricots should still be firm when served.) Have pound cake slices ready to serve, spoon on ice cream. Immediately heat rum in saucepan or a ladle just until first bubble forms; ignite and pour over apricots at table. Wait until flame dies to spoon apricots over ice cream and cake.

> **Tips:** 12 fresh apricots can be used for canned. Wash, cut in half and remove pits; cook over low heat in small amount of water until tender. Prepare as directed, adding extra sugar for sweeter sauce, if desired. Or use 2 to 3 fresh peaches or drained canned peach halves.
>
> To make ahead, slice pound cake. Place slices on cookie sheet; top with ice cream and freeze until serving time. Fruit can be made ahead and reheated just before adding rum.

STRAWBERRY SOCIAL

1⅓ cups sauce

>   1 cup dairy or imitation sour cream
>   ½ cup strawberry preserves
>   Pound cake, cut into sticks
>   2 to 3 bananas, cut into ½-inch chunks

BEFORE GRILLING: In small bowl, combine sour cream and preserves; refrigerate until ready to serve.

ON THE GRILL: Place cake on grill 6 to 8 inches from coals. Toast until lightly browned on all sides. Just before serving, cut bananas into chunks. To serve, dip cake and bananas in sauce.

Our version of a New Orleans specialty. Served flaming from the grill, it's perfect for evening and is certain to please when served on homemade ice cream.

BANANAS FOSTER

6 servings

¼ cup butter
6 bananas, cut into 2-inch pieces*
½ cup firmly packed brown sugar
¼ cup orange juice
1 teaspoon grated orange peel
½ cup rum
¼ cup sugar
½ cup brandy

ON THE GRILL: In large shallow fry pan or heat proof casserole, melt butter 6 to 8 inches from coals or over low heat. Add bananas, sugar, orange juice and peel. Stir gently, until bananas are well coated and slightly softened. Add rum; continue heating for about 5 to 10 minutes until bananas are tender, basting occasionally. Sprinkle sugar over bananas. In small saucepan or ladle, heat brandy just until first bubble forms; ignite and pour over bananas at table. Wait until flame dies before spooning into serving dishes. If desired, serve with ice cream.

> **Tip:** *Slightly green bananas are a better choice than ripe bananas since they will soften less quickly while heating. Bananas may be left whole, if desired.

DESSERT APPLES

6 servings

6 apples
⅓ cup raisins
⅓ cup chopped nuts
3 tablespoons brown sugar
2 tablespoons butter

BEFORE GRILLING: Wash and core apples; remove one inch of peel around top. Combine remaining ingredients in small bowl. Stuff center of each apple with 2 tablespoons mixture. Wrap each apple in heavy duty foil.

ON THE GRILL: Place apple packets on grill 4 to 6 inches from hot coals and cook for about 10 minutes, until tender.

> **Tip:** Apples can be baked in 375° oven for about 45 minutes.

COCOBANA CAKE

9-inch square cake

2 cups Pillsbury's Best All Purpose Flour*
1 cup sugar
½ teaspoon salt
1 teaspoon cinnamon
1 teaspoon nutmeg
¼ teaspoon ground cloves
½ cup butter or margarine
1 teaspoon soda
½ cup buttermilk or sour milk
¼ cup light molasses
2 medium ripe bananas, sliced
2 eggs
½ cup flaked coconut
½ cup chopped nuts

Preheat oven to 350°. Generously grease bottom only of 9-inch square pan. In large mixer bowl, combine flour, sugar, salt, cinnamon, nutmeg and cloves. Cut in butter until mixture is crumbly. Reserve ½ cup of crumb mixture. Add soda, buttermilk, molasses, bananas and eggs. Blend at low speed until moistened; beat 3 minutes at medium speed, scraping bowl occasionally. Stir in coconut. Pour batter into prepared pan, spreading to edges. Sprinkle with reserved crumbs, then nuts. Bake at 350° for 40 to 45 minutes until toothpick inserted in center comes out clean. Serve warm or cold.

> **Tips:** To sour milk, add 1½ teaspoons vinegar or lemon juice to ½ cup milk. Stir; allow to stand 10 minutes until soured.
>
> Cake can be baked as directed in 11x7-inch pan.
>
> *For use with Pillsbury's Best Self-Rising Flour, omit salt and soda.
>
> HIGH ALTITUDE ADJUSTMENT — 5,200 feet. Decrease soda to ¾ teaspoon. Bake at 375° for 30 to 35 minutes.

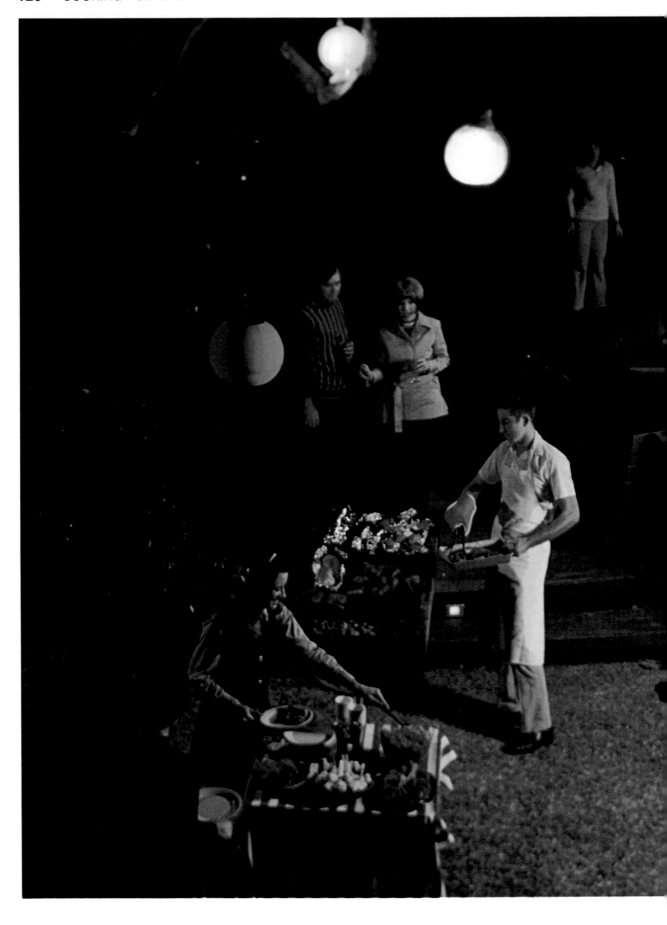

Cooking for Crowds

Getting families and friends together for a barbecue is summertime entertaining at its best. Any reason will do whether it's to welcome a new neighbor, to celebrate a family birthday or maybe just to show off a new barbecue grill!

The number of guests can grow and grow! There's something about summer with its large outdoor living space that gives each of us a generous spirit. Preparing a whole meal for a larger number of guests is not without special challenges. Meals of this type require a little more planning and organization, but are well within the skill of most homemakers.

We've developed this chapter full of hints and planning helps for three summertime entertaining situations with which you might be faced. Recipes for favorite summer foods are featured along with buying information, so there will always be plenty to eat for hearty appetites but without too many leftovers.

WEEKEND CHICKEN BARBECUE: The summer party away from home that you might give while on vacation. Planning and preparation involves one hostess with limited kitchen space.

FAMILY REUNION PICNIC: This one gets everyone together from youngsters to Grandpa. One person plans the menu, but everyone takes a hand in preparing this sit-down buffet dinner.

NEIGHBOR "PITCH-IN PARTY": Share in a fun-filled evening that's no chore — or expense for anyone. It's everyone's pot luck favorite with a plan!

Weekend chicken barbecue

Home away from home for more and more Americans on summer weekends is out in the country, up to the lake or off to a favorite campsite. Entertaining when you arrive at the same time as your guests (often after a long drive) can be challenging at best.

Even the most skillful and experienced hostess welcomes a few new tricks up her sleeve. And tricks we have, along with some good food ideas for a whole day or more.

Begin with some nourishing snacks the minute you arrive. Assorted cheese sandwiches with fruit and hot mugs of coffee are bound to put everyone into a better frame of mind. Since your guests are sure to volunteer their help, have some specific ideas in mind of things they can do. Smooth sailing ahead!

Another trick is the menu. With limited cooking and storage space away from home, simple foods are necessary. However, let one or two of the dishes have star status! In our menu, it's the chicken and slaw that get this distinction.

Regular grills usually aren't large enough to provide space for cooking a large amount of chicken all at once. Since you'll want everyone to eat at the same time, you can inexpensively put together a pit grill or, borrow or rent this type of equipment from groups in your community (see photograph, page 120).

A pit grill can be constructed with light-weight building blocks (heavy cement blocks are more likely to crack from the heat) with a grill top of 1x1-inch or 1x2-inch welded wire supported by small pipes or rods laid across the blocks (see diagram).

If some of your guests aren't arriving until the barbecue, invitations with clever maps attached are needed. When entertaining out of town, it's a thoughtful idea to let guests know who else is invited. That way, not everyone needs to drive. Give newcomers to your group an extra welcome by arranging for another couple to give them a lift to the barbecue.

Set a colorful table using paper tableware. Many colors and patterns are available to spark almost any entertaining mood. Plastic or wicker plate holders make eating from plates on your lap easier. For napkins, paper hostess towels or dampened terry towels will be welcomed by guests at any chicken barbecue!

Portability is the key in planning this menu. Consider foods that can be made at home and carried easily. Our grill is large enough to cook chicken, potatoes, corn and heat French bread. The corn and potatoes are not really necessary to the success of the meal, but are a nice accompaniment if space allows.

Menu

Chicken Madras, page 71
Overnight Crisp Slaw, page 128
Fresh Vegetable Relishes
Toasted French Bread
"Spiked" Watermelon
Cold Beverage

Buying Guide:

CHICKEN: Buy the number of halves or quarters desired for your group. Prepare sauce in advance; one recipe will be adequate for 6 servings; double recipe for 12; quadruple recipe for 24.

SALAD: Overnight Crisp Slaw is a good traveler in a tightly covered plastic container that can be used as the serving dish as well.

VEGETABLES: Depending on the variety of relishes you have and other foods in the menu, quantities needed will vary. The guide on page 123 will help. For corn, allow 1 or 2 ears per person. For baking potatoes, allow 1 per person. Crisp vegetable relishes can be prepared at home; store in ice water to keep them crisp. Slice tomatoes and pickles just before serving.

FRENCH BREAD: Allow 1 to 2 slices per serving. Cut loaves into serving sized portions. A 20-inch loaf makes about 10 slices. Cut only part of the way through and spread with seasoned butter. Wrap in foil for traveling — the unwrapped foil can be the serving basket later!

"SPIKED MELON": Cut a plug out of the side of a watermelon. Pour in orange-flavored liqueur, gin or other liquor, using ½ to 1 cup (or more if desired) for an average watermelon. Replace plug; chill thoroughly. This makes a great dessert for a summer barbecue.

AMOUNTS OF PICNIC FOODS TO PURCHASE

FOOD	FOR 6 SERVINGS	FOR 12 SERVINGS	FOR 24 SERVINGS
Salad greens (¾ cup serving)	1 quart (1 head lettuce)	2 to 3 quarts (2 to 3 heads lettuce)	5 quarts (4 to 5 heads lettuce)
Prepared salad dressing (2 to 3 tablespoons serving)	one 8-oz. bottle	two 8-oz. bottles	3 8-oz. bottles
Frozen, canned or fresh vegetables		See Green Beans, page 124	
Potato chips (¾ to 1 oz. per serving)	one 8-oz. bag	one 16-oz. bag	24 single serving-size packages or two 16-oz. bags
Watermelon		Allow about 1 lb. per person	
Cold cuts (2 to 2½ oz. per serving)	12 oz.	24 oz.	3 lbs.
Sandwich Bread (2 slices)	16-oz. loaf	24-oz. loaf	three 16-oz. loaves
Carrots for relishes (2 to 3 strips)	4 oz.	8 oz.	1 lb.
Radishes (2 each)	1 to 2 bunches	2 to 3 bunches	5 bunches
Pickles, olives	1 pint	1 quart	2 quarts
Layer or Bundt cakes		12 to 16 servings per cake	
13x9-inch cakes		12 to 15 servings per cake	
8-inch pies (6 servings per pie)		6 servings per pie	

Family reunion picnic

What fun it is on that summertime Sunday when the whole clan gets together for a family dinner. Planning for this meal that bridges generations requires some special thought . . . but it's one time you'll never be short of volunteers! Everyone will want to help.

With this plan, you are the organizer. Your job starts even months in advance when you decide to hold the reunion. Maybe it's an annual event — and the date and location are always the same. Even so, there still needs to be a letter with all the details sent to each family invited.

If this is a new idea for your family, take these added steps.

1. Decide who is to be included. The list can grow quickly if families are large. Trim the list, if necessary, to one you can handle. Recipes in this chapter are suited to 25, but up to 50 people is manageable, especially when you have the outdoors as your dining room!

2. A location is the next concern. If one of the families has a large enough yard — that's the answer. If not, choose a park area with adequate sanitary facilities such as running water, restrooms, picnic tables and benches.

3. Getting everyone and everything to the picnic spot can be a bit of an undertaking! If possible, get equipment together a few days ahead. Plan to have at least 2 of the men get the area set up before everyone else arrives so the meal can be served without too much waiting.

4. Take special consideration for young and old alike. Have plenty of comfortable patio chairs, shaded areas out of the sun, active and quiet games that include everyone, lots of cold drinks — and the inevitable first aid kit for bruised elbows, sunburn or insect bites. That first aid kit also needs something for upset stomachs — someone always eats just one too many pieces of Aunt Sue's homemade rhubarb pie!

Our meal plan is for serving at home. For a family reunion held in a park or other location away from home, follow the food suggestions given for the Weekend Chicken Barbecue.

Menu

*Honey Glazed Ham, page 59
*Scalloped Potatoes, page 129
 Green Beans with Almonds
*Basic Creamy Coleslaw, page 129
 Buttered Hot Rolls
 Homemade Ice Cream
 Cold Drinks

Buying Guide:

HAM: Allow ⅓ to ½ lb. per serving for boneless ham, ½ to ¾ lb. for bone-in hams. A fully cooked rolled or shaped ham can be cooked to a turn and served easily. You can even have your butcher slice and tie these hams ahead of time — and that means no carving!

GREEN BEANS: Fresh, frozen or canned can be used. Allow 3 to 4 oz. per serving — that's about ½ cup. For fresh green beans, you'll need to buy about 1½ lbs. for 6 servings; 3 lbs. for 12 servings and 5 to 6 lbs. for 24 servings. For frozen green beans two 10-oz. pkgs. serve 6; three 10-oz. pkgs. serve 12 and six 10-oz. pkgs. serve 24. Look for larger sized packages when serving groups — usually saves both money and time. For canned green beans, two 1-lb. cans serve 6; three 1-lb. cans serve 12 and six 1-lb. cans or one No. 10 can serves 24. Top with sliced or slivered almonds before serving.

BUTTERED HOT ROLLS: Allow 1½ to 2 rolls per person. Allow 1 lb. butter for 5 dozen rolls.

HOMEMADE ICE CREAM: Recipes for homemade ice cream in this book, pages 114-115, make 1 gallon. One gallon makes about 24 ⅔-cup servings.

COLD DRINKS: Take cold beverages in returnable bottles. Allow at least two bottles per person. Drink the cold beverages right from the bottle, so no cups or glasses are needed. A supply of straws would be a thoughtful gesture. For other cold drinks, such as fruit punch, lemonade or iced tea, 1½ qts. makes 6 servings; 3 qts. makes 12 servings and 1½ gal. makes 24 servings.

New neighbor "pitch-in-party"

Entertaining large groups costs — no doubt about it! But even if you're stretching dollars, you can share the fun of getting a group of friends together for a "pitch-in party" such as the one we planned to welcome new neighbors.

Even when everyone shares in supplying different parts of the menu, any party needs a host and hostess. You can fill that role!

There are a variety of ways to organize this kind of gathering. Easiest, of course, is simply "potluck". Most of us realize the disadvantages of this type of meal, especially for a group that's not too large. A better idea is to *plan* who brings what kind of dishes. Decide what you, as hosts, will provide for the party — drinks, meat, dessert or whatever.

For the barbecue in this plan, guests bring the meat of their choice plus one or two other dishes. Suggest possibilities for other dishes, but be flexible. Let each person exercise their own creativity. Even if Jan and Sara both bring a potato salad, chances are everyone will want to try each kind!

Whether you're hosting or attending a barbecue of this type, here are suggestions for some accompaniments you might provide:

SALADS:

Family Reunion Potato Salad, page 128
Red Pickled Potato Salad, page 92
Picnic Macaroni Bean Salad, page 93
Rice 'N Fruit Toss, page 94
Basic Creamy Coleslaw, page 129
Overnight Crisp Slaw, page 128
Celery Seed Coleslaw, page 93
Summertime Bean Salad, page 94
Creamy Lima Salad, page 94
Acapulco Pea Salad, page 95
Gelatin Salads
Tossed Salads

RELISHES:

Olives
Pickles — all kinds
Green onions
Radishes
Tomatoes, plain or vinaigrette
Cucumbers in sour cream or vinegar
Cauliflower
Carrots
Celery
Green pepper rings
Mushrooms
Confetti Corn Quickie, page 95

EGGS AND CHEESE:

Deviled Eggs
Cottage cheese

BREADS:

French bread
Rye bread
Pumpernickel bread
Cheesy Garlic Hot Roll Braid, page 102
Butterflake Herb Loaf, page 104
Tato Flake Cheese Buns, page 104
Onion Buns, page 105
Hard rolls
Smokey Barbecue Buns, page 103
One Step Supper Rolls, page 102
Cheese 'N Chili Corn Bread, page 103
Salted Bread Sticks

HOT DISHES:

DESSERTS:

Providing the beverage for the barbecue is usually assumed by the host. This is one of the big costs in entertaining, especially if you decide to serve liquor. Manning your own bar is one answer. That way you mix the drinks and have some control over the frequency with which they're served. Summer fruit drinks spiked with gin and rum are more economical than cocktails. Plenty of cold beer served right from an icy keg is another solution.

Chilled fruit-flavored wines mixed with carbonated beverages make refreshing summer drinks. Serve over ice in tall glasses; guests don't even need to know they contain no hard liquor!

Making coffee for a crowd is most easily done with a party-size electric urn. Many church or women's groups have one which you can probably borrow or consult the telephone book for rental equipment. Allow 1 lb. coffee for 40 cups. Consider using instant coffee, too. A 4-oz. jar plus 10 qts. of water makes 40 cups.

Iced tea is one of summer's most popular drinks. Brew extra strong hot tea. For 4 glasses, use 6 teaspoons tea (or 6 teabags) and 4 cups boiling water. Steep 5 minutes. Strain; add 1 quart fresh cold water. Pour over ice cubes and serve. Quantity can be doubled. For easier handling of tea, 4 regular teabags equals 1 *family-sized* tea bag. Loose tea can be tied in a cheese cloth bag to eliminate straining. IN A HURRY: Place 1 teaspoon instant tea in a tall glass. Fill three-fourths full with cold water. Add ice cubes.

To make 2 gallons, use a ¼-lb. package loose tea (16 *family-sized* tea bags); add 2 qts. boiling water. Prepare as directed. Add 6 qts. cold water.

If iced tea becomes cloudy, add a small amount of boiling water to clear — about ½ cup per quart. Many iced tea mixes in various sizes and flavors are available for making tea easily. These are handy for brewing a large quantity of tea, especially if away from home.

The sharing for this barbecue can include equipment and dishes, too! Small hibachis and portable grills were used for the steaks and hamburgers pictured below. Whatever sizes you use, it's a good idea to have enough grill space so that everyone eats at the same time.

Sturdy plates will be appreciated when it comes to eating steaks. Again, ask one of the neighbors for extra plates or glassware that you don't have or rent some.

FAMILY REUNION POTATO SALAD

Size of serving: ¾ cup

Ingredients	For 6 Servings	For 12 Servings	For 24 Servings
Diced cooked potatoes	4 cups (2 lbs.)	2 quarts (4 lbs.)	4 qts. (8 lbs.)
sliced celery	¾ cup	1½ cups	3 cups
hard cooked eggs, chopped	3	6	8
sliced radishes	⅓ cup	¾ cup	1½ cups
sliced green onions	4 (¼ cup)	1 small bunch (½ cup)	2 small bunches (1 cup)
salt	1 teaspoon	2 teaspoons	4½ teaspoons
pepper	Dash	⅛ teaspoon	¼ teaspoon
salad dressing	⅔ cup	1 cup	2 cups
prepared mustard	1 teaspoon	2 teaspoons	1 tablespoon
Yield	about 5 cups	about 2 quarts	4½ quarts

1. Combine potatoes, celery, eggs, radishes, onions and seasonings.
2. Combine salad dressing and mustard.
3. Add to potato mixture; mix lightly.
4. Chill.

Serving Suggestion: Line salad bowl with lettuce leaves; garnish with radish roses.

OVERNIGHT CRISP SLAW

Size of serving: ½ cup

Ingredients	For 6 Servings	For 12 Servings	For 24 Servings
Sugar	½ cup	1 cup	2 cups
celery salt	½ teaspoon	1 teaspoon	2 teaspoons
garlic salt	½ teaspoon	1 teaspoon	2 teaspoons
lemon juice	¼ cup	½ cup	1 cup (8 oz.)
vinegar	¼ cup	½ cup	1 cup (8 oz.)
shredded cabbage	1 small head	1 large head (2 lbs.)	4 lbs.
chopped celery	1 med. stalk	2 med. stalks	4 med. stalks
chopped green pepper	¼ cup	½ large (½ cup)	1 large
chopped green onions	2 (2 tablespoons)	4 (¼ cup)	1 small bunch
sliced radishes	¼ cup	8 to 10 (½ cup)	16 to 20 (1 cup)
Yield	3 cups	1½ quarts	3 quarts

1. Combine sugar, celery salt, garlic salt, lemon juice and vinegar.
2. Add to remaining ingredients except radishes; toss lightly.
3. Cover and chill overnight.
4. Just before serving, add radishes.

SCALLOPED POTATOES

Size of serving: ⅔ cup

Ingredients	For 6 Servings	For 12 Servings	For 24 Servings
thinly sliced raw potatoes	4 cups	8 cups (4 lbs.)	4 qts. (8 lbs.)
butter	¼ cup	½ cup (¼ lb.)	1 cup (½ lb.)
flour	¼ cup	½ cup	1 cup
salt	1 teaspoon	2 teaspoons	1 tablespoon
pepper	⅛ teaspoon	¼ teaspoon	½ teaspoon
milk	1¾ cups	1 qt.	2 qts.
Yield	1½-quart casserole or 8-inch square baking pan	one 13 x 9-inch baking pan	two 13 x 9-inch baking pans

1. Place potatoes in greased baking pan.
2. To make white sauce, melt butter in saucepan. Blend in flour, salt and pepper. Add milk. Stir and cook until thickened.
3. Cover potatoes with white sauce.
4. Bake, uncovered, at 350° 1½ to 2 hours until potatoes are tender.

Cheesy Onion Potatoes: Before baking, cover potatoes with shredded cheese and French fried onion rings (½ cup cheese and 1 can (3½ oz.) onion rings for 6; 1 cup cheese and 2 cans onion rings for 12; 2 cups cheese and 4 cans onion rings for 24.)

Butter Crumb Topped Potatoes: Before baking, cover potatoes with buttered bread crumbs. (½ cup for 6; 1 cup for 12; 2 cups for 24.)

Quick 'N Easy Scalloped Potatoes: Use Pillsbury's Scalloped Potato Mix. This will save time — no need to slice raw potatoes and measure ingredients. (1 package for 6; 2 packages for 12; 4 packages for 24.)

BASIC CREAMY COLESLAW

Size of serving: ⅔ cup

Ingredients	For 6 Servings	For 12 Servings	For 24 Servings
cabbage	1 small head	3 lbs.	6 lbs.
green onions	2	4	1 small bunch
sugar	1 tablespoon	2 tablespoons	¼ cup
salt	½ teaspoon	1 teaspoon	2 teaspoons
mayonnaise or salad dressing	½ cup	1 cup	2 cups (1 pt.)
vinegar	1 tablespoon	2 tablespoons	¼ cup
Yield	1 quart	2 quarts	4 quarts (1 gal.)

1. Shred cabbage; slice onions.
2. Combine remaining ingredients for dressing.
3. Just before serving, add dressing to cabbage; toss lightly.

Tip: For a crisp chilled coleslaw, heads of cabbage can be crisped in ice water before shredding, then chilled.

ZESTY PORK AND BEANS

Size of serving: ¾ cup

Ingredients	For 6 Servings	For 12 Servings	For 24 Servings
bacon	8 slices (⅓ lb.)	16 slices (⅔ lb.)	32 slices (1⅓ lbs.)
pork and beans in tomato sauce*	2 cans (1-lb. each)	4 cans (1-lb. each)	8 cans (1-lb. each)
brown sugar	½ cup	1 cup	2 cups
chopped onion**	¼ cup	½ cup	1 cup
leaf oregano	2 teaspoons	1 tablespoon	2 tablespoons
garlic salt	½ teaspoon	1 teaspoon	2 teaspoons
catsup	½ cup	1 cup (10-oz. bottle)	2 cups (1 lb. 4-oz. bottle)
Yield	1½-quart casserole	3-quart casserole	two 3-quart casseroles

*A 1-lb. can pork and beans contains 2 cups. Since several can sizes are available, use the can-size guide, next page, for additional help in choosing larger cans.

**Instant minced or frozen chopped onions can be used for fresh, see guide on page 21.

1. In fry pan, fry bacon until crisp; drain on paper towel. Reserve ¼ cup drippings for 6 servings (½ cup for 12; 1 cup for 24.)
2. Combine reserved drippings with remaining ingredients in casserole.
3. Sprinkle with crumbled bacon.
4. Bake at 350° for 25 to 30 minutes until bubbly and heated through.

LIGHT BAKED BEANS

Size of servings: ¾ cup

Ingredients	For 6 Servings	For 12 Servings	For 24 Servings
Great Northern or Navy beans	2 cups	3½ cups (1½ lbs.)	7 cups (3 lbs.)
boiling water	4 cups	1½ quarts (6 cups)	3 quarts (12 cups)
salt pork or bacon, cut into ½-inch pieces	½ lb.	¾ lb.	1½ lbs.
brown sugar	½ cup	¾ cup	1½ cups
chili sauce or catsup	¼ cup	⅓ cup	¾ cup
chopped onion	1 tablespoon	2 tablespoons	¼ cup
prepared mustard	1 tablespoon	1½ tablespoons	3 tablespoons
salt	1 teaspoon	1½ teaspoons	1 tablespoon
pepper	⅛ teaspoon	¼ teaspoon	⅜ teaspoon
Yield	1½-quart casserole	2½-or 3-quart casserole	two 3-quart casseroles

1. Wash beans. Cover with boiling water; let stand 1 hour or longer.
2. Add salt pork to beans in large saucepan. Cover; simmer until tender, about 1 hour.
3. Combine beans and liquid with remaining ingredients. Pour into casserole or bean pot.
4. Cover; bake at 350° 2½ to 3 hours until beans are completely tender, stirring occasionally and adding water, if necessary.
5. Remove cover during last 30 minutes of baking; do not stir.

BOSTON BAKED BEANS

Size of serving: ¾ cup

Ingredients	For 6 Servings	For 12 Servings	For 24 Servings
Great Northern or Navy beans	2 cups	3½ cups (1½ lbs.)	7 cups (3 lbs.)
water	4 cups	1½ quarts (6 cups)	3 quarts (12 cups)
salt pork, cut into ½-inch pieces	½ lb.	¾ lb.	1½ lbs.
molasses	½ cup	¾ cup	1½ cups
chopped onion	¼ cup	⅓ cup	¾ cup
brown sugar	2 tablespoons	3 tablespoons	¼ cup
dry mustard	2 teaspoons	1 tablespoon	2 tablespoons
salt	½ teaspoon	¾ teaspoon	1½ teaspoons
Yield	1 to 2-quart casserole	two 1½-quart casseroles or one 3-quart casserole	two 3-quart casseroles

1. Wash beans. Cover with water; let stand overnight.
2. Cover; simmer until tender, about 1 hour. Drain; reserve liquid.
3. Combine beans and salt pork in bean pot or casserole.
4. Add enough water to bean liquid to make 2 cups for 6 servings; 3 cups for 12; 4 cups (1 qt.) for 24. Combine with remaining ingredients. Pour over beans. Stir carefully.
5. Cover; bake at 300° 6 to 7 hours, stirring occasionally and adding water, if necessary.
6. Remove cover during last hour of baking; do not stir.

CAN SIZE GUIDE:

When preparing foods in quantity, it is sometimes easier to use larger can sizes than in the original recipe. The most common institutional can size is the No. 10 can which contains about 3 quarts. This amount is equal to that in seven 15½-oz. cans (No. 300); six 1-lb. cans (No. 303); five 1 lb. 4-oz. cans (No. 2); four 1 lb. 13-oz. cans (No. 2½) or two 46-oz. cans.

New England Clambake

The clambake — almost everyone has heard of that delectable feast, but fortunate are those who have actually partaken of such a delightful experience.

Modern technology has changed little of the ritual of assembling the clambake. First, round flat stones are collected to fill the shallow pit dug that morning for the occasion. An immense fire is built on top and carefully tended to ensure that the stones reach their maximum heating capacity. Meanwhile, the food is gathered, washed, and skillfully prepared for the steaming.

When all is ready and the stones are super hot, all rush to rake away the fire and a blanket of seaweed is laid atop the stones before they are allowed to lose any of their precious heat. Layers and layers of clams, onions, potatoes, corn, lobsters and other mouthwatering foods are piled on — appetites grow increasingly larger as aromatic smells continually escape from under the steaming tarpaulin which was spread over after the last ear of corn was tucked in. The waiting begins.

Finally someone lifts a corner of the 'tarp' to check the progress. The clams have opened! Like magic everyone suddenly surrounds the "bake," plate in hand, as the tarp is peeled away. The food is dished up, cupfuls of butter are passed around and all delve in, not wanting to be the last with the least.

With today's fast jets and modern refrigeration techniques, almost anyone, anywhere can have their own clambake as close as the nearest delicatessen grocery store. Even though you may have to order your supplies a few weeks in advance, New England wholesalers are able to supply you by air parcel post, the entire seafood package — steamer or quahog clams, lobsters and plenty of seaweed — enough for your own clambake.

1. Pry open the shell further if necessary. Grasp the clam and pull clam from shell.
2. Dip entire clam in butter.

We have listed three alternative methods depending on the facilities available to you and the number of people you wish to serve. We recommend you read through all directions before you begin as a few steps must be done the day before. Happy steaming!

About Clams

There are two types of clams which are generally found in clambakes — the hard-shell quahog clam and the soft-shell steamer. Both are best for steaming when they are small. Quahogs, especially, become tough when they get larger than 3 inches.

When preparing clams for steaming wash them several times and then leave in salt water for at least 12 hours to rid them of sand and any material in their stomachs.

If you do not dig your own clams, be very choosy when buying them in the store. Clams can live a long time out of water but once they die they spoil very quickly. Look for clams with their shells tightly closed. And reject any clams which do not open upon steaming.

To eat a clam, pry open the shell further to get a good grip on the clam. Pull forcefully to release the clam from the shell. Soft-shell clams have a black membrane around the neck which is often tough and should be discarded. The rest of the clam can be eaten, some prefer dipped in butter, to your enjoyment.

Handling the Lobster

Eating a whole lobster to retrieve every last bite and still looking graceful takes a little dexterity and a bit of practice. Start by breaking off the tail and claws. The claws will need to be cracked with a nutcracker to get at the delicious meat inside. The smaller tail pieces

1. After twisting the claw off the body, use a nutcracker to break the hard shell.
2. Snap the tail off the lobster, make a horizontal cut at the end of the tail and insert your thumb or other instrument to push the meat out in one piece.

on the end can be broken off and the meat sucked out. When ready to eat the larger meaty section, use a small knife and make a short cut in the underside by the tail section. Insert the thumb or other blunt narrow object into the slit and push meat out.

There are still edible portions to be found in the smaller claws, legs and main body. Use the nutcracker again on the smaller claws. Pull the legs off the body and suck out the meat inside as with a straw. The meat in the body can be removed easiest by peeling the outer shell away from the body. Some consider the lung membrane, red coral (eggs) and green liver as better parts of the lobsters, while others prefer not to eat any part of the main body. Use your own taste.

TRADITIONAL CLAMBAKE *15-20 servings*

4 bushels of seaweed (rockweed is best)
100 hard-shell or 200 soft-shell clams
40 ears of corn
20 lobsters
20 medium size potatoes
10 medium size onions

BEFORE GRILLING: The day before, scrub clams and cover with salt water (⅓ cup salt for each gallon of water) for at least 12 hours to rid them of sand and help to eliminate the material in their stomachs. Starting about 4 hours before eating time, dig a hole approximately 3 feet across and 1 foot deep. Line the hole with smooth round stones. (Be sure they have not been heated before.) Build a fire on the stones and keep it burning for 2½ to 3 hours to heat the stones thoroughly. Feed the fire often. Gather and wash seaweed. Soak in salt water for at least 45 minutes. Husk all but the inside layer on the corn. Remove the silk but make sure the last layer of husks still protects the corn. Save outer husks for laying on the bake. Scrub potatoes and lobsters. Peel onions, and if large, quarter them; otherwise leave onions whole.

3. Break off each leg and suck the meat out like a straw.
4. Pull back the shell to get at the main body organs.

ON THE GRILL: When all food is ready for the bake, rake away the fire. Quickly cover stones with a layer of seaweed, about 6 inches deep. Start layering the foods beginning with the clams, then add the potatoes, onions, lobster and corn. Cover the foods with the corn husks and another layer of seaweed. Sprinkle the entire mound with a bucket of water. Quickly cover with a wet tarp that extends the pit area by at least 1 foot. Weigh tarp down on the edges with stones. Steam for about 1 hour. To test for doneness, lift tarp carefully at one corner. If the clams are opened, that is a good sign the rest of the food is done. Serve with salt, lemon, and lots of melted butter.

If you do not wish to dig up your back yard and are planning on serving fewer people, here are two alternative methods of approximating the traditional Clambake.

"GARBAGE CAN" CLAMBAKE

6-8 servings

2 bushels seaweed
80 soft-shell, or 40 hard-shell clams
16 ears of corn
8 lobsters
8 medium size potatoes
8 medium size onions

BEFORE GRILLING: Heat enough stones to heavily layer the bottom of your can. Prepare foods as in the traditional clambake.

ON THE GRILL: Place hot stones in the bottom of your can, and layer with 6 inches of seaweed. Layer the foods beginning with the clams, add potatoes, onion, lobsters and corn. Top with corn husks and additional seaweed. Cover can tightly with lid and allow to steam about 1 hour. When clams have opened the food should be ready.

Tip: To do on the grill or stove top, half the ingredients. Clean and prepare foods as in traditional method. Line bottom of wash boiler or very large metal kettle with a layer of seaweed. Add 2 quarts water to kettle. Place kettle on very hot grill. Bring water to boil. Drop in potatoes and onions and cook, covered, for 30 minutes. Add corn, lobsters and clams last. Continue steaming, covered for an additional 15 to 20 minutes until clams open.

Texan Barbecue

Probably the greatest feature of the Texan Barbecue is the mounds of food. Texans, known for their generosity, have no limits in the quantity of food — just keep it coming! More often than not there is more than one main dish which guests may choose from, however, most try it all.

Menu

*Barbecued Brisket
 Polish Sausage
*Citrus Honey Barbecued Chicken, page 67
*Basic Creamy Coleslaw, page 129
*Family Reunion Potato Salad, page 128
 Beef and Bean Supper Dish
*Sourdough Biscuits
 Baking Powder Biscuits
 Cornbread
*Southern Pecan Pie
 Watermelon

BARBECUED BRISKET

8 to 12 servings

  4-6 lbs. fresh brisket
  1 bay leaf
  1½ teaspoons salt
  1 teaspoon peppercorns

Barbecue Glaze

  ½ cup chili sauce or catsup
  1 tablespoon prepared mustard
  1 tablespoon vinegar
  1 tablespoon Worcestershire sauce
  ½ teaspoon chili powder

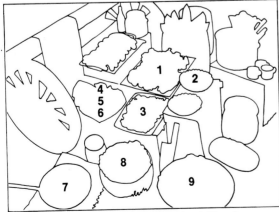

1. Citrus Honey
   Barbecued Chicken
2. Southern Pecan Pie
3. Barbecued Brisket
4. Cornbread
5. Sourdough Biscuits
6. Baking Powder Biscuits
7. Beef and Bean Supper Dish
8. Family Reunion Potato Salad
9. Basic Creamy Coleslaw

BEFORE GRILLING: Put brisket in large covered pot or Dutch oven. Add enough water to cover brisket. Add bay leaf, salt and peppercorns. Simmer 3 to 3½ hours.

BARBECUE GLAZE: Combine all ingredients.

ON THE GRILL. Place brisket on the grill 4 to 6 inches away from hot coals. Basting brisket with barbecue glaze occasionally, cook 45 to 60 minutes.

Tips: Cooked brisket may be barbecued in oven. Preheat oven to 350°. Spread barbecue glaze on cooked brisket and bake, uncovered, 45 to 60 minutes, basting occasionally with pan juices.

Brisket may be cooked the day ahead and refrigerated until ready to use. Increase barbecuing time by about 30 minutes.

SOURDOUGH STARTER

This Sourdough is made from a combination of milk and flour. As the mixture sours, yeast develops in the milk's natural sugar, giving off carbon dioxide bubbles which cause products to rise and be light.

To make your starter, place one cup milk in a small crock or jar. Let stand at room temperature about 24 hours. Stir in 1 cup flour and let stand, uncovered, 2 to 4 days or until bubbles begin to form. Cover and keep refrigerated. This makes about 1½ cups starter.

Each time you use a portion of starter, leave at least ½ cup remaining and replenish it by adding equal amounts of flour and milk. If you use 1 cup starter for a recipe, add about 1 cup flour and 1 cup milk; if you use ½ cup, add ½ cup each flour and milk. Let the starter stand, covered, at room temperature 8 to 12 hours. Then, return to the refrigerator.

The starter needs to be replenished about every 10 days to keep the yeast alive and active. When not replenished at this frequency, the yeast may absorb all the sugar and perish from lack of food. If this happens, discard at least half the starter and add ½ to 1 cup milk and flour and let stand, covered, overnight. Refrigerate until ready to use.

The starter can be used alone as the leavening or in combination with yeast or soda. Additional yeast helps yeast breads rise faster as the sourdough works very slowly in the stiff breads. Often soda is added to help the leavening process. Soda also neutralizes the flavor; so the more added, the less sour the finished bread tastes.

SOURDOUGH BISCUITS

12 to 16 Biscuits

½ cup sourdough starter
2 cups unsifted Pillsbury flour*
1 cup milk
1 tablespoon sugar
1 teaspoon baking powder
½ teaspoon salt
½ teaspoon soda
¼ cup butter, margarine or oil

The night before baking, combine starter, 1 cup of flour and milk; mix until smooth. Cover and let stand overnight or about 8 hours. Next morning, add remaining 1 cup flour, sugar, baking powder, salt and soda to sourdough mixture and mix until dough clings together. (if necessary, add additional flour.) Knead 10 to 12 times on floured surface. Roll pat dough to ½ to ¾-inch thickness. Cut biscuits with biscuit cutter. Melt butter in 8 or 9-inch square or 9-inch round pan. Place biscuits in baking pan, turning to coat with butter. Cover and let rise in warm place about 30 minutes or until light. Bake in preheated 375° oven 25 to 30 minutes or until golden brown.

> **Tips:** Recipe may easily be halved, baking in 8-inch pie pan.
> If desired, use up to half whole grain flour.

BEEF AND BEAN SUPPER DISH

4 to 6 servings

1 lb. ground beef
1 medium onion, sliced
½ teaspoon salt
¼ teaspoon pepper
3¼ cups (1 lb. 12-oz. can) pork and beans
½ cup catsup
2 tablespoons brown sugar
½ tablespoon Worcestershire sauce
1 tablespoon vinegar
¼ teaspoon Tabasco sauce

In large fry pan, brown ground beef and onion, stirring occasionally; drain excess fat.

Add remaining ingredients; mix well. Simmer, covered, 20 to 30 minutes or until flavors are well blended.

> **Tip:** If desired, Beef and Bean Supper Dish may be served as a sandwich filling on buns.
> Recipe may be doubled for larger groups.

Make sure your guests save room for this finale to your barbecue. It is a rich, filling dessert but one that nobody would want to miss.

SOUTHERN PECAN PIE

6 to 8 servings

9-inch unbaked pastry shell
4 eggs
1¼ cups dark corn syrup
⅓ cup brown sugar
½ tablespoon flour
1¼ teaspoons vanilla
¼ cup butter or margarine
1 cup chopped pecans*

Preheat oven to 350°. Prepare unbaked pastry shell. In large mixing bowl, combine eggs, corn syrup, brown sugar, flour and vanilla; beat well. Melt butter; add to egg mixture along with pecans. Pour into pastry shell. Bake until center of pie is puffed and golden brown. Cool. Serve plain or with whipped cream or ice cream.

> **Tips:** Pecan pie may be frozen, but is best if reheated at 350° for 15 minutes during or after thawing.
> Light corn syrup can be used for dark corn syrup, but the flavor will be milder and less rich.
> If desired, add ½ to 1 cup drained, crushed pineapple, semisweet chocolate pieces or chopped dates with pecans.
> For a more decorative topping, use pecan halves instead of chopped pecans. Mix filling according to directions, omitting pecans. Pour into pie shell and arrange pecan halves on top.

Midwest Harvest Feast

Lucky is the hunter who returns bountifully laden with tantalizing wild game. And the Midwest provides ample opportunity with its grain fields and lush forests. Only one note of caution: wild game does not have the layer of fat domestically raised animals do and, thus, must be treated with special care on the grill. We suggest covering the game with a pseudo layer of salt pork that protects the meat from the drying heat and adds a subtle flavor. Frequent basting can also help save the precious juices.

Menu
*Cucumber in Vinegar and Oil
*Corn Relish
*Roast Goose
*Wild Rice Casserole
*Baked Acorn Squash
*Pumpkin-Eggnog Pie

CUCUMBERS IN VINEGAR AND OIL
5 to 6 servings

- ½ cup oil
- 1 cup vinegar
- 2¼ tablespoons sugar
- 1 teaspoon salt
- ¼ teaspoon pepper
- 2 cucumbers, thinly sliced
- 2 small onions, thinly sliced

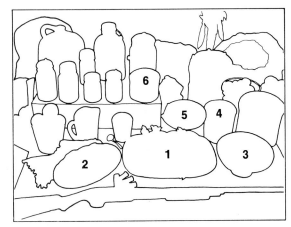

1. Roast Goose
2. Maple Flavored Acorn Squash
3. Pumpkin-Nog Pie
4. Cucumbers in Vinegar and Oil
5. Wild Rice Casserole
6. Corn Relish

In a bowl combine all ingredients. Cover and chill 1 to 2 hours.

Tip: Prepared onion dressing and a little salt make a good marinade for cucumbers.

CORN RELISH
2½ cups Relish

- 2 cups (1-lb. can) drained whole kernel corn
- ⅓ cup pickle relish
- ⅓ cup chopped pimiento
- ⅓ cup chopped green pepper
- ¼ cup sugar
- 1 small onion, chopped
- ¼ cup vinegar
- 1 teaspoon cornstarch
- ½ teaspoon celery seed
- 1 tablespoon prepared mustard

In saucepan, combine all ingredients, mixing well. Cook, stirring occasionally, until mixture comes to a boil and thickens slightly. Cool before serving. Store, covered, in refrigerator for 2 to 3 weeks.

Tips: For longer storage, fill jars to within ½ inch of top with hot relish; seal with vacuum-seal lids.

Fresh corn can be used for canned; cover, bring to boil and simmer about 5 minutes.

ROAST GOOSE
5 to 6 servings

- 8 lb. gosling
- ½ cup honey
- ¼ cup butter, melted
- salt, pepper

BEFORE GRILLING: If using a domestic goose, sprinkle cavities with salt and pepper and, if desired, fill loosely with favorite dressing. Allow 1 cup of dressing for each pound of goose. If using a wild goose, which is low in fat content, fill as directed with favorite dressing. Cover goose with slices of salt pork about ¼-inch thick, or thick sliced fat bacon.

Be sure to cover all parts of the bird, paying special attention to the surfaces which are highly exposed. Tie in place with kitchen string.

ON THE GRILL: Arrange coals for roasting meat; use method B, page 5. Center meat on grill with drip pan in place. Cover. Roast over slow fire, about 6 inches from coals until meat thermometer registers 190° internal temperature. During last ½ hour of cooking baste liberally with honey-butter sauce (remove fat strips from wild goose).

> **Tips:** Goose can be roasted as directed in 350° oven.
>
> For the most tender roast goose, it is very important that your bird be no more than 1 year old. If in doubt, do not barbecue, but braise in the conventional method.

WILD RICE CASSEROLE

5 to 6 servings

    1¼ cups wild rice
     3 cups water
     2 teaspoons salt
     ½ cup (4-oz. can) drained sliced
        mushrooms
     1 medium onion, sliced
     2 tablespoons butter or margarine
     ½ teaspoon leaf thyme

Preheat over to 350°. Wash rice. In 2-quart casserole, combine all ingredients. Cover and bake 1¼ to 1½ hours or until rice is tender, stirring occasionally during last half hour.

> **Tip:** For the fluffiest rice, soak rice in water several hours or overnight before cooking as directed.

MAPLE-FLAVORED ACORN SQUASH

5 to 6 servings

     3 small acorn squash
     6 tablespoons butter
     6 strips of bacon, cut in 3 pieces each
     6 tablespoons maple-flavored syrup
        or brown sugar

BEFORE GRILLING: Wash squash and cut in half lengthwise. Scoop out seeds with tablespoon. Wrap each squash half individually in foil, sealing tightly.

ON THE GRILL: Place squash cut side up either directly on the coals or on a close grill. Bake 45 to 60 minutes or until squash is fork tender. Meanwhile, partially fry bacon pieces. Remove squash from grill and open foil. Place one tablespoon of butter, one tablespoon of maple-flavored syrup or brown sugar and three pieces of bacon in each half. Place squash back on grill, with foil open on top, for another 15 minutes. Be careful not to tip the squash, allowing the butter to run out.

> **Tip:** To bake in your oven, preheat oven to 400°. Prepare squash as directed. Place squash cut side down on baking sheet. Bake 40 to 60 minutes until tender. Turn squash halves right side up and fill each half with remaining ingredients. Bake 10 to 15 minutes longer.

PUMPKIN-NOG PIE

5 to 6 servings

        9-inch unbaked pastry shell
     ½ teaspoon pumpkin pie spice
     2 eggs
     1 can (1 lb. 2 oz.) pumpkin pie mix*
     1 cup prepared egg nog

Egg Nog Topping

     ½ cup (1 envelope) whipped topping mix
     ¼ cup milk
     ¼ cup prepared egg nog
     1 teaspoon vanilla

OVEN 400°

Prepare 9-inch unbaked pastry shell, adding ½ teaspoon pumpkin pie spice to flour mixture. In large mixing bowl, combine eggs, pumpkin pie filling and egg nog. Beat until thoroughly blended. Pour into unbaked pastry shell. Bake at 400° for 45 to 50 minutes until knife comes out clean when inserted near center. Cool. Just before serving, spoon Egg Nog Topping around edge of pie.

Egg Nog Topping: In small mixer bowl, combine all ingredients. Beat at medium speed until peaks form.

> **Tip:** *This is the pumpkin pie mix with sugar and spices added; you add eggs and liquid.

Colorado Picnic

Crisp mountain air and a cool rushing stream provide unforgettable memories, but even in your back yard you can duplicate the camping scene. Have your party a Sunday morning brunch outdoors, since who can resist a fresh trout and potato fry? We've selected meal accompaniments to enhance the outdoor atmosphere. And don't forget this menu when you are really out enjoying the wilds.

Menu
* Wild Green Toss Salad
* Cheese Stuffed Trout
* Quick Potato Browns
* Herb Toast
* Fresh Fruit Shortcake

WILD GREEN TOSS SALAD

That "something different" for your next salad could be in your back yard or the field across the way. We've listed a few greens that grow wild but are common throughout the country. On your next camping trip, save a little space and leave the lettuce head at home. Your salad is out there waiting for you.

Dandelion greens — Leaves are best when young and tender. Wash thoroughly after picking, discarding wilted or bruised leaves, and trim off any clinging roots.

Asparagus — grow both wild and in cultivated gardens. The wild ones are found often near streams and springs. Look for the tiny spears poking up in the early spring (they become woody by summer). Cut spears with a sharp knife just below soil level when they are 2 to 3 inches tall. Use them raw for a crunchy addition.

Daisies — are often considered weeds in many lawns, but the tender young leaves have a celery-like flavor that can spark up any salad.

Watercress — is found growing in the water where springs bubble up. Although quite tart, you will be pleased with the taste it adds to your salad.

Combine the greens you wish, alone or mixed with torn lettuce. Serve lightly tossed with a simple vinegar and oil dressing (¼ cup vinegar, ½ cup oil, ¼ teaspoon salt, dash pepper) to enhance the green flavors.

There is nothing like fresh fish frying to perk up an appetite. The delicate flavor of trout is enhanced by the hint of onion in the stuffing.

CHEESE STUFFED TROUT
4 to 5 servings

> ½ cup sliced fresh mushrooms
> ¼ cup chopped green onion or fresh white onion
> 2 tablespoons Parmesan cheese
> 2 lbs. whole trout

BEFORE GRILLING: Spoon onion, mushrooms and cheese into cavity of fish as stuffing. Season with salt and pepper. Secure with toothpicks or metal nails (as used on a stuffed turkey).

ON THE GRILL: Broil or grill over hot coals about 8 minutes per side until fish flakes.

> **Tips:** Fish fillets can be used for whole fish. Coat fillets with flour or pancake mix. Saute onion and mushrooms in small amount of fat until slightly tender; push to side of skillet. Add fillets and fry until fish flakes. Serve fillets topped with onion and mushrooms; sprinkle with Parmesan cheese just before serving.
>
> To prepare in skillet, stuff fish and dip in flour. Fry in small amount of hot fat.

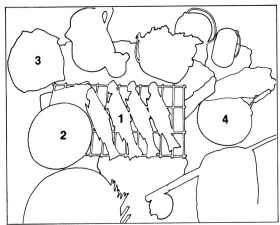

1. Cheese Stuffed Trout 3. Herbed French Bread
2. Quick Potato Browns 4. Fresh Fruit Shortcake

A super fast way to have fried potatoes without fuss. Great to take camping, for an early morning breakfast.

QUICK POTATO BROWNS
3 to 4 servings

2 tablespoons butter or margarine
2 cups (15-oz. can) drained small
    whole potatoes
½ teaspoon salt
Dash pepper
1 medium onion, sliced

In medium fry pan, brown potatoes in butter over medium heat, seasoning with salt and pepper during cooking. (Since canned potatoes are already cooked, all they need is browning.) Add onion near end of browning. Continue cooking until tender. Serve hot.

Tips: If desired, garnish with chopped parsley, dill weed or toasted sesame seeds.

For Quick Home Fries or Hash Browns, slice or chop potatoes before frying.

Leftover, boiled potatoes may be used for canned potatoes.

HERBED FRENCH BREAD

1 loaf French bread
1 pkg. dry Italian salad dressing mix
¼ cup butter, melted

BEFORE GRILLING: Cut slices diagonally one inch apart in French loaf, nut cutting quite through bottom of bread. Combine butter and salad dressing mix. Spreading slices apart slightly, brush melted butter mixture on each slice. Wrap entire loaf in foil, pinching edges tightly to seal.

ON THE GRILL: Place loaf on the grill about 6 inches away from coals. Turning once or twice to prevent scorching, heat 20 to 30 minutes until bread is warmed through.

Tip: Bread can be heated in 350° oven for 20 minutes.

Light, tender, and delicious warm or cold, this is the ultimate for any ending to a barbecue feast. Any favorite fruit goes well—strawberries, raspberries, blueberries or peaches, to name a few.

FRESH FRUIT SHORTCAKE
6 to 8 servings

2 cups unsifted Pillsbury flour*
⅓ cup sugar
1 tablespoon (3 tsp.) baking powder
½ teaspoon salt
½ cup butter, margarine or shortening
¾ cup milk
2 eggs, slightly beaten

Preheat oven to 375°. In mixing bowl, combine flour with sugar, baking powder and salt. Cut in butter until crumbly. Combine milk and eggs. Add to dry ingredients all at once; stir until all dry particles are moistened. Spread dough in greased 9-inch round or 8-inch square pan. Bake 25 to 30 minutes or until golden brown. Serve warm, split and filled with sweetened fruit and whipped cream. Or, cut into wedges or squares and split; fill and top with sweetened fruit and whipped cream.

Tips: Recipe may be halved using 3 tablespoons sugar. Bake in greased 8-inch round pan 20 to 25 minutes. Or, make 4 individual shortcakes.

For INDIVIDUAL SHORTCAKES, drop dough by rounded tablespoonfuls 2 inches apart on greased baking sheet. Bake at 450° for 10 to 20 minutes or until golden brown.

*With self-rising flour, omit baking powder and salt.

Hawaiian Luau

One of the finest symbols of hospitality is the Luau which has been a feast of celebration to the Pacific islanders for generations. The Kalua pig is always the center of attraction surrounded by several kinds of fruit, steamed rice and a great assortment of finger foods. If your guest list and budget do not support the purchase of a pig, we have provided an alternative pork loin recipe. But whatever your main course, remember, fruits, flowers, palms and drinks all provide the little touches that make a super party!

Menu

* Hot Bacon Appetizers
  Island Fruit Salad
* Roast Suckling Pig
* Almond Currant Rice
  Baked Sweet Potatoes
* Minty Fruit Ice

How could something this simple be that good? Assemble these in advance and refrigerate to allow the marinade to permeate. Pop on the grill (or into the oven) just before the guests arrive.

HOT BACON PINEAPPLE APPETIZERS

25 to 40 appetizers

6 to 10 servings
  1 lb. sliced bacon
  1 fresh pineapple
    Hawaiian, Casino or Catalina
    salad dressing

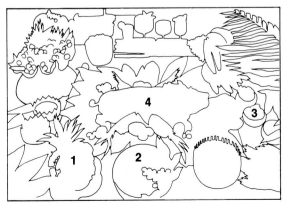

1. Hot Bacon Pineapple Appetizers
2. Quick Almond Currant Rice
3. Minty Fruit Ice
4. Suckling Pig

BEFORE GRILLING: Partially cook bacon strips; drain. Cut cooked bacon slices in half. Cut pineapple into bite size chunks. Wrap each pineapple chunk with a half-slice of bacon. Secure with wooden pick. Dip in salad dressing and marinate in refrigerator for ½ hour to 8 hours if desired.

ON THE GRILL: Arrange appetizers on skewers, place on rack over hot coals and grill 3 to 5 minutes until bacon is crisp, turning once. Baste with more dressing if desired. Serve hot.

> **Tip:** Appetizers can be baked in preheated 400° oven for 5 minutes or until bacon is crisp.

SUCKLING PIG

  18-20 lb. suckling pig
    Salt
    Pepper
  1 cup honey
  ½ cup butter
  ¼ cup soy sauce

BEFORE GRILLING: Order a whole pig from your butcher. Be sure to have him clean the pig, remove eyes and prepare it for the oven. Season the pig inside with salt and pepper. Make basting sauce by heating honey, butter and soy sauce together in small sauce pan until butter melts.

ON THE GRILL: Arrange coals for roasting meat; use method B, page 5. Center pig on grill with drip pan in place. Insert thermometer in thickest portion of meat. Cover. Roast over slow fire until thermometer registers 140°. Continue roasting, basting about every 15 minutes with sauce. Thermometer should read 170° when pig is done. Allow about 30 minutes per pound.

Toasted almonds and plump currants peek out from the heaping pile of snowy white rice, adding color and an intriguing flavor addition.

QUICK ALMOND CURRANT RICE

4 servings

>   2 cups quick-cooking rice
>   2 tablespoons butter or margarine
>   ¼ teaspoon salt
>   ¼ cup diced roasted almonds
>   ¼ cup currants

Prepare rice as directed on package, adding butter and salt. Just before serving, stir in almonds and currants.

>   **Tips:** If desired, ¼ cup chopped almonds that have been browned in 1 tablespoon butter or margarine can be used for the diced roasted almonds.
>
>   Regular, processed or converted white rice may be used in place of the quick-cooking rice. Use ⅓ cups regular rice and cook as directed on package. Proceed with remaining directions.
>
>   Raisins may be substituted for currants.

A refreshing ending to a filling meal, sherbet makes a pretty dessert any time. Use your imagination with garnishes and serving dishes.

MINTY FRUIT ICE

4 servings

>   4 slices pineapple
>   1 pint (2 cups) lemon sherbet
>   ¼ cup mint jelly

Place pineapple slice or ring in individual bowls or dishes. Top with ½ cup sherbet and 1 tablespoon jelly. Serve cold. If desired garnish with mint leaf.

>   **Tips:** Other flavors of sherbet can be used. We particularly like lime and raspberry.
>
>   Creme de Menthe may be used in place of mint jelly. Drizzle over sherbet just before serving.

Served on a platter covered with ti leaves and surrounded by mounds of fresh fruit, this could be an excellent substitution to the traditional pig. Allow at least one chop per person.

BARBECUED PORK LOIN

12 to 16 servings

>   8 lbs. boneless pork loin roast
>   Salt
>   Pepper

Barbecue Sauce

>   ½ cup (1 medium) chopped onion
>   1 clove garlic, minced or ⅛ teaspoon instant minced garlic
>   2 tablespoons oil or shortening
>   1 cup catsup
>   ½ cup water
>   ¼ cup firmly packed brown sugar
>   1 teaspoon salt
>   ¼ teaspoon crushed leaf thyme
>   3 tablespoons Worcestershire sauce
>   2 teaspoons prepared mustard
>   1 lemon, thinly sliced
>   Dash Tabasco sauce

BEFORE GRILLING: Sprinkle meat with salt and pepper. Prepare barbecue sauce by sauteing onion and garlic in oil in fry pan until tender. Add remaining ingredients. Bring to a boil and simmer for 5 minutes.

ON THE GRILL. Run spit through center of meat, making sure it is evenly balanced. Secure to rotisserie with heavy cord. Insert meat thermometer so tip is in center of roast but not resting in fat or on rod. Arrange coals for roasting meat; use method B, page 5. Grill over hot coals for 2 hours until meat thermometer reaches 140°. Continue grilling, brushing with Barbecue Sauce every 20 minutes, until roast reaches 170° internal temperature, about 1½ to 2 hours longer.

Barbecuing Units

BARBECUING UNITS

As you have probably realized by now, the variety of barbecuing units available on the market is endless. If you have not already purchased a unit or if you are considering purchasing a new unit, there are some basic points you should consider:

How much food do you generally barbecue at one time—this will determine the size unit you should buy. If you serve a large number of people or your entire meal is prepared on the grill you will probably want to invest in a larger unit than if you only plan to do hamburgers for the family.

Where do you do most of your cooking—an electric rotisserie would be of little value to you on a hiking trail.

Where will you be storing your unit—there are collapsible models available if you are limited for space.

How much are you willing to spend—the cost varies considerably, however, we suggest avoiding the cheap, poorly constructed units, no matter what you budget. You will want your unit to last more than one summer.

Before you buy, examine a wide variety of units since each have their own advantages and disadvantages. We briefly cover the basics of the more popular units available on the following pages, but only by close evaluation and comparison can you make a wise investment to last you many years.

THE SMALLER PORTABLES

These are terrific for broiling hamburgers for a family, steak for two or three, or appetizers for a crowd. One of the most popular of these smaller units are the hibachis. They are usually made of cast iron or aluminum and generally have a grill which can be adjusted to a few different heights. Hibachis often come with a double cooking surface. This allows the chef to cook two different foods at one time or one large piece of food when fires are lit in both compartments.

Although hibachis can be very heavy for their size they are still very portable and small enough to store and be transported easily.

The other most common portable grill is the scaled down version of the barbecue brasier. They are lighter than hibachis and their "foldability" makes them one of the easiest units to carry and store.

Almost all types of these small portables are table-top models. If you are seriously considering this type of unit be sure you will be cooking dinners for only a few people or you will have your guests eating in shifts. Their greatest assets are portability and cost.

THE TYPICAL BRASIER

These are lightweight floor models with three or four legs, and two wheels for easy transport. The simplest brasier is just a shallow bowl with a grid on top. This is more than adequate for simple broiling of fish, steaks, hamburgers, and pieces of poultry. Since they are larger than the hibachis they can service more people and grill more food at one time. If your cooking gets more sophisticated later on, many units can be fitted with optional adjustable grills, half hoods, wind screens and rotisseries. Check to see if the model you are interested in is easy to assemble and disassemble if you plan on frequently carting your grill to places other than your own back yard.

THE COVERED GRILL

These units are becoming increasingly popular as barbecue chefs experiment beyond the usual steak and hamburger routine. With dampers to control the temperature, cooking roasts and other larger pieces of food becomes easier, and the efficient heat control provides a kitchen on wheels—grill, broiler, oven and smoker all in one unit.

The kettle shaped model is one of the more popular covered barbecues and also one of the more inexpensive (as far as covered units are concerned). They are designed with a damper on the bottom and one on the top dome lid. These dampers can be opened to raise the heat or closed to lower it. The reflective heat provided by the dome roasts and browns the top of the meat in much the same way an oven does.

Another variation is the covered box which can be found on wagons or in a permanent type installation. These are generally one of the largest barbecue units available. Their size and features also make them one of the most expensive units on the market, but their versatility is unlimited. Most are equipped with grill thermometers mounted on the dome so there is no guesswork involved in roasting. The grills and fire grates can be raised and lowered to control the temperature as well as the use of dampers. Some units come equipped with a built in electric fire starter, and some have fire doors to allow more fuel to be added without letting any precious heat escape.

Look for units made with heavy metal that can withstand high temperatures. Many brands of both the kettle and wagon models have optional equipment—specially designed food racks, extra grills, shish-kabob cookers, even a wok for the kettle unit—that allows you to expand their use as needed. A wise investment for the serious barbecue chef.

GAS AND ELECTRIC UNITS

Continually growing in popularity, mainly because of their easy maintenance, these units are also more economical to use than the conventional barbecue units. And despite what some traditionalists try to argue, they do indeed give a definite barbecue flavor to the foods cooked on them. All gas and many electric units use their fuel source to heat a layer of volcanic or ceramic rocks which then radiate the heat to the food. The drippings from the food flare and smoke on the rocks, giving the food its barbecue look and flavor. Some other electric units have only the coils under a heavy metal grill. Both methods produce an evenness in heat unobtainable by the charcoal method.

When purchasing a gas grill look for the American Gas Association (AGA) certification or look for the Underwriter's Laboratory (UL) seal of approval when purchasing an electric grill. They are your assurance that the unit complies with national safety standards.

The gas and electric barbecue grills have another advantage over the charcoal grilling method as they can be hot and ready to cook on in a mere 10 minutes. They are also excellent for indoor barbecuing since they require a less powerful ventilating system.

Their main disadvantages are cost and portability. If you plan on doing a lot of barbecuing away from home keep in mind you may also be far away from gas or electric sources. There are a few gas models which use a tank of LP gas, however, most models are designed for permanent installation.

Handy Utensils

A quick glance through your local department store should convince you there are innumerable tools and utensils available to today's barbecue. Which ones to buy? That is a question only you can answer. Think about how often do you barbecue. Is it just for the family or do you serve a large number of guests? What types of food do you most often cook? Are ribs your specialty; if so, a rib rack might be just the answer to your needs. Where do you barbecue — on the patio with electrical outlets in easy reach or do you prefer a lonely stretch on a sandy beach?

Only by careful analysis can you choose the right equipment to suit your needs and budget. (Very few tools are needed if they are well-chosen.) With some preplanning, you can achieve the optimum in convenience with the least strain on the pocketbook and help make your barbecuing the fun experience it should be.

We have listed for you some of the more widely used utensils. The first *three* are those which are considered to be essential to most barbecues, even the more primitive. The others are designed for special tasks. Choose among them to suit your purposes.

TONGS — are much preferred over forks for the handling of meat and vegetables. Forks pierce the food, allowing precious juices to escape. The well-equipped outdoor cook has two pair — one for foods, the other for arranging coals. Long handled ones are best for keeping hands away from direct heat.

BASTING BRUSHES — are convenient to have in two sizes, a small one for kabobs, fish and appetizers and a larger one for steaks, roasts and other main course foods. The special long-handled barbecue basters are nice. However, a good paint brush (one without plastic bristles) makes an excellent baster at often less cost. Cotton or sponge dish mops make good daubers for large surfaces.

Choose a basting brush large enough to give quick coverage to a surface without being so large it spatters the sauce all over the grill causing waste, mess and flame flareups.

ALUMINUM FOIL — is the tool with the greatest versatility. Its uses are limited only by the imagination of the user and the emergency needs. Remember, there is a shiny and a dull side to foil. The shiny side reflects the heat — always keep it facing the food.

- Lining the grill (with the shiny side up) helps to reflect the heat toward the food and aids in coal cleanup, not to mention a cleaner grill.

- Wrapping foods in foil acts as a steamer. If you do not wish to have a crisp and charred surface on your foods, wrap in foil when cooking (keeping the shiny side in). The foil helps keep the moisture from escaping. Keep in mind that the foil does not protect your food permanently. Check food occasionally and turn often to prevent burning especially with food placed directly on the coals and those which must remain on the grill for long periods of time. If you find your foil wrapped food cooking faster than the rest of your dinner, you may remove from the coals without unwrapping and later return to heat.

- Foil makes an excellent disposable drip pan. Using heavy-duty foil, tear off a piece twice the length of your roast plus 12 more inches. Fold the foil in half the short way, making a double thickness. Turn up all four edges 1½ inches, pinching the corners to the sides of the pan to hold in all drips.

- To make a wind break, fasten a band of foil completely around the grill edge. This also helps to reflect the heat.

- Don't have a covered cooker? Cover your cooker with a sheet of extra wide heavy-duty foil allowing for a few spaces for air to keep the fire going.

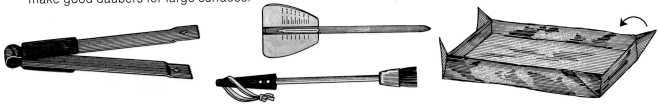

- When camping or picnicking away from home, always bring a roll of aluminum foil. It can substitute for many a forgotten utensil and save the meal from disaster. Many cooks have fashioned sauce pans, griddles and fry pans from foil in an emergency.

WATERING BOTTLE — is needed for those times when excess dripping from fat or marinade causes a flare-up. We found clothes sprinklers or spray bottles to work very satisfactorily. Just aim at the flare-up spot, being careful not to wet the food. Usually, only one or two squirts will be sufficient as you do not want the coals to lose their heat.

PAPER TOWELS — are almost as indispensable as aluminum foil for helping out in a crisis. Wet paper towels wrapped around freshly husked ears of corn before they are wrapped in foil will help keep the corn juicy while it is cooking. And of course, wet or dry, they speed up clean-up.

THERMOMETERS — are even more of a necessity cooking outdoors than indoors, as charcoaling heat may vary considerably. They are the only way you can be sure your roast is done to your desired perfection.

There are basically two types of thermometers to be used in barbecuing. The grill and spit thermometers can tell you the temperature at the height your rack or spit is at. They are the most accurate way of deciding if you are the correct level for fast or slow cooking. The second type is a meat thermometer — the same type as used in oven roasting. To test the doneness of your roast insert the thermometer into the thickest portion of the meat, making sure the bulb of the thermometer doesn't rest in either a fat portion or on bone.

ASBESTOS MITTS — are flame proof padded mitts than can save many a hand from unnecessary burns and pain. Although there are many styles and colors to choose from, we would strongly urge you to purchase a pair specifically labelled as asbestos (usually recognized by the silver metallic color). An accidental brush directly on the coals could burn a hole in an everyday cloth mitt.

BASKET GRILLS AND HINGED BROILERS — are best used with smaller pieces of meat and foods which require frequent turning and are bothersome to handle individually. The hinged broiler has a smaller grid, which makes them invaluable for pieces of food which might fall through to the fire on the normal rack. Basket grills have been designed deep enough to hold pieces of chicken and other irregular shaped foods. They are also great for food which requires constant turning and tossing.

RIB RACKS — are designed to increase the amount of cooking capacity by standing the ribs at an angle to the heat source.

VEGETABLE RACK — fits around the outside of the grill to keep the vegetables, especially corn and potatoes, close enough to the fire for cooking but out of the center where the meat is being prepared. Some cooks prefer this to laying the vegetables on the rack or coals which block heat and use valuable space.

ELEVATED HALF GRILL — allows the barbecuer to cook more than one type of food which requires different cooking temperatures. With this utensil, an additional 50% cooking space is created, as the half rack rests on feet above the main cooking grill.

SKEWERS AND SKEWER RACK — come in a variety of lengths and materials, from six-inch bamboo sticks to long elaborate brass-handled swords. The most functional are steel with heat resistant wooden handles to ease when turning. The skewer rack, although not necessary, aids in the constant turning needed to cook a perfect kabob.

ROAST HOLDERS — are used with the covered kettle grills to stand the otherwise bulky roast in the most favorable cooking position. It also aids in transporting the roast

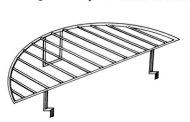
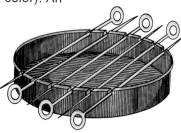
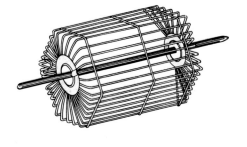

Cuts of Beef and Pork

STEAKS (tender)

T-bone Steak: The bone, which has the distinct T shape, separates the large loin muscle from the small tenderloin muscle. This cut comes from the loin area.

Rib Steak: The rib bone identifies this cut easily. It is cut from the rib area — similar to the Rib Roast, only cut into 1 to 2-inch thick steaks. If it is sold without bone or outside fat trimming, it is called Rib Eye Steak.

Tenderloin Steak: This cross-section of the tenderloin muscle has no bone and very little fat. It is also sold as Filet Mignon.

Sirloin Steak: A large, tender steak that contains several large muscles. It may be boneless or may contain a small wedge or flat bone. The top (largest) muscle is sometimes separated and sold as Top Sirloin Steak.

Club Steak: This steak is similar to the Rib Steak, but sometimes includes a small portion of the tenderloin muscle. It is cut from the rib area and may or may not contain a rib bone.

Porterhouse Steak: Similar to a T-Bone Steak but larger in size. The tenderloin muscle is larger in this cut than in other steaks.

STEAKS (less tender)

Round Steak: This steak may have the characteristic round bone with 1 large muscle above the bone (often separated and sold as Top Round) and 2 smaller muscles below the bone (often separated and sold as Bottom Round). The smallest muscle is occasionally separated and sold as Eye of Round Steak. Family Steak and Swiss Steak are usually cut from this same rump area. Unless pretendered, they should be cooked with liquid.

"Cube" Steak: These are less tender pieces of meat that are made tender by mechanical cubing (cutting through the fibers). They are also sold as Minute Steaks.

Flank Steak: This long boneless steak comes from the less tender flank area. It is also called London Broil or Plank Steak. It can be very tender and flavorful if simmered with liquid or if tenderized, broiled rare and carved across the long muscle into thin slices for serving.

ROASTS (cooked without liquid)

Standing Rump Roast: A triangular-shaped roast that contains the rump bone, the tail bone and usually part of the round leg bone. It is from the rump area and may be boned, rolled, tied and called Rolled Rump Roast. It can be roasted or cooked with liquid.

Rolled Rump: A boneless, rolled roast with several layers of meat interspersed with small amounts of fat and covered with a thin layer of fat. This is from the rump area so it is less tender than a Rib Roast; but if it is from high quality meat, it is very good roasted.

Rolled Rib Roast: A Standing Rib Roast which has had the bones removed and has been rolled and tied.

POT-ROASTS (cooked with liquid)

Blade Bone Roast: This cut is really a pot-roast and includes several meat muscles, the blade bone and sometimes part of the backbone. Cut from the shoulder (chuck) area near the rib section, it is usually less expensive than arm bone roasts, contains slightly more bone and waste, and is sometimes referred to as Chuck Roast. Occasionally it is boned, rolled and tied and called Boneless Chuck Pot Roast. If cut into 1 to 2-inch slices, it is called Blade Steak.

Sirloin Tip: A small tip of the sirloin is included in this roast from the round steak area. If it is from high quality meat, it can be roasted just like some of the more tender cuts.

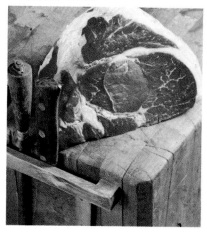

Heel of Round: This wedge-shaped or triangular cut is from the end of the round steak (rump) area where there is no bone. It is less tender than the Rump Roast and should be cooked with liquid unless it has been pretendered.

Arm Bone Roast: This cut contains the arm bone and sometimes cross sections of the rib bones — unless they are removed by the retailer — and is from the shoulder (chuck) area. You can tell it from the round steak because the bone is nearer the center of the cut and includes several small meat muscles. It is sometimes called Chuck Roast. If cut into 1 to 1½-inch slices, it is called Arm Steak.

Beef Brisket: This cut contains the breast bone and portions of the ribs, although it is frequently boned and sold as Boneless Brisket. It comes from the breast and rib area and requires long simmering in liquid for tenderness.

Short Ribs: Cut from the boney tip of the ribs near the brisket. These cuts contain a cross section of rib bone with alternate layers of meat and fat. They are cut from the boney tip of the ribs and should be cooked with liquid for tenderness.

PORK ROASTS

Pork Loin Roast: A roast from the loin or rib section. It is sometimes boned and tied and sold as a roll. Rib sections from two loins are sometimes tied together to form a Crown Roast. Loin and rib chops are also cut from this section. The loin is sometimes cured and smoked — for roasts or chops.

Shoulder Roasts: These include: Arm Roast (cut from the arm section of the shoulder and identified by the round arm bone), Fresh Boston Shoulder (contains the blade bone exposed on two surfaces and is sometimes called Boston Butt), and Boneless Rolled Roast. These make tender roasts, but unless boned, they contain bone and more fat than a Loin Roast.

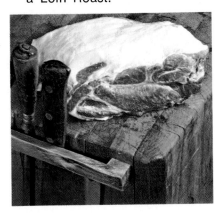

CHOPS AND STEAKS:

Loin Chops: These chops have two muscles (one on each side of the T-shaped bone) and are cut from the loin area. They are also sometimes cured and smoked and are sold as Smoked Pork Chops.

Canadian-Style Bacon: This cut is the boneless loin muscle (which would otherwise be a Loin Roast) that has been cured and smoked. It is available whole, cut into sections or sliced; it is also available "fully-cooked" or "cook-before-eating".

Pork Tenderloin: The lean muscle that runs along the back; this is considered the most tender cut of pork.

Spareribs: A thin covering of meat surrounds these bones that come from the top of the rib section and breast area. Country-style ribs are a leaner cut and come from the rib section of the loin area. Country-style ribs and Spareribs can usually be used interchangeably in recipes.

Rib Chops: These have only one muscle and come from the rib area. They are sometimes cut extra thick and a cut made into the rib side for stuffing. These chops are occasionally cured and smoked and are sold as Smoked Pork Chops.

HAM CUTS: Hams are available fully-cooked (need no further cooking) and cook-before-eating (partially cooked in processing but need further cooking).

Smoked Ham: Ham cuts have the characteristic single round bone. Hams are from the back leg of pork and have been cured and smoked. They are available as bone-in, semi-boneless, boneless and shaped or rolled. In addition, they can be sold whole, halved, or as pieces. The shank half is the lower half (extending down the leg); the butt half is the upper half.

Index